FUNDAMENTAL PRINCIPLES OF LAW

The Law of Contract

AUSTRALIA
Law Book Co.
Sydney

CANADA and USA
Carswell
Toronto

HONG KONG
Sweet & Maxwell Asia

NEW ZEALAND
Brookers
Wellington

SINGAPORE and MALAYSIA
Sweet & Maxwell Asia
Singapore and Kuala Lumpur

FUNDAMENTAL PRINCIPLES OF LAW

The Law of Contract

by

Sir John Smith, C.B.E., Q.C., LL.D., F.B.A.
Honorary Bencher of Lincoln's Inn;
Honorary Fellow of Downing College, Cambridge
Emeritus Professor of Law
University of Nottingham

Fourth Edition

LONDON
SWEET & MAXWELL
2002

First Edition 1989
Second Impression 1990
Second Edition 1993
Second Impression 1995
Third Edition 1998
Fourth Edition 2002

Published in 2002 by
Sweet & Maxwell Limited of
100 Avenue Road, Swiss Cottage,
London NW3 3PF
(http://www.sweetandmaxwell.co.uk)
Typeset by YHT Ltd, London W13 8NT
Printed in England by MPG Books Ltd, Bodmin, Cornwall

ISBN 0–421–78170X

A CIP catalogue record for this book
is available from the British Library

No natural forests were destroyed to make this product.
Only farmed timber was used and re-planted.

PREFACE

This new edition is necessary primarily because of the enactment of the Contracts (Rights of Third Parties) Act 1999 which makes important changes to a central aspect of the law of contract. The effect of the Act and some of the problems it creates are described in the chapter on Privity of Contract which becomes the largest and probably the most complex in the book. Some possible effects of the Act on other parts of contract law are noted elsewhere. There has been the usual crop of significant cases. *Barry v. Davies* at last confirms the *obiter dicta* of 1859 in *Warlow v. Harrison* (auction sales without reserve). *Shogun Finance Ltd. v. Hudson* applies the established principles concerning mistake of identity in offer and acceptance but provokes a dissent from Sedley L.J. which could portend the first scrutiny by the House of Lords of this controversial area of the law for more than a century. Two House of Lords decisions on implied terms—*Malik v. BCCI* and *Johnson v. Unisys Ltd.* indicate both an expanding role for this device and some limitations. *Attorney-General v. Blake* required a new section on "Accounting for profits obtained by breach of contract". The section on undue influence has been completely re-written in the light of *Royal Bank of Scotland v. Etridge (No.2)* and in an attempt to clarify the confusing use by the courts of the concepts of presumptions and burdens.

I have retained the terms "plaintiff" and "writ" in discussing cases in which they were used. It would be confusing for the reader who is diligent enough to read a case in the law reports if this book called them "claimant" and "claim". It is bad enough that these much less informative and precise terms have to be used in respect of later cases. Regrettably, we are out of line with the rest of the common law world whose citizens are not deemed to be too thick to understand terminology which has been in common use by intelligent laymen for centuries.

The book is cross-referenced to Smith & Thomas, *A Casebook on Contract*, (11th ed., 2000) where the reader will find extracts from the great majority of the cases referred to and the important statutes and regulations.

I am indebted to my colleague, Horton Rogers, for our discussion of many points of contract law; and to the publishers for their courteous, swift and efficient handling of this edition.

John Smith
January 2002

CONTENTS

TABLE OF CASES

TABLE OF STATUTES

CHAPTER ONE

Contractual Rights and Duties

We all make contracts every day. Each time we buy anything—a railway ticket, a pair of shoes, a meal—we make a contract. Many of us spend most of our lives performing contractual obligations owed to our employers. We may be conscious of contracting only when we enter into some important transaction, like buying a house or a new car. But the law of contract is always there, to be invoked when something goes wrong: there is an accident on the railway, the shoes prove defective or the meal causes food poisoning.

The same general principles govern commercial contracts as the everyday transactions mentioned. A case concerning the employment of a prima donna may be an important precedent in a dispute about the hiring of a ship. An advertiser's promises concerning the therapeutic qualities of his smoke ball may be governed by the same principles as the promises of a shipper of goods to the stevedore who will load them. These general principles are almost all principles of the common law. They are not to be found in any code or statute but are derived from precedent. Consequently, any study of the law of contract must be, to a large extent, a study of the cases which made it. There are some important statutory modifications of the common law principles, particularly by the Frustrated Contracts Act 1943, the Misrepresentation Act 1967, the Unfair Contract Terms Act 1977 and the Contracts (Rights of Third Parties) Act 1999, all of which are examined in this book. In addition, there is a vast amount of legislation relating to particular types of contract. For example, the contract of employment is now heavily regulated by statute.

Such contracts are now necessarily the subject of specialised works. But generally this legislation assumes the existence of the principles of the common law. They continue to apply, except in so far as the statute expressly or impliedly modifies them. An understanding of these principles is therefore essential to an understanding of the specialised law. Moreover, questions under almost any other branch of the law may depend on the law of contract. A petrol company's offer to supply a "world cup coin" of minute value to a motorist buying four gallons of petrol is unlikely to give rise to an action for breach of contract; but the effect of the offer in the law of contract determined whether the company was liable for a very large sum in purchase tax.[1] It would hardly be worth suing a chocolate company for its failure to fulfil its promise to supply a record of "Rockin' Shoes" for 1s 6d and three chocolate wrappers; but, on the answer to the question whether the wrappers were part of the contractual price depended the rights to substantial sums by way of royalties on the record.[2] The outcome of many actions in the law of tort turns on issues of contract. Even in the criminal law, many cases relating to property offences can be properly understood only in the light of contractual principles. The law of contract is then a basic subject which must be grasped by anyone who aspires to understand or apply the law.

UNDERTAKINGS OR PROMISES

The distinguishing feature of contractual obligations is that they are not imposed by the law but undertaken by the contracting parties. The name of the old common law form of action was *Assumpsit*—"he undertook." The plaintiff alleged that the defendant undertook to do something and did not do it, or did it badly; or that he undertook that something was so (*e.g.* the horse was sound) and it was not so. Many duties are imposed on us by the law whether we like it or not. If I drive my car on the road I owe an inescapable duty of care to all other road users and if, in breach of the duty, I negligently cause injury to one of them, he may sue me in the tort of negligence. But the only reason why I am bound to go to work in the morning is that I have given an undertaking to my employer to do so; and his undertaking is the only reason why I am entitled to my pay at the end of the month.

Contractual and tortious duties frequently overlap, especially where negligence is concerned. A carrier of passengers in a vehicle on the road will of course owe them the duty which he

1 See the *Esso Petroleum* case [1976] 1 All E.R. 117; S. & T. 16.
2 *Chappell & Co. Ltd v. Nestlé Co. Ltd* [1960] A.C. 87; S. & T. 210.

owes to all other road users in tort; but, if he is carrying them under a contract, it will be an implied term of the contract that he will exercise due care. The content of the two duties will be the same, so that free riders will be no worse off than those riding under a contract. But contractual duties are often stricter. If the diners in a restaurant are poisoned by the food, notwithstanding the fact that the restaurateur and his staff exercised all proper care, those who have contracted to buy the food have a remedy because the restaurateur has impliedly undertaken that the food is reasonably fit for eating, and it is not. But any guests who are not parties to a contract have no claim except in the tort of negligence and the restaurateur has not been negligent.

The distinction between contractual and tortious duties is less clear cut than it may so far have been made to appear, since, by statute, some contractual duties are now inescapable. For example, a seller cannot exclude the undertaking implied by section 14 of the Sale of Goods Act 1979 that the goods will be reasonably fit for their purpose where the buyer is a "consumer."[3] So, just as the motorist who drives on the road cannot evade the obligation to use care to other road users, the restaurateur who invites the public to buy food in his restaurant cannot evade the obligation to supply food fit for eating. But the former is a duty in tort and the latter remains a duty in contract.

The law of contract then is about undertakings or promises. It determines which promises are, and which are not, binding in law; and it prescribes the remedies available to a person who complains that a binding promise has been broken. The word, "promise," is generally used in ordinary speech to refer to acts to be done in the future and most contracts contemplate future performance by one or more of the parties. In the law of contract, "promise" is used in a wider sense to include undertakings about existing facts, as where the seller of a car promises that it is roadworthy or the occupier of premises promises that he has taken reasonable steps to make them safe. In many contracts the only, or the only significant, promises relate to a matter of fact, as where goods are bought in a shop for cash. The acts which the seller and buyer perform—delivery of the goods and payment of the price—are, for all practical purposes, coincident with the formation of the contract and the only promises likely to be relied on in a dispute between the parties are those of the seller relating to the quality of the goods.

---

3 See below, p. 180.

DEEDS, WRITTEN AND ORAL PROMISES

It would be impracticable to make all promises binding in law and therefore English law, like all other systems, has rules to define the promises which are binding. A promise is not binding unless it is made in "a deed" or given "for consideration." A person may make any lawful promise binding in law by executing a deed. At common law a deed was a document which was "signed, sealed and delivered" but, since section 1 of the Law of Property (Miscellaneous Provisions) Act 1989 came into force on September 27, 1989, the execution of a deed by an individual (as distinct from a corporation) no longer requires a seal. It is sufficient that the document:

(i)   makes it clear on its face that it is intended to be a deed, by describing itself as a deed or expressing itself to be executed and signed as a deed, or otherwise; and

(ii) it is signed (and "signed" includes making one's mark) either (a) by the maker in the presence of a witness who attests the signature or (b) at the maker's direction and in his presence and the presence of two witnesses who each attest the signature; and

(iii) it is "delivered" as a deed by the maker or his agent. "Delivery" is widely defined to include any act by the maker which indicates that he considers the deed to be binding.

The 1989 Act has simplified the making of a deed but the great majority of promises have never been made in this formal way. If the promise is not in a deed, it is binding only if it is given for consideration. Usually, it makes no difference whether the promise is oral or in a document which does not amount to a deed. Contracts of the greatest importance—the sale of diamonds worth a million pounds—may be made by word of mouth or any other conduct signifying an intention to contract. The only question is whether the promise was made for consideration. There are exceptional cases where statute provides (i) that a contract is not valid unless it is made *in* writing or (ii) it is not enforceable in a court of law unless it is *evidenced* in writing. These are considered in Chapter 20, below.

BARGAINS

The "doctrine" of consideration is considered in detail below but it is so fundamental that it must be outlined immediately.

The general idea is that a promise to make a gift is not binding but a bargain is. A promise is given for consideration when the promisor asks for something in return for his promise and gets what he asks for. The promise is binding because the promisee has "bought" it by giving "the price" asked. "I promise that I will give you my car" is a promise which may be seriously intended and may impose a moral obligation on the promisor but it is not capable of becoming a contractual promise as the promisor has asked for nothing in return. A prompt "acceptance" by the promisee makes no difference. "I promise that I will give you my car for your motor-bike," on the other hand, is an offer capable of becoming a contract. The promisor has specified what he wants in return for his promise and, when the promisee accepts the offer by giving it to him, a contract is made.

An offer to make a contract is a promise with a price-tag.

BILATERAL AND UNILATERAL CONTRACTS

Sometimes what the promisor wants is a promise from the other party. When he gets what he wants, *i.e.* the other party's promise, his own promise is binding. So too is that of the other party. O promises A that he will employ him from January 1 next year at a salary of £10,000 a year. On October 1, A accepts the offer. He is, of course, thereby promising to perform the duties specified in the job description. Both parties are now bound. O has received consideration in the form of A's promise to do the work specified. A has received consideration in the form O's promise to pay his salary and fulfil all the other duties of an employer. This is called a "bilateral" contract because each of the two parties has made contractual promises.

Sometimes the offeror asks, not for a promise, but for an act, in return for his promise. The typical example is the offer of a reward. "£10 to anyone who returns my lost dog." The offeror is not seeking promises, but action. If A finds the dog and returns it to O he is entitled to the reward. He has paid the required price for the promise. This is called a "unilateral" contract, because only one side has made a promise. A has not promised to do anything. He has done all he has to do when he returns the dog. Of course, there are two parties to a unilateral contract, but only one promisor.

OFFER AND ACCEPTANCE

Contracts are bargains and the natural way to make a bargain is for one side to propose the terms and the other to agree to them. So contracts are almost invariably made by a process of offer and acceptance. The law looks for an offer and acceptance, not because of some technical legal requirement, but because this is the way in which contracts are in fact made. The lack of offer and acceptance does not preclude the existence of a contract, if it can be discerned from the facts in some other way. Suppose that a Yacht Club invites its members to take part in a race on the terms that "Each competitor agrees with every other competitor that he will be liable for all damage caused by him through any breach of the rules in the course of the race." When the race begins, there is a series of contracts between each competitor and every other competitor; but it is impossible to say that one rather than the other is the offeror or the acceptor. This hypothetical example is based on *Clarke v. Dunraven*.[4] In this case each competitor made a written agreement with the Club when he entered the race. Each competitor had certainly made a contract with the Club that he would pay an injured competitor for damage he caused in breach of the rules. However, it was not the Club which sued[5] the defaulting yacht-owner, but the injured competitor. The action succeeded. A possible explanation is that each person to enter the race made an offer to any subsequent entrants and accepted the offer already made by any previous entrants. It is sometimes possible to discern an offer and acceptance in rather unpromising material; but this would not be possible in the hypothetical case put above because there is nothing between the invitation by the Club and the race. The parties have agreed, "I will be bound by the rules if you will"; there is a bargain, but no offer and acceptance.

Much attention has been devoted to the problem of "cross-offers"—*i.e.* X and Y each posts an offer in identical terms to the other. Is there a contract when both offers arrive? In the one case in which the matter has been considered[6] five judges out of six thought, *obiter*, that there is not. Some seem to have thought offer and acceptance essential and, of course, there was no acceptance. Others stressed the practical inconvenience of holding there to be a contract: parties in this situation would not be clear where they stood, so the right course was to say that there was no contract until one of them had accepted. Until then the transaction lacks the quality of a bargain.

4 [1897] A.C. 59; S. & T. 28.
5 The Club would presumably have been able to recover only nominal damages from a defaulting competitor, because the Club had suffered no loss. The injured competitor could not, at that date, rely on the contract between the defaulting competitor and the Club because of the doctrine of privity of contract. It might be different since the Contracts (Rights of the Third Parties) Act 1999 came into force, below p. 111.
6 *Tinn v. Hoffman* (1873) 29 L.T. 271; S. & T. 27.

OFFER AND PROMISE

The first requirement of an offer is that it should contain a promise by the offeror. If there is no promise, there is no offer. In *Gibson v. Manchester City Council*[7] a letter from the Council stated, "The corporation may be prepared to sell the house to you at the purchase price of £2,725 . . . If you would like to make a formal application to buy . . ." It was held that this was not an offer to sell the house, capable of acceptance by Gibson. No reasonable reader of the letter could suppose that the Council was promising to sell the house. They were inviting Gibson to offer to buy it. Their letter was what is commonly called "an invitation to treat." It did not indicate that present willingness to be bound which is essential to an offer. The use of the word "offer" does not necessarily mean that an offer in the contractual sense is being made. In *Spencer v. Harding*[8] a circular issued by the defendants began, "We are instructed to offer to the wholesale trade by tender the stock in trade . . ." and went on to state that payment must be made in cash, and the time when the tenders would be opened. The plaintiffs made the highest tender but the defendants refused to let him have the goods. It was held that there was no contract. The question in such a case is whether the reasonable reader of the circular would have supposed that the defendants were promising to sell to the highest bidder. Did they really intend to do so, however low that bid might be? The answer must be in the negative. It would be different, as Willes J. said, "If the circular had gone on, 'and we undertake to sell to the highest bidder.'"

The test is not one of the actual intention of the alleged offeror but of his intention as it would have appeared to a reasonable man. If the reasonable man would have thought the offeror was promising to be bound, then he is promising to be bound; but otherwise not. This "objective"[9] approach leads to something approximating to rules of law in particular common situations; but they are rules which give way to an expression of a contrary intention. The display of goods in a shop window or in a self-service shop is not an offer to sell the goods but an invitation to the customers to offer to buy them—unless the shopkeeper in some way makes it clear that he does intend the display to be an offer. In *Pharmaceutical Society of Great Britain v. Boots*[10] the question was whether the sale of certain drugs was taking place,

---

7 [1979] 1 W.L.R. 294, HL; S. & T. 7.
8 (1870) L.R. 5; C.P. 561; S. & T. 9, Common Pleas.
9 See below, p. 12.
10 [1953] 1 Q.B. 401, CA; S. & T. 17.

as required by law, under the supervision of a registered pharmacist. The Society contended the display of the goods in a self-service shop was an offer to sell the goods which was accepted by the customer when he took an article off the shelves and put it in the wire basket provided. The argument was rejected. The customer offered to buy the goods at the cash point and the cashier, supervised by the pharmacist, could then accept or reject the offer as appropriate. One argument that was found persuasive by the court was to the effect that, if the Society was right, a customer who took an article from the shelves, having contracted to buy it, would have to pay for it. He would not be able to put it back and take something else instead. But no reasonable person would suppose he had bought the thing as soon as he put it in the wire basket. This was a good answer to the case as put by the Society; but it is not a conclusive argument against holding the display to be an offer. The court might have held, as some American courts have done,[11] that the display is an offer which is accepted by presenting the goods to the cashier, and not till then. That, however, would have produced a different result in the case; and the law is settled that the mere display is not an offer—unless the shopkeeper clearly indicates that it is.

The law in respect of auction sales is also well settled. The auctioneer who "offers" goods for sale is, in law, merely inviting the potential bidders to make offers to buy them, offers which he may or may not accept. Consequently a bidder may retract his bid at any time before the auctioneer signifies his acceptance by the fall of the hammer, or in another customary manner.[12] Where the auctioneer advertises that the sale shall be without reserve, the recent case of *Barry v. Davies*[13] decides that he is bound to sell to the person who attends and makes the highest bid. The advertisment is an offer by the auctioneer to the whole world, inviting them to attend and bid. The contract is made with a bidder when it is clear that no one is going to make a higher bid than his. This is not a contract of sale. The bidder could still withdraw his bid. If the auctioneer does not accept the bid, the contract of sale is never made. But the auctioneer has broken his contract to sell to the highest bidder and is liable in damages. In *Barry v. Davis* the auctioneer, D, said that certain machines were worth £28,000. B made the only bid of £400. D refused to accept it, in breach of his promise to sell to the highest bidder. B was awarded damages of £26,000. The contract is described as

11 S. & T. 19–20.
12 Sale of Goods Act 1979, s.57, S. & T. 20, codifying the common law.
13 [2000] 1 W.L.R. 1962, C.A.

"collateral" to the contract of sale, though the latter contract (which would have been made between the owner of the machines through the agency of the auctioneer and B) was never concluded. The advertisement that the sale is to be without reserve is an inducement to attend and bid. The auctioneer obviously wants to attract as many potential bidders as possible so attendance in response to the advertisement is consideration for the auctioneer's promise that the sale shall be without reserve. In *Barry v. Davies* the court at last confirmed the fully considered but technically obiter opinions stated as long ago as 1959 in *Warlow v. Harrsion*.[14]

The auctioneer's implied promise is *"If I put the good up for sale, the sale shall be without reserve"*. he does not promise that they will be put up for sale.

In *Harris v. Nickerson*[15] an auctioneer advertised in terms similar to those in *Warlow v. Harrison* but the goods were not put up for sale at all. The plaintiff, who had travelled from London to Bury St Edmunds to bid for the goods, failed in an action for breach of contract to recover his expenses. The advertisement, thought the court, was a mere declaration of intention to put the articles up for sale, not a promise to do so. *Warlow v. Harrison* was distinguished. In the light of the two cases, the auctioneer who advertises that he will sell goods without reserve is saying, in effect, "I intend (but do not promise) to put these articles up for sale; and, if I do so, I promise that the sale shall be without reserve—*i.e.* I will accept the highest bona fide bid." Auctioneers might be a little surprised at the complexity of the matter.

An important distinction is that there can be only one highest bona fide bidder but many people may attend the auction in response to the announcement that the goods are to be sold. It would be "excessively inconvenient" if the auctioneer were liable to all of those attending to bid for some item which had been withdrawn. Reasonable men would not suppose that the auctioneer intended to undertake any such liability and so the promise was not to be imputed to him.

Tenders

Whether an invitation to tender amounts to an offer depends on the terms of the invitation, as *Spencer v. Harding*[16] shows. If it asks for tenders for the supply of goods of a specified type, "such

---

14 (1859) 1 E.& E. 309; Exch. Chamber; S. & T. 21.
15 (1873) L.R. 8, QB 286; S. & T. 24.
16 Above, p. 7.

as we may think fit to order," for one year,[17] it is clearly not an offer because there is no promise to order anything. A tender stating the prices at which the tenderer will supply the goods, however, is, in the absence of contrary words, an offer which may be accepted by the placing of an order. A "general acceptance," not ordering any goods, appears to be no more than an expression of satisfaction of the invitor with the prices proposed. As the offer is to remain open for a year and may be accepted from time to time, it is known as a "standing offer." Each time an order is placed for goods, there is a new contract. It seems clear that the offeror may, at any time during the year, revoke the offer, not, of course, so as to affect acceptances already made, but for the future. He has received no consideration for any promise to keep the offer open for the year—unless, by a general acceptance of his tender, he can be said to have been promised—"If we order any goods (and we do not promise to do so) we promise to order them from you."

If on the other hand, the invitation to tender states that the invitor *will require* certain goods and asks for tenders to supply them, a tender will, prima facie, be an offer capable of a once-for-all acceptance by the invitor.

Where the invitation to tender is a firm offer, can it be accepted by a "referential bid"—a bid which says "I will pay £1000, or £10 more than any other bid, whichever is higher"? The answer given by the House of Lords in *Harvela Investments Ltd v. Royal Trust Co. of Canada Ltd*[18] is that it cannot. If everyone made referential bids, it would be impossible to determine which was the highest. If a referential bid were effective, a buyer who made only a fixed bid would be deprived of the chance of success; the invitor's object of obtaining the best price bidders were prepared to pay would be frustrated and other bizarre results might follow. In the *Harvela* case, the invitor thought the referential bid was a valid acceptance and acted accordingly; so the court held that he did not understand the nature of the offer he had in fact made. An "objective" meaning is given to the offer. Because of the unhappy consequences to which referential bids would lead, we must take it that the reasonable offeree would say, "He cannot be supposed to have intended referential bids to be acceptable." But if the invitor says, "Referential bids welcome," they must surely be valid and he must take the consequences. It is for him, and not for any court, to determine the conditions of his offer to contract.

A tenderer may incur substantial expense in responding to an

17 *cf. Great Northern Railway v. Witham* (1873) L.R. 9; C.P. 16.
18 [1986] A.C. 207, HL; S. & T. 13.

invitation to tender. If his tender is not accepted, this expenditure will be wasted. If the tender has been fairly considered and rejected, he has no complaint. That is the chance he takes. But what if the tender, though submitted before the deadline stipulated and complying in all respects with the invitation, is not even considered? If tenders have been solicited from selected persons known to the invitor and there is a prescribed procedure for submission, then he will have an action for breach of a contract to consider his tender. He is, it seems, reasonably entitled to suppose that the invitor was impliedly promising, "If you will submit a tender in accordance with these conditions, I promise to consider it." He accepts this offer of a unilateral contract by submitting a tender conforming with the conditions.[19] There are difficulties about the amount of damages: how do we assess the value of the opportunity for consideration of the tender which may, or may not, have been accepted? But the courts (see below, p. 223) are not deterred by this difficulty from making the attempt.

19 *Blackpool and Fylde Aeroclub Ltd v. Blackpool Borough Council* [1990] 1 W.L.R. 1195; S. & T. 11.

CHAPTER TWO

The Objective Meaning of Promises

It sometimes happens that a person's actual intention differs from his apparent intention. He may in fact make a particular promise when his intention is to make a promise of a different kind, or, perhaps, not to make a promise at all. In such a case he will be bound by the promise he in fact made if it has become part of a bargain. He will protest in vain that this was not his real intention. If O makes an offer which can reasonably bear only one meaning and A accepts, O cannot escape liability by saying that he intended it to mean something else. This judgment of intention by the words and other conduct of a person is known as the "objective test." Where the inquiry is directed to ascertaining a person's real state of mind, the test applied is "subjective." It is sometimes necessary to determine a person's real state of mind for the purposes of the law of contract, as will appear; but generally the law applies an objective test. If this were not so, no one could ever act safely on a contract which he reasonably believed he had made. There is always the possibility that the other party might be under some undisclosed, undiscoverable misapprehension as to the existence or nature or effect of the contract. If he is, that is his misfortune.

If any reasonable observer of the promisor's conduct would have supposed, and the promisee did suppose, that the promisor was making a particular promise, say X, then the promisor will be bound by promise X if it is comprised in a bargain with the promisee. In *Tamplin v. James*[1] the defendant attended an auction

1 (1880) 15 Ch.D. 215, *affirmed* 15 Ch.D. 219, CA, S. & T. 113.

to buy "The Ship" inn which was put up for sale as "Lot 1." The particulars of sale and the plan, to which the auctioneer drew attention, made absolutely clear the extent of the property. Lot 1 was not sold at the auction but, immediately afterwards, the defendant made an offer for it which was accepted. Later it emerged that he made the offer under the mistaken belief that Lot 1 included two adjacent plots. He had known the property from a boy and observed that these plots had always been occupied by the occupier of the inn. He declined to complete unless these two plots were conveyed to him. It was held that he was bound by his contract to buy Lot 1 and, indeed, that an order of specific performance be made requiring him to carry out that contract. Clearly there was no actual "meeting of minds" or *consensus ad idem*—a notion to which the older cases pay much lip-service— for the defendant intended to buy the inn and the two plots and the plaintiff intended to sell only the inn. But there was a contract.

Conversely, if the owner of adjacent properties, X and Y, decided to sell X and invited offers on the basis of a plan and description which, by an error, included both properties, he would be bound by a contract to sell both to an offeror who made his offer on the reasonable supposition that both were for sale and whose offer was accepted.

It is sometimes said that the basis of the law is the doctrine of estoppel. This takes a variety of forms and is encountered on several issues in the law of contract. Estoppel in its simplest and most common form is a rule that where one person (the representor) makes a statement of fact to another (the representee) in reliance on which the representee reasonably supposes he is intended to, and does, act to his detriment, then in any litigation which later takes place between them, the representor will not be allowed to say (*i.e.* he will be estopped from saying) that his representation was untrue, even if it is certain that it was in fact untrue. In applying the objective test, judges sometimes use similar language. In *Tamplin v. James* Baggallay L.J. said "I think [the defendant] is not entitled to say to any effectual purpose that he was under a mistake."

It is clear, however, that the basis of the objective test is not estoppel because it applies even though there has been no action by the other party in reliance on the "representation" of intention to contract on certain terms. In one case a person who had signed a contract to sell a two-acre plot of land under the belief, not induced by fraud or misrepresentation, that the contract related to only half an acre of the plot, was held bound although he tore up the agreement within minutes of signing it.[2]

2 *Hasham v. Zenab* [1960] A.C. 316, PC.

The only act which the party relying on the objective test need have done is to enter into the contract, and this may be very far from an act to his detriment.[3]

WHERE A KNOWS, OR OUGHT TO KNOW, THAT O'S OFFER DOES NOT REPRESENT HIS REAL INTENTION

In *Tamplin v. James*, the vendor reasonably believed that the purchaser meant what he said. It is otherwise if A knows, or ought to know, that O's real intention is different. In *Hartog v. Colin and Shields*[4] the defendants offered to sell 30,000 skins to the plaintiff at prices per pound. The previous negotiations had been carried on (as was customary in the trade) by reference to the price per piece. The value of a piece was about one-third that of a pound. The price stated was absurdly low and the defendants said that they had written "pound" in error for "piece." Singleton J. dismissed an action for damages, saying, "The plaintiff could not reasonably have supposed that the offer contained the offeror's real intention." The plaintiff knew, or ought to have known, that the defendant did not really mean to say what he had in fact said. It would have been different if the plaintiff had reasonably believed the defendant was mistaken only as to the value of the skins. If that had been his only mistake, his words would have truly represented his intention and the law would not preclude the buyer from taking advantage of the mistake which he knew the seller was making.

WHERE THE OBJECTIVE FACTS ARE AMBIGUOUS

In *Tamplin v. James*, the objective facts were unambiguous. The reasonable observer being aware of all the facts except the defendant's secret thoughts could have been in no doubt that they were contracting about Lot 1 as described. It is different where the objective facts are ambiguous. The party responsible for the ambiguity cannot enforce the contract in the sense in which he intended it, if the other party intended it in the other sense. In *Falck v. Williams*[5] the plaintiff sent an offer in code by telegram. Because he did not use enough words, the offer was ambiguous; it might be taken to refer to one or other of two

---

3 *Centrovincial Estates plc v. Merchant Investors Assurance Co. Ltd* [1983] Com.L.R. 158, CA; S. & T. 118.
4 [1939] 2 All E.R. 566, Q.B.
5 [1900] A.C. 176, PC; S. & T. 119.

contemplated transactions. Falck intended a contract for the carriage of copra from Fiji to the United Kingdom. Williams accepted, intending to contract for the carriage of coal from Sydney to Barcelona. Falck's action to enforce the contract in the sense in which he understood it failed. Lord MacNaghten said, *obiter*, that if Williams had been maintaining his construction of the contract he would equally have failed. This is more arguable. Suppose, being in no doubt that the ambiguous telegram bore the meaning he attributed to it, he had taken expensive action in reliance on the contract he believed he had made. Should the author of the ambiguity be allowed to say, "You ought to have spotted it"?

Where the ambiguity is the fault of neither party and they understand the contract in different senses, there is certainly no contract. In *Raffles v. Wichelhaus*[6] there was a written agreement for the sale by the plaintiffs to the defendants of 125 bales of cotton, "to arrive ex Peerless from Bombay." Unknown to the parties, there were two *Peerless's*, one leaving Bombay in October and the other leaving Bombay in December. The seller's cotton was on the December *Peerless* but the buyer thought it was on the October *Peerless*. The buyer refused to accept the cargo of the December ship and the seller sued him. The court rejected the argument that it was immaterial by which ship the goods should come. No doubt it was important for the buyer to know when he could expect delivery. It was, or purported to be, a contract for the sale of a specific cargo, not simply a contract for the sale of 125 bales of cotton of a particular description. If it had been the latter, it was clear that the seller was ready and willing to perform it and was entitled to his damages. But, as it was intended to be the sale of a specific cargo, it was essential to determine which cargo was the subject of the contract; and that was impossible, because each cargo fitted the contract description equally well. Nor was it clear that the ambiguity was the responsibility of the one rather than the other.

If both parties had interpreted the telegram in *Falck v. Williams* in the same sense, and if both parties in *Raffles v. Wichelhaus* had had the same *Peerless* in mind, it is clear that there would have been a valid contract, notwithstanding the objective ambiguity. In such cases, therefore, it may be necessary to determine the actual state of mind of the parties—to apply the subjective as well as the objective test. In *Raffles v. Wichelhaus* the seller admitted that the buyer was thinking of the other ship, so there was no need to prove it by evidence.

6 (1864) 2 H. & C. 906; S. & T. 123.

WHERE A KNOWS THAT O IS MISTAKEN AS TO THE TERMS OF THE CONTRACT

We have already noticed that A is not precluded from enforcing the contract because he knew that O was making a grave mistake as to the value of the subject-matter of the contract. The same is true where A knows that O is making other material mistakes of *fact*. But it is different if A knows that O is mistaken as to the terms of the contract; he knows that O thinks the contract contains term X and that in fact it contains not term X but term Y. It is clear that O cannot then enforce the contract in the sense of Y, though it undoubtedly says "Y." Probably—though this is less clear—A can enforce the contract against O in sense X.

All these propositions are illustrated by *Smith v. Hughes*.[7] The plaintiff sued the defendant on a contract for the sale of a specific parcel of oats. The defendant said that he had contracted for old oats, whereas these oats were new and useless to him. He refused to pay the price. The jury found a verdict for the defendant but, because there were unresolved questions of fact, it is necessary to consider the case on three hypotheses.

(i)   *The word "old" was used in the discussion leading to the oral contract of sale.* If this was the case, then the jury's verdict was right because it was a contract for the sale of old oats. The seller could not perform it by delivering new oats.

(ii) *The word "old" was not used but the seller knew that the buyer believed that the oats were in fact old.* If that was the case, the verdict was wrong. So long as he did nothing to induce or encourage it, the law allowed the seller to take advantage of the buyer's mistake of fact. "The passive acquiescence of the seller in the self-deception of the buyer," said Cockburn C.J., did not "entitle the latter to avoid the contract." The question was not "what a man of scrupulous morality or nice honour would do under such circumstances." *Caveat emptor*—let the buyer look out for himself.[8]

(iii) *The word "old" was not used but the seller knew that the buyer believed that the seller was contracting that the oats were old.* In that case, the verdict was right.

7 (1871) L.R. 6 Q.B. 597; S. & T. 124.
8 Though this principle is as firmly established in the law as any, there are difficulties in reconciling it with the decision of the Court of Appeal in *Solle v. Butcher*, below, p. 193, and its successors.

The difference from (ii) is that here the seller knows that the buyer is making a mistake, not merely of fact, but as to the terms of the contract. He cannot enforce the contract in a sense different from that which, as he knew at the time of contracting, the buyer intended. It was not necessary for the court to go further and the decision leaves open the question whether the seller fails because—as some have argued—the contract is void or because there is a contract for the sale of old oats which the seller cannot perform. It is submitted that the latter is the better view and that strongly persuasive authority for it is provided by *Roberts v. Leicestershire County Council.*[9]

The plaintiffs, building contractors, signed a contract in which they undertook to build a school in a period of 30 months. They had not read the contract and believed that the relevant period was 18 months, which would have been to their advantage. It was the period proposed in their original tender but had been changed during the negotiations. The officers of the Council knew that the plaintiffs were under this misapprehension as to the contents of the contract when the Council sealed the contract. Pennycuick J. held that the contract should be rectified by substituting 18 for 30 months. Now a court orders rectification of a written contract only when it is satisfied by "irrefragable evidence" that the written words do not represent the true contract between the parties. This was an 18-month contract because the defendants knew at the time of contracting that the plaintiffs believed it was an 18 month contract—just as (on hypothesis (iii), above) the seller in *Smith v. Hughes* knew that the buyer believed it was a contract for old oats.

OBJECTIVISM AND WRITTEN SIGNED CONTRACTS

"When a document containing contractual terms is signed, then, in the absence of fraud, or . . . misrepresentation, the party signing it is bound and it is wholly immaterial whether he has read the document or not." The law was thus stated by Scrutton L.J. in *L'Estrange v. Graucob.*[10] The party is bound although he does not really in his mind assent to the particular terms in the document, because he does not know what they are. Here again, it has been suggested that estoppel is the basis of the law—that the signer represents that he knows what is in the document and cannot now deny it because the other has acted in reliance on the representation. But this is clearly not so because the other party

9 [1961] Ch. 555; S. & T. 131.
10 [1934] 2 K.B. 394, CA; S. & T. 135.

may know very well that the signer has not read the document—that was so in *L'Estrange v. Graucob*, but the signer was bound by the unread document. It seems that the position is simply that the party who signs the document unread expresses his assent to the terms in it, whatever they may be.

If a person is induced to sign by fraud or misrepresentation, the contract is at least voidable—he may rescind it if he acts promptly.[11] If, however, before the contract is avoided a third person acquires rights under it for value and in good faith, the contract cannot be avoided for fraud or misrepresentation as against him. The party signing is bound unless he can show that the contract he signed was not merely voidable, but void—a nullity. In that case the third party could acquire no rights. A signed document might be held void under the doctrine of *non est factum*.

NON EST FACTUM

This doctrine applies where:

(i) A's signature has been procured by the fraud of B;
(ii) B's fraud was such as to lead A to believe that the contents of the document were fundamentally different from the fact; and
(iii) A was not guilty of negligence in so signing.

The doctrine originated in cases where illiterate or blind persons were induced to make deeds by fraud as to the nature of the document. The signer could plead *non est factum*—"it is not my deed"—against the innocent third party, because he never intended to sign any such deed. Where an elderly man was induced to sign a bill of exchange by a fraudulent representation that it was a guarantee, it was held that the plea was good against an innocent person who had given value for the bill relying on the signature, provided that the signer was not guilty of any negligence in so signing—which was then a question for the jury.[12] There the document signed was of a class entirely different from what it was represented to be; but it is now clear that the document need not be in a different class, provided that it is "fundamentally" or "radically" or "totally" different. So the doctrine might apply if B had told A that the document was a promissory note for £10 and it was a promissory note—but for £10,000.

11 Below, pp. 146–147.
12 *Foster v. MacKinnon* (1869) L.R. 4; C.P. 704.

The difference must be one which is material to the signer; *i.e.* he would certainly not have signed, had he known the truth. In the leading case of *Gallie v. Lee*[13] Mrs Gallie, an elderly widow who could not read because she had broken her spectacles, signed a document which she believed to be a deed of gift of her house to her nephew Parkin, to whom she was devoted, but which was in fact a deed of sale of the house to Lee for £3,000, the receipt of which she acknowledged in the deed but did not in fact receive. This certainly looks like a fundamental difference; but one must have regard to the "object of the exercise." The document was put before her by Lee in the presence of Parkin, and she knew that the transaction was intended to divest her of her interest in the house in pursuance of a joint project of Lee and Parkin to raise money on the security of it. The document in fact carried out the object she intended it to carry out. It was therefore not void. The case illustrates the reluctance of the courts to allow a person to avoid, as against an innocent purchaser, in that case, the building society which had advanced money in reliance on Mrs Gallie's signature on the deed, the effect of a document which she has in fact signed.

"Negligence" in this context means simply carelessness. Once again the notion of estoppel is sometimes invoked, but it is not a true estoppel though the careless person may be said to be "precluded" from denying that it is his deed. A business man who signs "blind" a pile of letters put before him by his trusted secretary for signature is perhaps not negligent and may be "exercising a wise economy of his time and energy;" but if the secretary has slipped in a guarantee of her overdraft, it seems that the signer will be liable to the bank which allows her to overdraw. He takes the chance of a fraudulent substitution.

The defence of *non est factum* is narrowly construed. There is a heavy onus on a person seeking to escape liability on a document that he has signed. If A grants a power of attorney to B, whom he knows or ought to know is incompetent, he cannot successfully plead *non est factum* when B, exercising the power of attorney, signs a document which she does not understand.[14]

OBJECTIVISM AND WRITTEN UNSIGNED CONTRACTS

The signature of a written contract is the means by which the parties declare their willingness to be bound by the written

13 [1971] A.C. 1004, HL; S. & T. 138.
14 *Norwich and Peterborough Building Society v. Steed (No. 2)* [1993] Ch. 116, CA; S. & T. 146.

terms. The parties may declare their willingness in other ways. Evidence that the parties agreed orally that the document should be the contract is just as effective as signature. Delivery by O to A of a paper containing the terms, or some of the terms, on which O is willing to contract has the same effect, if it is made quite clear to A that these are O's terms. A's acceptance concludes a contract on those terms. Does the rule in *L'Estrange v. Graucob* apply in its full rigour to these written but unsigned contracts? It appears from the *Interfoto* case[15] that the rule must be qualified. If the paper contains a particularly onerous or unusual term, that term will not be part of the contract unless A has taken some exceptional step to make clear that it is. For example, terms (i) and (iii), which are commonplace in contracts of that character, will be part of it; but term (ii), the onerous term, will not.

In *Interfoto* the plaintiffs had a library of photographic transparencies. The defendants inquired about photographs of the 1950's. The plaintiffs sent 47 transparencies with a delivery note which was plainly a contractual document containing the plaintiffs' terms of business. A contract was made, either when the defendants had the opportunity to read the terms or, at the latest, when they telephoned to say that some of the transparencies could be of interest and they would call back. But then the matter was overlooked and all the transparencies were retained for 28 days. The term in question provided that all transparencies must be returned within 14 days of delivery and that a holding fee of £5.00 plus VAT per day would be charged for each transparency retained beyond that time. Consequently, the defendants received a bill for £3,783.50 which they declined to pay. Applying authorities[16] which had previously been applied only to exclusion clauses, the Court of Appeal held that insufficient notice had been given of this particularly onerous term and that it was not binding on the defendants.

If the holding fee had been 5p instead of £5, the clause, though printed with no greater degree of prominence, would undoubtedly have been incorporated into the contract. If the reasonable recipient of the delivery note would have known of the existence of the 5p clause, it is hard to see why he would not also have known of the £5 clause. The court strained the device of reasonable notice to exclude what they judged to be an unfair term. But if this is right for unsigned documents, is it not also right for signed contracts? Suppose the plaintiffs had obtained the defendants' signature to the unread delivery note. Perhaps

---

15   *Interfoto Picture Library Ltd v. Stiletto Visual Programmes Ltd* [1988] 1 All E.R. 348, CA; S. & T. 156.
16   See below, pp. 162–166.

the next step is a modification of *L'Estrange v. Graucob*, holding that, even in a written and signed contract, the onerous clause is not incorporated unless printed in red or something of that sort.

THE OBJECTIVE MEANING OF THE CONTRACT

A contract will be enforced in its objective sense at the suit of either party unless there has been misrepresentation or there are grounds for rectification. And if a written contract is the contract they intended to write down, there are no grounds for rectification merely because they were both making a mistake. In *Rose v. Pim*[17] the written contract was for the sale of "horsebeans." The buyer had been asked by a third party for "feveroles" which are a different sort of bean. But the seller told the buyer that feveroles were just horsebeans and that he could supply them; so they entered into a contract for the sale of horsebeans. The buyer might have rescinded that agreement on the ground of misrepresentation[18] if he had acted promptly enough; but there were no grounds for rectification because the parties, though under a misapprehension, did in fact intend to buy and sell horsebeans. However, it is going too far to say, as Denning L.J. did, that one does not look into the "inner minds of the parties" in the formation of a contract. If the parties had been aware of the distinction between horsebeans and feveroles but had agreed to use "horsebeans" to mean "feveroles," evidence to that effect would surely have been admissible. The court is entitled to take account of the circumstances with reference to which the words were used and the object, appearing from those circumstances, which they had in view; but it may not look at the negotiations leading to the contract, such as earlier drafts which were rejected or amended.[19]

It is also said to be well-settled that it is not legitimate to use as an aid to construction of the contract anything the parties did or said after it was made. "Otherwise one might have the result that a contract meant one thing the day it was signed, but by reason of subsequent events meant something different a month or a year later."[20] This, however, is subject to the effect of estoppel.

---

17 *Rose (Frederick E.) (London) Ltd v. Pim (William H.) Jnr. & Co. Ltd* [1953] 2 Q.B. 450, CA; S. & T. 128.
18 Below, p. 146.
19 *Prenn v. Simmonds* [1971] 1 W.L.R. 1381.
20 *Miller (James) v. Whitworth Estates* [1970] 1 All E.R. 796 at 798, *per* Lord Reid.

Estoppel and the construction of the contract

Suppose that one of the parties, X, misunderstands the agreement and misleads the other, Y, as to its meaning. If Y acts to his detriment in reliance on that misinterpretation, X will be estopped from denying that this is the true construction of the contract. The meaning of the contract will have been effectively changed.[21] The law, however, goes further. Where there is no misrepresentation but the parties have mutually agreed that the contract bears a particular meaning (which is not the true, objective meaning), and they act on that assumption, both will be estopped from denying that it has the meaning assumed. This is known as "estoppel by convention".[22] But, while the doctrine applies to mistaken interpretation of a contract, it cannot operate so as to defeat a rule of law. Where the parties to an agreement for a lease intended it to have retrospective effect, the landlord could not be estopped from denying that it had that effect. It is a rule of law that a grant of land cannot take effect retrospectively.[23]

---

21 *Sarat Chunder Dey v. Gopal Chunder Lala* (1892) 19 Ind.App. 203, P.C., and *Calgary Milling Co. Ltd v. American Surety Co. of New York* [1919] 3 W.W.R. 98, PC, both relied on by Robert Goff J. in *Amalgamated Investment, etc. v. Texas Commerce* [1981] 1 All E.R. 923, affirmed [1982] Q.B. 84, CA; S. & T. 266.
22 See the *Amalgamated Investment* case, above.
23 *Keen v. Holland* [1984] 1 W.L.R. 251, CA.

CHAPTER THREE

The Formation of Unilateral Contracts

O makes an offer of a unilateral contract to A when he promises A that he will do something (or that something is so) *if* A will do a specified act, other than the making of a promise to O. A may then accept the offer by doing that act. O promises A £100 if A will walk to York. The promise becomes binding only when A reaches York. If A falls in a faint five yards from the city boundary and completes the journey in an ambulance, he is entitled to nothing. Nor has A committed a breach of contract. He did not promise to do anything. He was entirely free not to start on the walk or to abandon it any time.

Whether an offer is an offer of a unilateral or of a bilateral contract is a question of the construction of the offer. Would a reasonable person think he was being asked to promise to do the act or simply to go ahead and do it? If the latter, A cannot turn the offer into a bilateral contract by promising to do the act. A's promise would be irrelevant.[1] It would not be an acceptance. It is for O, and him alone, to prescribe the mode of acceptance; and he has prescribed the doing of an act.

The classic case on unilateral contracts is *Carlill v. Carbolic Smoke Ball Company*.[2] The Company advertised that they would pay £100 "reward" to any one who caught influenza after having used the smoke ball three times daily for two weeks, according to

---

1 Although Lord Simon has described such a case as a second "type" of unilateral contract; S. & T. 301–304.
2 [1893] 1 QB 256, CA; S. & T. 35.

the printed directions supplied with each ball. Mrs Carlill used the ball as prescribed and then caught influenza. It was held by the Court of Appeal that she was entitled to the reward. The act requested, and therefore the consideration supplied by her, was the use of the ball for two weeks. As soon as she had completed that act she had a contract with the company which continued to exist at least as long as she persisted in using the ball three times daily. Of course, the company was not obliged to do anything until she caught 'flu; but catching 'flu was a condition of their liability, not part of the consideration—clearly, it was not something which the company asked people to do. It was rather like a contract of insurance. The "premium" was using the smoke ball three times daily for two weeks. Catching 'flu—far from being something that the offeree was asked to do—was "the accident," on which compensation was payable. The terms of the offer made it clear that it was the use of the smoke ball, not the purchase of it, which was the consideration. It made no difference whether Mrs Carlill had bought the ball or been given it as a present, or had borrowed it. Of course, it was the sales that the company was interested in but balls could not be used unless they were first bought by someone.

The traditional examples of unilateral contracts are of a trivial domestic nature—walking to York, using the smoke ball, digging gardens, etc.—but the concept plays a large and useful part in commercial transactions. If a shipper of goods says to a firm of stevedores, "If you will load my goods on to the ship, I promise you that your liability shall be limited to £500," and, in consequence, the stevedores do load the goods on the ship, it is clear that there is a unilateral contract and that the stevedores' liability is accordingly limited.

Where A knows of the offer and does the act requested he has a contract although his motive in doing the act may have been something quite different from obtaining the consideration offered by O. In *Williams v. Carwardine*[3] a woman, who (it was assumed) knew of the existence of an offer of a reward for information leading to the conviction of a murderer but who gave that information, not to get the reward, but only because she thought she was going to die and to ease her conscience, was entitled to the reward. Mrs Carlill would have been no less entitled to the reward if it had appeared that her sole reason for using the ball was to avoid catching 'flu.

Where, however, A does the act in ignorance of the offer, it seems that there is no contract. In an Australian case[4] it was held

<hr/>

3 (1833) 5 C. & P. 566; S. & T. 41.
4 *R. v. Clarke* (1927) 40 C.L.R. 227; S. & T. 41.

that, where A had once known of the offer but had forgotten its existence when he did the act requested, there was no contract. A contract, it was said, could not be made in ignorance of the offer; and forgetting about it was the same as never hearing of it. Where an offer is made to the whole world it is arguable on grounds of public policy that anyone who does the act requested, whether he has heard of the offer or not, should be entitled to recover. The argument may be made in relation to the offers of rewards for information leading to the apprehension of criminals. The public-spirited citizen who gives the information as soon as it comes to his attention may be at a disadvantage compared to the selfish person who waits to see if a reward has been offered. But the argument is not convincing. The offeror should only have a liability imposed on him if he can properly be said to have undertaken it; and he will usually have made the offer, not out of a desire to reward the worthy citizen, but in order to induce him to do something. The law treats the person who knows of the offer as an acceptor even though he is not in fact induced because his motive is something else, but it would seem wrong to go further.

When must the offeree know of the offer? *Gibbons v. Proctor*[5] suggests that it is sufficient that he knows at the moment before the act of acceptance is complete. A reward had been offered by O for information. A, a policeman, being unaware of the offer, gave the information to a fellow-officer, B, who gave it to a superior, C, who gave it to O. When C gave the information to O, A knew of the offer. That was enough. It would follow that if A posted a letter to O containing information, being unaware that O had offered a reward for that information, A would be entitled if he learned of the offer before the letter arrived. Similarly, if Mrs Carlill had learned of the offer only when she had used the ball three times daily for 13 days—the contract would have been complete on the fourteenth day. Indeed, it would presumably have been enough that she should have learned of it after the fourteenth day but before she caught 'flu, provided she was continuing to use it in accordance with the directions.

REVOCATION OF THE OFFER OF A UNILATERAL CONTRACT

It is clear that O's offer becomes a binding contract only when A completely performs the act requested. It appears at first sight then that O may revoke his offer at any moment before the act is complete. Clearly, A may abandon performance at any time and

5 (1891) 55 J.P. 616.

so it has been argued that O should be equally free to call the whole thing off. This may, however, seem very unfair where A has expended time, money and effort in reliance on the promise. Does the law really allow O to drive by in his Rolls Royce, as A toils along the last hundred yards into York, and call out, "Offer revoked"? Could the Smoke Ball company really have revoked their offer when Carlill was embarking on the fourteenth day of sniffing?

A preliminary point may be disposed of. If A has conferred a benefit on O before O revokes, then A may recover the value of that benefit in a quasi-contractual action of *quantum meruit*. So, if the request was to dig the whole of O's garden and O, without justification, told A to get out when the job was nearly done, A would be entitled to the value to O of the service rendered—which might be more or less than the reward offered. But this would be of no help in the walking to York or the Smoke Ball case because no discernible economic benefit has been conferred on the offeror.

The most common, and most attractive, solution that has been proposed is to hold, where appropriate, that there is a second, implied, promise by O that, if A embarks on performance, O will not revoke the offer. When O says to A, "I will pay you £100 if you walk to York," he is making two promises—(i) the express promise to pay £100 when the walk is complete and not before and (ii) an implied "collateral" promise not to revoke his offer if A sets out on the walk. By making a start, A accepts the second offer. He supplies consideration for the implied promise by starting to walk. If O then "revokes" his offer to pay £100 while A is on his way, A can probably treat the revocation as inoperative[6] and proceed to earn the £100 or at least recover damages for the loss of the opportunity to earn that sum.

The courts will, however, imply a promise only when it is necessary to do so to give "business efficacy" to the transaction—*i.e.* to make it work—or because the parties, as reasonable men, *must* have intended such a promise—it was something that went without saying. In the examples discussed above, such a promise might well be implied—what reasonable person would expect to embark, or expect another to embark, on some arduous endeavour to earn a reward on the basis that the offeror could, at a whim, call the whole thing off? But this is not necessarily always so in the case of offers of unilateral contracts. In *Luxor (Eastbourne) Ltd v. Cooper*[7] O offered A £10,000 if A introduced a party who should buy O's two cinemas. A introduced X who

6 *Mountford v. Scott* [1975] 2 W.L.R. 114, CA; S. & T. 80.
7 [1941] A.C. 108; S. & T. 47.

agreed, subject to contract, to buy, and remained throughout ready and willing to buy, the cinemas. O declined to proceed with the sale. The consideration for O's promise was supplied when A introduced X. So it follows that the contract between O and A was made then. The sale of the cinemas was a condition (like the catching of 'flu in *Carlill*), an event, outside the control of A. O prevented the event from happening. A's action for the commission failed because the commission was payable only on the completion of the sale which never occurred. A's action for breach of an alleged implied promise by O to do nothing to prevent the completion of the sale also failed. The House of Lords held that there was no room for the implication of such a promise. It was not necessary to imply such a promise to give business efficacy to the contract—A was taking a risk in the hope of substantial remuneration (the equivalent, the House observed, of the Lord Chancellor's salary for a year) for a comparatively small exertion (eight or nine days' work). The prospective bargain was a very reasonable one without the implication of any such term. Many a reasonable man would have been glad to take the chance. It was quite otherwise in *Errington v. Errington*.[8] A father bought a house in his own name for his son and daughter-in-law to live in. He paid part of the price in cash and borrowed the rest from a building society. He left the couple to pay the instalments and told them that the house would be theirs when all the instalments were paid. Denning L.J. treated this as an offer of a unilateral contract—"If you will pay off the instalments, I will convey the house to you." The couple were not bound to pay the instalments but, if they did, they would be entitled to the house. However, before that was done, the father died and the widow claimed possession. The Court of Appeal dismissed her action, Denning L.J. on the ground that there was an implied promise by the father not to revoke his offer once the couple entered on performance, so that they were entitled to remain in possession. The widow, as personal representative, could be in no better position. An arrangement which would have allowed the father to turn the couple out when they had paid almost all the instalments on his house was (it may be thought) one which no reasonable couple would expect, or be expected, to agree to.

If this is the right approach, there is no universal rule as to the revocability of offers of unilateral contracts. Everything depends on the circumstances of the particular case. This has the disadvantage of uncertainty but the corresponding advantage of flexibility. It enables the court to reach a just solution when a

8 [1952] 1 K.B. 290; S. & T. 45.

rigid rule—either that such offers are always revocable or that they are always irrevocable—would not do so.

COMMUNICATING ACCEPTANCE OF OFFERS OF UNILATERAL CONTRACTS

Whether communication of an acceptance is required depends on the terms of the offer. Communication is for the benefit of the offeror so he can dispense with it if he wishes. In the case of many offers of unilateral contracts, it is obvious from the nature of the offer that communication is not required. No reader of the Smoke Ball company's advertisement would have supposed that he was expected to write and advise the company that he was using the ball and accepting their offer of a reward in the event of his catching 'flu. The same will be generally true of offers made to the public—though in the case of offers of rewards for information, the act of acceptance is obviously the communication of the information—not necessarily to the offeror. Communication to the police, for example, might be the acceptance. The test must be, as always, how would the reasonable reader of the offer understand it?

CHAPTER FOUR

Formation of Bilateral Contracts

Since bilateral contracts consist in an exchange of promises, there must be a strong presumption that communication of an acceptance is required. O makes promises to A in return for promises to himself which he requests from A. Clearly this normally requires A to communicate to O his willingness to promise. To decide to accept an offer is not the same thing as to accept it. If a committee resolves to accept the offer of a candidate for employment, that resolution will not make a contract. It will have to be communicated, and intentionally communicated. If the candidate happened to be listening at the door and overhear the committee's resolution to appoint him, he could not successfully claim to have a contract. If the decision were communicated to him by an unauthorised person he would be no better off[1]—unless that person had "ostensible authority"—that is, he was a person whom A had led O to believe to have authority to speak on A's behalf.

Even in the case of bilateral contracts, however, the principle that the offeror can, if he chooses, dispense with communication, applies. The offeror can prescribe the mode of acceptance and, if he chooses to prescribe something other than communication, then he is bound by that and there is a contract when that other thing is done.

It is clear that O cannot force a contract on A by writing, "If I do not hear from you within X days I will assume you have

---

1 *Powell v. Lee* (1908) 99 L.T. 284; S. & T. 48.

agreed to my terms." A may, with impunity, put such a letter in the waste-paper basket and ignore it. It would be the same if O said that he would assume that A agreed if A did some commonplace act—like going to his usual place of work on Monday morning. O cannot restrict A's liberty to do such an act except at the price of finding himself bound by a contract. What, however, if A takes O at his word and, with the intention of accepting the offer, remains silent or does the commonplace act as the case may be? If A later seeks to enforce the contract, O's defence must be, "But you did not communicate your acceptance to me." A may then, surely, fairly reply, "But that was because you told me I need not communicate." The famous case of *Felthouse v. Bindley*[2] affords some authority against this view. An uncle wrote to his nephew, saying that there had been a misunderstanding as to the price at which he was to buy the nephew's horse. He had thought it was £30, the nephew that it was 30 guineas. Uncle offered to split the difference, writing, "if I hear no more about him, I consider the horse mine at £30 15s." Nephew decided to accept this offer. He did not communicate with uncle but directed the auctioneer, who was to sell his farming stock, to keep this horse out of the sale, "as it had already been sold." The auctioneer, by mistake, put up the horse with the rest of the stock and sold it. The uncle sued the auctioneer in conversion, alleging that it was his horse that the auctioneer had wrongly sold. The action in the Court of Common Pleas failed for two reasons. (i) There was no contract for the sale of the horse to the uncle because the nephew had not communicated his acceptance. (ii) Even if there were such a contract, it was not enforceable on the day of the auction because it was a contract for the sale of goods of the price of more than £10 and, on that day, there was not in existence a written memorandum of the contract as required by the Statute of Frauds 1677.[3] The Court of Exchequer Chamber affirmed the judgment of the Common Pleas, but on the second ground. The Statute of Frauds had not been complied with and, for that reason, the ownership in the horse had not vested in the plaintiff. That particular provision of the Statute of Frauds was re-enacted in the Sale of Goods Act 1893 but was repealed by the Law Reform (Enforcement of Contracts) Act 1954. If the case came before the courts today, it would be necessary to decide whether the first ground given by the Common Pleas was right or wrong. It is submitted that it was wrong. If the horse had died after the nephew had directed the auctioneer to keep it out of the sale, and

2   (1862) 11 C.B. (N.S.) 869, *affirmed*, 7 L.T. 835; S. & T. 50.
3   See below, p. 243.

before that sale, surely the uncle could not have resisted his nephew's claim for the price on the ground that nephew had never communicated his acceptance to him. The uncle had dispensed with his right to have acceptance communicated to him. In that case it was clear that the nephew intended to accept because of his direction to the auctioneer. It would be more difficult where A simply did nothing. If A denied that he intended to accept, it would probably be impossible to challenge that denial effectively. If A asserted that he intended to accept, O would be in equal difficulty. It might be replied that the difficulties are all of his own making. It should, however, be noted that in a case[4] where a written offer provided that it should become binding only upon its being signed by A, Lord Denning said that there was no contract until A signed the document *and* notified the offeror. Otherwise, "[A] would be able to keep the form in the office unsigned, and then play fast and loose as [A] pleased. [O] would not know whether or not there was a contract binding them . . . " The other judges did not find it necessary to express an opinion on this point. Where the offer is ambiguous, these considerations should weigh in deciding whether it really does dispense A from the need to communicate; but, if O's expressed intention is clear, should he not have to live with the consequences?

Similarly, "Where the *offeree* himself indicates that an offer is to be taken as accepted if he does not indicate to the contrary by an ascertainable time, he is undertaking to speak if he does not want a contract to be concluded," said Peter Gibson L.J., *obiter*, in *Re Selectmove*,[5] adding that there was no reason in principle why in such a case the offeree's silence should not be an acceptance. It seems, however, that in the case envisaged, the offeree might be taken by his "indication" to have accepted the offer conditionally on his not speaking before the end of the ascertained time.

O may dispense with communication impliedly as well as expressly. It appears that, in the case of motor car insurance, the provision of a temporary cover note is an offer to insure for the future. Though the point has not been decided, it seems that the offer can be accepted by conduct without communication. The insurance company expects the driver to take his car on the road in reliance on the note, without communication. By doing so he impliedly agrees to pay the premium, at least for the period of the note. If there is no such contract, many people must have been trapped by the cover note into committing a serious offence by driving in reliance on it. If the driver does not intend to renew

---

4 *Robophone Facilities Ltd v. Blank* [1966] 1 W.L.R. 1428 at 1432, CA.
5 [1995] 2 All E.R. 531 at 535–536, CA; S. & T. 53 and 240. [Author's italics.]

his insurance with that company and is not acting in reliance on the note, then he has no contract with that company.[6] This is another of those instances where the court would have to attempt to look into A's mind and determine his actual intention at the time he used the vehicle.

CONTRACTS MADE THROUGH THE POST

Where the parties are in each other's presence, it is usually easy to infer that at a particular moment they are in agreement in the same terms on the same subject matter. Where they have negotiated through the post, this is not so. There must be a substantial interval between any expression of willingness to be bound by one party and the concurrence of the other. The former may have changed his mind before the latter expresses his concurrence. To meet his difficulty the courts in the nineteenth century developed a rule ("the rule in *Adams v. Lindsell*"[7]) that acceptance is complete, and the contract is made, when A posts the letter of acceptance. The rule was carried to its logical conclusion in a case[8] which decided that the contract is good even though the letter of acceptance is lost in the post and never arrives. The courts justified this decision on the theoretical basis that the post office was O's agent to receive the acceptance. This is obviously a fiction. A pillar box is no more an agent than a hollow tree. And the post office's duty is simply to transmit the letter unread. The rule is in fact simply one of business convenience. The law might equally have hit upon the moment of delivery of the acceptance as the moment of the formation of contract, but it would have been necessary to decide whether that moment was when the letter was delivered to the premises or when it was—or, perhaps, ought in the normal course to have been—read. The moment of the posting of the acceptance has the advantage of being precise and relatively easy to prove and of being the earliest moment at which it is possible to hold that a contract is in existence, thus making for expedition in business transactions.

It is important to note the narrow limits of the rule. It is strictly confined to the acceptance of offers. It has no application to the making of, or revocation of, offers, or any other element in negotiations for a contract. This demonstrates the fictional nature of the agency theory. The post office is not deemed an agent to

---

6 As in *Taylor v. Allon* [1966] 1 QB 304; S. & T. 51.
7 The rule is conveniently described thus as *Adams v. Lindsell* is the case in which it first appeared; (1818) 1 B. & Ald. 681.
8 *Household Fire Insurance Co. v. Grant* (1879) 4 Ex.D. 216, CA; S. & T. 53.

receive any of these other communications. So most of the hypothetical cases put by Bramwell L.J. in his dissent in *Household Fire Insurance Co. v. Grant* to demonstrate the absurdity of the rule laid down by the majority, are not in point.[9]

If I write to my landlord, offering to sell him some hay and he replies accepting my offer and in the same letter (ungratefully!) gives me notice to quit, the contract of sale is concluded when the letter is posted but the notice to quit is not valid unless and until it arrives. Modern judges have fallen into the same trap as Bramwell L.J. in their attempts to ridicule the rule. "Is a stockbroker who is holding shares to the order of his client liable in damages because he did not sell in a falling market in accordance with the instructions in a letter which was posted but never received."[10] Of course he is not liable. The client's letter is not a letter accepting an offer of a contract. The rule in *Adams v. Lindsell* has no application.

The operation of the rule can always be excluded by O if he wishes. If he indicates, expressly or impliedly, that acceptance must actually be communicated, then the contract is not complete on posting but only when the acceptance arrives. Where an option to purchase freehold property (which is an offer) provided that it was exercisable (*i.e.* could be accepted) "by notice in writing to [O]," it was held that the phrase, "notice . . . to" required actual communication.[11] It was not necessary to decide whether the contract was made when the letter came through O's letter box or when he read, or when he ought, in the normal course, to have read it. The case reveals some judicial unhappiness with the rule in *Adams v. Lindsell* and the opinion that "it probably does not operate if its application would produce manifest inconvenience and absurdity." The courts may therefore be more easily persuaded that the circumstances of the case are such that A, as a reasonable man, would have known that O did not intend the rule to apply. General principle would suggest that the test ought to be, "Would the reasonable man who received the offer realise that the offeror required actual communication?" This approach is, however, difficult to apply in this context because, unlike most of the principles governing the formation of contract, we are here dealing with an arbitrary and artificial rule which the ordinary person who has never studied law is probably unaware of.

The application of the rule in *Adams v. Lindsell* is not confined

---

9 See S. & T. 55–56.
10 *Holwell Securities Ltd v. Hughes* [1974] 1 W.L.R. 155; S. & T. 57 at 60, *per* Lawton L.J.
11 *ibid.*

to the case where the offer is made through the post. It has been said that it applies "Where the circumstances are such that it must have been within the contemplation of the parties that, according to the ordinary usages of mankind, the post might be used as the means of communicating the acceptance of an offer ...",[12] so the rule was held to apply when A, who lived in Birkenhead was handed the offer in O's office in Liverpool and took it away with him. A contract was made when the acceptance was posted in Birkenhead. O must have contemplated that A might send his acceptance by post. The above dictum was uttered when there was probably more enthusiasm for the rule in *Adams v. Lindsell* than today. Possibly the rule would now be less readily applied in similar circumstances.

As noticed at the outset, the reason for the rule in *Adams v. Lindsell* was the substantial delay which necessarily occurs in expressions of intention through the post. There is no reason to apply the rule to instantaneous communications and it has been decided that it does not apply. In the case of communications through telex or fax or e-mail which are, and are intended to be, virtually instantaneous, the general rule that acceptance must be communicated applies. So when O in London made an offer by telex to A in Holland and A's acceptance was received on O's telex machine in London, the contract was held to be made in London, because it was made when and where the acceptance was received.[13] When A posts a letter, he is adopting a means of communication which does not usually fail but he has no means of knowing whether the letter will arrive or, later, whether it has arrived; but when A sends a telex or fax or e-mail message to O during O's business hours, he will usually receive an immediate acknowledgment and, if he does not, he will know there is something wrong. He cannot reasonably act on the assumption that his acceptance has arrived or (unlike the postal acceptor) will arrive. He must get through again. So there will be no contract unless and until the acceptance is actually received. The only exception would be where O leads A to suppose that the acceptance has been received when it has not. O would then be estopped from denying that there was a contract.

This is the position when the communication is, and is intended to be, instantaneous. But a telex, fax or e-mail communication may be neither instantaneous nor intended to be so. It may be sent or received through third parties. Lord Wilberforce has said,[14] "No universal rule can cover all such

---

12 *Henthorn v. Fraser* [1892] 2 Ch. 27 at 33, *per* Lord Herschell.
13 *Entores Ltd v. Miles Far East Corporation* [1955] 2 Q.B. 327, CA; S. & T. 63.
14 *Brinkibon Ltd v. Stahag Stahl* [1983] 2 A.C. 34 at 42; S. & T. 66.

cases; they must be resolved by reference to the intentions of the parties, by sound business practice and in some cases by a judgment where the risks should lie." If then, A sends an acceptance to O at an hour when he knows O's office is closed and that the message will not be read for some hours, the position is not settled. It is similar in some respects to the case where the letter of acceptance is posted.

The rule in *Adams v. Lindsell* has no application to the revocation of an offer. If O has made an offer to A through the post and he wishes to revoke it, he must actually communicate his revocation to A. This was settled in the case of *Byrne v. Van Tienhoven*[15] where Lindley J. held that the principle that the post office is an agent did not apply to the withdrawal of an offer. As the rule in *Adams v. Lindsell* was by then well-settled, it would have made no practical sense to hold that a revocation was effective on posting. One of the virtues of the *Adams v. Lindsell* rule is that A, once he has posted his letter, can act in absolute confidence that he has made a binding contract. But if a revocation were effective on posting, he could never know whether or not there was a revocation in the post. He would not know how he stood, nor would O because, when he posted his revocation he could not know whether or not an acceptance had already been posted. As it is, A, at least, can act, confident of his position, though O cannot.

PARTIES BECOME BOUND WHEN THEY INTEND TO DO SO

O may lay down his own rules as to how his offer may be accepted. If he chooses to stipulate some eccentric act as the only manner in which his offer may be accepted—place your letter of acceptance in the hollow tree before midnight—that is effective. If he stipulates that acceptance must be by notice in writing to himself, O, notice to his solicitor is ineffective.[16] However, unless O makes it quite clear that only the specified method of acceptance will do, the court is likely to interpret the offer to mean that any other method of acceptance which is no less advantageous to him will conclude the contract. Presumably, once again, the test should be, how would a reasonable person interpret the offer?

" . . . parties become bound by contract when, and in the manner in which, they intend and contemplate becoming

15 (1880) 5 C.P.D. 344; S. & T. 62.
16 *Holwell Securities Ltd v. Hughes*, above, p. 33.

bound."[17] This is a fundamental principle. We have noticed that the offeror may dictate the terms on which he is prepared to be bound but, if both parties have proceeded on the basis that the contract shall be concluded in a particular time and manner, then the contract can be made only at that time and in that manner. In *Eccles v. Bryant* the court was concerned with a contract for the sale of land which was being negotiated by their solicitors. There is a well established practice among solicitors that contracts for the sale of land become binding only when the two copies of the contract, signed by the vendor and by the purchaser respectively, are exchanged. Though each party to the contract has signed a contractual document in identical terms, the contract is not concluded until the two documents are exchanged—because the parties, through their solicitors, do not intend it to be binding until then. In *Eccles v. Bryant* both parties had signed the contract, the purchaser had posted his part and it had been received, but the vendor declined to deliver his part and repudiated the agreement. There was no contract. The earliest time at which a contract could come into existence, thought Lord Greene, is when the later of the two documents is actually put into the post. This is the rule in the Law Society's *Conditions of Sale*, 2.1.1 (1995) in accordance with which solicitors commonly act.

It follows from the broad principle stated in *Eccles v. Bryant* that the exchange rule does not apply if the conduct of the parties indicates that they do not intend it to apply. In *Storer v. Manchester City Council*[18] the Council wrote to the plaintiff, a council house tenant, "I understand you wish to purchase your council house and enclose the Agreement for Sale. If you will sign the agreement and return it to me I will send the agreement signed on behalf of [the Council] in exchange." The plaintiff signed and sent back the agreement but, before the town clerk returned it, Labour gained control of the Council which then declined to proceed. It was held that there was a specifically enforceable contract. The Council had made a firm offer to sell which the plaintiff had accepted by signing and returning the agreement as requested. It was immaterial that the town clerk did not intend to be bound, except on exchange. He had not evinced that intention. On the contrary, he had expressed a willingness to be bound before exchange.

The exchange principle is a valuable one because it ensures that neither party is bound until he has a document of title in his hands; but it has caused particular difficulties where, as is common, there is a chain of contracts for the sale and purchase of

---

17 Lord Greene M.R. in *Eccles v. Bryant* [1948] Ch. 93; S. & T. 70 at 71–72.
18 [1974] 1 W.L.R. 1403.

houses. For example, X and Y have agreed, subject to contract, on the sale of Y's house to X; but X cannot afford to bind himself to buy until he has a contract for the sale of his own house to W; and Y may be unwilling to bind himself to sell the house to X until he has secured a firm contract with Z to buy Z's house. The chain of contracts contemplated may be represented as follows:

$$W \longleftrightarrow X \longleftrightarrow Y \longleftrightarrow Z$$

If the procedure envisaged in *Eccles v. Bryant* is followed and each contract is concluded only when an exchange through the post is complete, there is a grave risk that X may find that he has committed himself to buy but that W has changed his mind so that X has two houses on his hands. And Y may find that he has committed himself to sell to X, but Z has changed his mind, so Y is left without a house at all. The risks are inevitable because of the delay involved in the process of exchange. If the solicitors of all four parties could meet together and exchange the signed parts of the contracts virtually simultaneously, all risk could be eliminated; but it will usually be impracticable for them to meet. A solution has been found in a system of "exchange" by telephone. If all the contracts have been signed and all the parties are ready to proceed, W's solicitor may agree to hold the contract signed by W to the order of X's solicitor who in turn will agree to hold X's signed contract to sell to W to the order of W's solicitor. X's solicitor will also agree to hold X's signed contract to buy from Y to the order of Y's solicitor—and so on down the chain. Some of the contracts may have been physically delivered in advance and held to the order of the delivering solicitor until the time agreed for the "constructive" (or notional) transfer. But it seems that there need be no physical delivery at all. In the leading case of *Domb v. Isoz*[19] Buckley L.J. said: "Exchange of a written contract for sale is in my judgment effected so soon as each part of the contract signed by the vendor or the purchaser as the case may be, is in the actual or constructive possession of the other party or of his solicitor." When W's solicitor agreed to hold the contract signed by W to the order of X's solicitor, that document, though physically held by W's solicitor, was in the "constructive" possession of X's solicitor. This, in Buckley L.J.'s words,[20] satisfies "the essential characteristic of exchange of contracts"—that "each party shall have a document signed by

19 [1980] Ch. 548 at 557; S. & T. 72.
20 *ibid.* at 557; S. & T. 72.

the other party in his possession or control so that, at his own need, he can have the document available for his own use." The assumption is that a client is no worse off when a document is held on his behalf by someone else's solicitor than when it is held by his own solicitor. The system assumes the integrity of solicitors. When a solicitor is instructed by a vendor or purchaser, he has, in the absence of instructions to the contrary, authority to carry the transaction through in accordance with the custom and practice of the profession, including the procedure of exchange and now the procedure of exchange by telephone. The Law Society's Conditions of Sale, 2.1.2 (1995), provide:

> "If the parties' solicitors agree to treat exchange as taking place before duplicate copies are actually exchanged, the contract is made as so agreed."

THE DURATION OF AN OFFER

An offer continues in existence for so long as the offeror intends it to continue. If he states, "This offer is to remain open until noon on April 1," it remains open until that moment and then ceases to exist. It may be that the offeror specifies no time for the termination of the offer but it is highly improbable that he intended it to last for ever and the reasonable person would not suppose that he did. The offer therefore comes to an end after the lapse of a reasonable time. The most obvious explanation for this is that there is an implied term to that effect in the offer—any reasonable observer would assume that this is what the offeror in fact intended, though he did not trouble to say so. But in one case Buckley J. suggested a different explanation—that the failure to accept within a reasonable time amounts to an implied rejection which equally brings the offer to an end.[21] The practical difference was thought to be that the implied term theory involves an inquiry into what the parties as reasonable men would have thought to be a reasonable time *when the offer was made*; whereas the implied rejection theory required the court to take into account events occurring after the offer was made, enabling it to make an objective assessment of the facts and to decide whether, in fairness to both parties, the offeree should be regarded as having refused the offer. As Buckley J. wanted to take into account events occurring after the offer was made, he preferred the latter theory.

21 *Manchester Diocesan Council for Education v. Commercial and General Investments Ltd* [1970] 1 W.L.R. 241; S. & T. 68 and 85.

REJECTION AND COUNTER-OFFER

An offer comes to an end when the offeree rejects it. This is because, on receipt of the rejection, the offeror will naturally regard himself as free to make inconsistent offers to others, free from the liability to become bound to the first offeree; and the offeree, as a reasonable person, must know this. A counter-offer has the same effect as a rejection. O offers to sell A his farm for £1,000. A replies, offering to buy the farm for £950. O refuses this counter-offer. A then "accepts" the offer to sell for £1,000. He is too late. That offer terminated when O received the counter-offer.[22] Again, the reason would appear to be that, on receipt of the counter-offer, O was entitled to suppose that A was not interested in the offer to sell for £1,000 and to regard himself as free to offer the property elsewhere. Whether he in fact offers it elsewhere is immaterial.

It is necessary to distinguish between a counter-offer and a mere inquiry. An inquiry is not an offer and therefore not a counter-offer and it leaves the offer standing. So where O offered to sell A some iron for 40s, specifying no time for delivery, and A replied "Please wire whether you would accept 40 for delivery over two months, or if not, longest time you would give," it was held that this left the offer intact and a subsequent acceptance of it was valid.[23] It will be noted that A was not offering to buy at 40s for delivery over two months and that his message did not contradict any express term in the offer.

It follows logically from these principles that all the terms of the contract must be contained, expressly or impliedly, in the offer. An acceptance which purports to add something to the terms is, by definition, a counter-offer and does not create a contract unless and until it is accepted. Attention should, however, be drawn to "The Uniform Law on the Formation of Contracts for the International Sale of Goods" in Schedule 2 to the Uniform Laws on International Sales Act 1967. This provides (para. 2) that—

" . . . a reply to an offer which purports to be an acceptance but which contains additional or different terms which do not materially alter the terms of the offer shall constitute an acceptance unless the offeror promptly objects to the discrepancy; if he does not so object, the terms of the contract shall be the terms of the offer with the modifications contained in the acceptance."

22 *Hyde v. Wrench* (1840) 3 Beav. 334, S. & T. 75.
23 *Stevenson v. McLean* (1880) 5 Q.B.D. 346; S. & T. 78.

While this is the law of England where the parties choose the Uniform Law of Sales as the law of the contract, it does not necessarily follow that it is the law for any other type of contract governed by English law. When O has made an offer on particular terms, he should not have different or additional terms forced upon him. It is for him, not for the court, to say whether any modification is "material" or not. To impose on O the obligation promptly to object if he does not wish to be bound seems to be contrary to the principle of *Felthouse v. Bindley*.[24] If, however, O proceeds to act on the proposed contract after receiving A's modified acceptance, then he might properly be held to have agreed to the modification proposed; that would simply be an acceptance by conduct of A's counter-offer.

This problem is of practical importance in what has become known as "the battle of the forms." Two businesses have standard forms of agreement but in different terms and each is anxious that the proposed contract shall be governed by his conditions and not the other side's. X makes an offer on his form. Y replies purporting to accept, but on his form. Clearly X cannot preclude Y from offering different terms by including in his offer a statement that his terms are to prevail over any terms in Y's reply.

If Y does reply, offering different terms and X accepts— expressly or by conduct—the contract is made on Y's terms. In the leading case, *Butler Machine Tool Co. Ltd v. Ex-Cell-O Corporation (England) Ltd*,[25] X signed and returned a tear-off slip on Y's form, "We accept your order on the terms and conditions stated thereon" and, though they added, referring back to their own form, "Your official order . . . is being entered in accordance with our revised quotation on 23rd May," the return of the slip made it clear that the contract was made on Y's terms. Lord Denning said he thought that "In many of these cases our traditional analysis of offer, counter-offer, rejection, acceptance and so forth is out-of-date," but the majority thought it was the right way to proceed and, indeed, Lord Denning himself appears to have applied it.

REVOCATION OF OFFERS

A promise to keep an offer open for a specified period, like promises in English law generally, is enforceable only if it is in a deed or given for consideration. If O offers to sell property to A and says that he will keep the offer open for six weeks, he may,

---

24 Above, p. 30.
25 [1979] 1 W.L.R. 401; S. & T. 75.

at any time within the six weeks, revoke the offer by giving notice to A.[26] The rationale is that A is not bound in any way, so why should O be bound? The rule has been criticised and may give rise to injustice where A acts in reliance on the offer, for example by entering into other contracts on the assumption that he can call on O to perform the contract he has offered to make.

If O accepts consideration from A in return for a promise to keep the offer open, A has an effective remedy. In *Mountford v. Scott*[27] O, in consideration of the payment of £1, granted in writing an option to A to purchase O's house for £10,000, exercisable within six months. Within the six months and before the option was exercised, O purported to withdraw his offer. A then exercised the option. The Court of Appeal held that A was entitled to specific performance of a contract for the sale of the house. Though the court held that the trial judge had wrongly concentrated on the question whether the option agreement was specifically enforceable, the decision seems, in effect, to be that the option agreement *was* specifically enforceable. The offer continued in existence notwithstanding O's purported revocation of it. A was not restricted to damages for breach of the option agreement.

Where the offer is made to a particular person or persons it can be revoked by communicating with that person or persons but where it is made to the public, communication with everyone is impracticable. The question of the revocation of such an offer does not seem to have arisen in England. In the United States, the solution is that the offer may be revoked by giving the same notoriety to the revocation as was given to the offer.[28] If that is done the offer is revoked. It is immaterial that A, who thereafter purports to accept, was unaware of the revocation. On the assumption that it ought to be possible for a person who has made an offer to the public to be able to revoke it, this seems to be the only practicable solution. It is not free from difficulty. If the offer has been made by a full page advertisement in *The Times*, it can be revoked by a full page advertisement in *The Times*, but when is it revoked? Perhaps the answer is, when ordinary readers of *The Times* might reasonably have been expected to see it—which would mean, of course, that it will be revoked somewhat later in Aberdeen than in London.

O revokes his offer by making it clear to A that he is no longer willing to be bound on the terms specified in the offer. If he does this, it is immaterial that his communication is not in terms of the

26 *Routledge v. Grant* (1828) 4 Bing. 653; S. & T. 79.
27 [1975] 2 W.L.R. 114.
28 *Shuey v. United States* (1875) 92 U.S. 73; S. & T. 82.

42   *Formation of Bilateral Contracts*

revocation of an offer. In one case, O was wrongly under the impression that his offer to buy a car had been accepted, but he did not wish to go through with the supposed contract, and he returned the car offering to forfeit his deposit. In fact, his offer to buy had not been accepted and it was held to be revoked. O thought he was offering to rescind what he believed to be a contract but he had made it clear that he did not wish to be bound by his offer and, as it was still unaccepted, that was enough to revoke it.[29] If O does something inconsistent with the continued existence of his offer and A has notice of this, A can no longer accept. In effect, the offer is revoked. If O offers to sell property to A and then sells it, or enters into a binding contract to sell it to B, and A receives notice of this fact, A cannot accept O's offer. This was the decision in *Dickinson v. Dodds*.[30] In an unguarded example Mellish L.J. appeared to suggest that the mere sale of the property by O to B was sufficient to revoke his offer to A. This, however, is clearly not so, and it is certain that Mellish L.J. did not intend to say so. If A were to accept within the time specified in the offer to him, in ignorance of the fact that O had already sold to B, O would be bound to both A and B and would necessarily break his contract with one of them.

EXPRESS OR IMPLIED TERMS TERMINATING OFFER

If O states that his offer is to terminate on the occurrence of a specified event and that event occurs, the offer is at an end. A can no longer accept whether he is aware of the occurrence of the event or not. An offer may be subject to implied as well as express conditions. An actual contract will be terminated by the occurrence of certain events under the doctrine of frustration.[31] It is obvious that any event which would frustrate the proposed contract, had it been entered into, must also terminate the offer when the event occurs before the offer is accepted. O offers to let his theatre to A for a performance on April 1, but on February 1, before A has accepted, the theatre is burnt down. Or, O offers to let rooms to A to view a procession on May 1, but on April 10, before A has accepted, the procession is cancelled. In such cases the offer must be terminated because, even if it been accepted, the contract would have been frustrated. The question is whether an offer might be "frustrated" in circumstances in which the contemplated contract, had it been made, would not. In

29 *Financings Ltd v. Stimson* [1962] 1 W.L.R. 1184; S. & T. 83.
30 (1876) 2 Ch.D. 463; S. & T. 83.
31 Below, p. 197.

Financings Ltd v. Stimson, in the interval between O's offering to buy a car and A's acceptance of that offer, the car was stolen and badly damaged. It was held that the acceptance was not effective. The offer had come to an end. There was an express provision in the offer that the buyer had examined the car and satisfied himself that it was in good order and condition. The court held that the offer was impliedly conditional on the car remaining in substantially the same condition until the moment of acceptance. If the contract had been concluded, it is not clear that the damage to the car, after the contract was made but before delivery, would have amounted to frustration.

Suppose O offers to buy A's garage business for £100,000, the offer to remain open for seven days. Two days later, plans are announced for a by-pass which will divert the bulk of the traffic from the garage. Realising that O will no longer want the garage, or at least will not want to pay so large a sum for it, A immediately posts a letter of acceptance. If the contract had been made, the announcement would not have frustrated it, but there seem to be good grounds for argument that the offer should no longer be regarded as open. If A must, as a reasonable person, have realised that, in the changed circumstances, O would no longer wish his offer to stand, it is arguable that it should be regarded as at an end.

Death of the offeror

The effect on the offer of O's death depends on the nature of the offer. If it is to render personal services of some kind, it terminates. If O, having written to A offering to write a book, dies, A cannot accept and sue O's personal representatives for damages when the book fails to materialise. The offer died with O and it is quite immaterial whether A knew of O's death when he purported to accept. Where the contract is not one for personal services and is capable of performance, notwithstanding O's decease, as, for example, where it merely involves payment of money, A may accept so long as he is unaware of O's death. In *Bradbury v. Morgan*[32] O asked A to extend credit from time to time to X and promised to guarantee payment of the balance of X's account. O died but A, unaware of the death, continued to extend credit to X. O had made a standing offer. Each time A gave credit to X he accepted the offer. It was held that A was entitled to claim the money from O's executors on the guarantee. Bramwell B. thought the offer would not come to an end until the executor of the offeror gave notice; but later cases

32 (1862) 1 H. & C. 249; S. & T. 87.

hold that such a guarantee comes to an end when the offeree has notice that the guarantor is dead. This amounts to notice of trusts which, if the guarantor has made a will, may be, and if he has died intestate, will be,[33] incompatible with the continuance of the guarantee.

These principles apply to the case of a simple offer. It may be different if the deceased has contracted to keep the offer open, for then that contract is binding on his personal representatives. It will be recalled that in *Errington v. Errington*[34] the offer which Lord Denning held to have been made by the father was not revoked by his death, though, obviously, the offerees knew he had died. But there the father had contracted in his lifetime to keep the offer open and that contract was binding on his personal representative. In *Lloyd's v. Harper*[35] a father promised Lloyd's that, if they would admit his son as an underwriter, he would be responsible for all his engagements. That was an offer of a unilateral contract which was concluded when Lloyd's admitted the son. When, after the father's death, the son ran into financial difficulties, it was held that the contract was binding on his personal representatives. The guarantee, having been given for a once-for-all consideration, was irrevocable in the guarantor's lifetime and was not revoked by his death.

These cases all concern unilateral contracts. Offers of bilateral contracts are less likely to survive the death of the offeror because impossibility of performance on either side will nullify the offer and the process of exchanging promises may bring to the notice of the offeree the fact that the offeror is dead. But there seems no reason in principle why offers of contracts not requiring personal performance by the offeror should not survive his death.

Death of the offeree

If knowledge of the other party's death precludes the conclusion of a contract, it follows that the offeree's death will generally bring the offer to an end. Unlike cases like *Bradbury v. Morgan*, the act of acceptance cannot be done in ignorance of the death of the other party because it is to be done by the party who is dead. Moreover, any authority of an agent to conclude the contract on his behalf is revoked by his death.

---

33 *Re Whelan* [1897] 1 I.R. 575 (Chatterton V.C.).
34 Above, p. 27.
35 (1880) 16 Ch.D. 290.

CHAPTER FIVE

Contract as an Agreement

A CONCLUDED BARGAIN

"To be a good contract there must be a concluded bargain and a concluded contract is one which settles everything that is necessary to be settled and leaves nothing to be settled by agreement between the parties."

Viscount Dunedin stated this fundamental principle in *May and Butcher v. R.*[1] Until the parties have agreed on everything which they consider requires agreement, there is no contract. They are still in the course of negotiation. It is sometimes said that a contract is precluded only if there is some *essential* term yet to be agreed. But any term, however trivial it may appear to others, is "essential" if the parties consider it requires agreement and they have not agreed on it. That must apply equally when one of the parties considers that it requires agreement, provided that he has made this clear to the other party. If an otherwise complete contract states that there is some matter yet to be agreed between the parties, that will preclude the conclusion of the contract, at least while it remains "executory."[2] In *May and Butcher* the parties had entered into an elaborate arrangement for the sale of tentage but it provided that "The price or prices to be paid, and the date or dates on which payment is to be made shall be agreed upon from time to time between [the sellers and the buyers]." This precluded a contract, for there was yet no

1 (1929) [1934] 2 K.B. 17n, HL; S. & T. 89.
2 See below, p. 46.

concluded bargain. The arrangement included a clause requiring all disputes to be submitted to arbitration but that did not help to solve the problem because, like the rest of the clauses in the proposed agreement, it would become binding only when the bargain was concluded and that had never happened. The parties had never agreed on any price or date for payment.

It would probably have been different if the clauses had made no mention of the price or date. It is quite common for people to make contracts for the supply of goods or services without specifying the price to be paid. If they have done all the agreeing they intend to do, then there is an enforceable contract to pay a reasonable price. The law presumes that this is what the parties must have intended. It is the same with many other terms. If no time is specified for delivery or other performance, then it must be done within a reasonable time. But if the parties should specify, "Time of delivery to be agreed," then it must be agreed before the contract becomes effective. One or other of the parties, or both, might not have been willing to agree upon what a court would consider to be the reasonable time, or the reasonable price, or whatever the matter left for agreement is.

Executed and executory agreements

A distinction has to be made between an arrangement which is still wholly executory and one which is executed by one or both parties. An agreement is "executory" when performance lies in the future. Nothing has yet been done to carry the arrangement out. This was the position in *May and Butcher*. It is "executed" when it has been performed by one party or the other. Suppose we have an arrangement like that in *May and Butcher* but tentage is delivered and accepted and perhaps resold without any agreement as to the price. It would be outrageous if the buyer did not have to pay for it because there was no contract. In such a case "the law will say that there is necessarily implied, from the conduct of the parties, a contract that, in default of agreement, a reasonable sum is to be paid." This was stated by Denning J. in *British Bank for Foreign Trade v. Novinex*.[3] The plaintiffs had a friend with access to large quantities of oilskin suits. The defendants, who wanted to acquire oilskins, wrote to the plaintiffs (in effect) "If you will put us in direct touch with your friend we undertake to pay you an agreed commission on any business transacted with him." The plaintiffs put the defendants in direct touch with their friend. The defendant later declined to pay any commission. The Court of Appeal (reversing Denning J.

3 [1949] 1 K.B. 623; S. & T. 95.

who had stated the principle accurately but failed to apply it) held that the plaintiffs were entitled to a reasonable commission on transactions between the defendants and the plaintiffs' friend. The commission had never been "agreed" as the defendants' offer required, but it was an offer of a unilateral contract which was accepted, and wholly performed by the plaintiffs when they put the defendants in touch with the friend.

Unilateral contracts, of course are never "wholly executory," because there is no contract until the offeree has done his part. In *Foley v. Classique Coaches*[4] the contract was bilateral. The plaintiff agreed to sell some land to the defendants for a coach station in consideration of the defendants' agreeing to buy all their petrol from him. The agreement concerning the sale of the land and that concerning the sale of the petrol were put into separate documents, the former stating that it was conditional on the defendants' entering into the latter and the latter stating that it was supplemental to the former. It was a single bargain and the two parts stood or fell together. The petrol agreement provided that the petrol was to be sold "at a price to be agreed by the parties in writing and from time to time." It would appear that when both documents were signed, there was no contract, the case being indistinguishable from *May and Butcher*. But the land was conveyed and petrol was bought and sold for three years. The defendants then repudiated the petrol agreement. It was held that it was binding. The principle stated by Denning J. many years later was applicable. The agreement had been substantially executed on both sides and it would have been very remarkable indeed if, after all that, the court had held that there had never been a contract at all.

"LOCK-OUT" AGREEMENTS AND AGREEMENTS TO NEGOTIATE

An agreement by B for consideration supplied by A that, for a specified period, he will not negotiate with anyone except A for the sale of his (B's) property is a good contract. Such an agreement, known as a "lock-out" agreement, may be thought by A to be desirable where he is unable to assess what he is prepared to offer for B's property without considerable expenditure. A may be unwilling to incur this expenditure unless he is assured that the property will not be disposed of before he is in a position to make an offer for it. In the leading case, *Walford v. Miles*,[5] it was said that a term specifying the

4 [1934] 2 K.B. 1; S. & T. 91.
5 [1992] 2 A.C. 128, HL; S. & T. 97.

duration of the agreement is an essential and that a term limiting it to a reasonable time could not be implied; but there does not seem to be any reason in principle why a lock-out agreement, as described above, should not be impliedly limited to the time necessary for A to make the proposed assessment of the property. *Walford v. Miles* decides that a valid lock-out agreement operates only as a negative agreement—*i.e.* an agreement not to negotiate with anyone else—and that it does not imply a positive agreement to negotiate with A. On the contrary, an express agreement to negotiate is not binding because, like an agreement to agree, it lacks the necessary certainty. The argument that B was under an obligation to negotiate "in good faith" was rejected as being repugnant to the adversarial nature of negotiation: a negotiator must be free to threaten to withdraw if he is not offered terms better than those on the table. A "good faith" restriction would be unworkable because neither the negotiator nor the court could know when it operated. An agreement by B in a contract with A to "use all reasonable endeavours to obtain [for A] the right of first negotiation" from a third party is enforceable. That agreement is not an agreement to negotiate and it is clear what B is obliged to do.[6]

TERMS TO BE SETTLED OTHERWISE THAN BY AGREEMENT

Leaving something to be settled by agreement between the parties precludes an executory contract but leaving it to be settled in some other way does not. An agreement that the price be fixed by the buyer (or the seller) is a valid, though perhaps rash, contract. No further agreement is required. An agreement that a lender of money may vary the interest rate at his discretion is valid at common law and under the Consumer Credit Act 1974;[7] but it may be subject to an implied term that the discretion would not be exercised for an improper purpose, dishonestly, capriciously, or as no reasonable lender would.[8] The Sale of Goods Act 1979, s.8, stating a principle of the common law which is applicable to contracts generally, provides that "The price . . . may be left to be fixed in the manner thereby agreed, or may be determined by the course of dealing between the parties"; and section 9 recognises that the price may be fixed by the valuation of a third party. If the parties agree that the price shall be fixed by

---

6 *Lambert v. HTV Cymru (Wales) Ltd, The Times*, March 17, 1998.
7 *Lombard Tricity Finance Ltd v. Paton*, [1984] 1 All ER 918, applying *May and Butcher v. R.* [1934] 2 K.B. 17 at 21; S. & T. 91.
8 *Paragon Finance plc v. Nash*, [2001] 2 Com All E.R. 1025, CA.

X, that is a perfectly good contract. It does not require any further agreement between the parties. If X fixes the price in good faith, the parties are bound by the price he has fixed, however unhappy either of them may be about that price and however much it may depart from the reasonable price. The parties did not agree to buy and sell for a reasonable price, but for a price to be fixed by X. If X is being paid by the parties for this service, he owes both parties a duty to act with reasonable care and skill and, if he has not done so, the injured party may sue him for damages.[9] Of course, if there were fraud or collusion with one of the parties, the price will not be binding on the other.

The proper interpretation of this situation seems to be that there is a contract as soon as the parties have agreed on all the matters which they consider require agreement, including the term that the price is to be fixed by X. The Sale of Goods Act, s.9(2) provides that if one of the parties then prevents X from fixing the price, the other may sue him for damages. This too is, no doubt, a principle of the common law, the basis of it being that there is necessarily implied an undertaking by each party that he will do nothing to prevent the price being fixed.[10] The contract would lack "business efficacy" if either party were at liberty to prevent X fixing the price. If, without the intervention of either party, X for any reason, does not fix the price, the contract is, as the Sale of Goods Act, s.9(1) has it, "avoided." The parties have made a contract for sale at a price to be fixed by X and such a contract is now, without the fault of either, impossible to perform. It is frustrated.[11]

Agreement that the price shall be fixed by the parties precludes a contract; but leaving it to be agreed by two valuers, one to be nominated by each of them, or, in default of such agreement by an umpire appointed by the valuers is different. In *Sudbrook Trading Estate Ltd v. Eggleton*[12] the House of Lords, Lord Russell dissenting, held that this was, in effect, a contract for sale at a fair and reasonable price. The parties had done no more than specify the machinery for ascertaining the fair and reasonable price. Lord Scarman asked, "What was the object of their contract? A fair and reasonable price? Or a price reached only by the means specified?" He held that the former was the correct interpretation. When one party refused to appoint a valuer claiming that the contract was void for uncertainty, it was held that the contract (for the sale of land) could be specifically

9 *Campbell v. Edwards* [1976] 1 W.L.R. 403.
10 See below, p. 128.
11 Below, p. 197.
12 [1983] 1 A.C. 444; S. & T. 93.

enforced, the price to be fixed by a valuation ordered by the court.

In *May and Butcher* the parties expressly left something to be agreed. Parties may do so impliedly and that is equally fatal to the existence of a contract. The courts can often fill in the gaps in a quite skeletal agreement through the device of the implied term—we have noticed that the court will imply, in a contract for the sale of goods that the price is to be a reasonable one and that delivery is to be within a reasonable time—but there must be a certain minimum without which the court cannot say what the contract is. If called on to enforce an agreement falling short of that minimum, the judges do not know what it is they are supposed to enforce. In *Scammel (G.) and Nephew Ltd v. Ouston*[13]O agreed to by from S a new motor van but stipulated that "this order is given on the understanding that the balance of the purchase price can be had on hire-purchase terms over a period of two years." The House of Lords held that this sentence was "so vaguely expressed that it cannot, standing by itself, be given a definite meaning—that is to say, it requires further agreement to be reached between the parties before there would be a complete *consensus ad idem*." Hire purchase agreements can take a wide variety of different forms and there was no means by which the court could determine what terms the parties intended to apply, or would have agreed to. It might have been different if there had been any well-known "usual terms" in such a contract—the court might then have assumed that the parties intended these to apply—but there were not. In the case of a contract for the sale of land, it is sufficient that the parties, the property and the price are specified. The parties will usually wish, and will usually be well-advised, to reach agreement on many other matters but, if they are content to leave the matter there and have evinced an intention to be bound without further agreement, the law will imply the other terms which are necessary for the transaction to be carried out.

More usually, parties negotiating for the sale of land will agree to buy and sell at an agreed price, "subject to contract." There is no rule of law as to the meaning of this phrase but generally it means that there is further agreement yet to be reached between the parties. The effect, of course, is that there is no binding contract. The parties will expect their solicitors to negotiate and agree upon the further terms for their approval. In the meantime, either party is free to withdraw at will. The phrase, like all other words in contracts, must be read in context; the words mean what the parties appear to have intended them to mean and the

prima facie meaning—"there is more agreeing to be done"—
may be displaced by words showing a contrary intention. The
parties to an agreement subject to contract are both vulnerable in
that either may go to a great deal of trouble and expense, relying
on the expectation that a binding contract will be concluded,
only to find that the other party withdraws. The purchaser,
however, has one means of protection. He may, for consideration, make an independent contract with the vendor that the
latter will not, for a specified period deal with anyone else. If the
vendor breaks that "lock-out" agreement, he is liable in damages
to the purchaser for his wasted expenditure.[14]

While an agreement to agree is unenforceable because no one
can say what the parties would have agreed to if they have not
agreed in fact, there may be a perfectly good contract to make a
contract. A contract to grant a lease is a common and obvious
example. The lease itself is a contract, imposing obligations to
pay rent, to repair, etc. The difference is that in a contract to
make a contract all the terms of the second contract are to be
found, express or implied, in the first contract. There is no
further agreeing to be done.[15] The second contract merely puts
into proper legal form and language that which has already been
agreed, though perhaps not expressed in words. There may
sometimes be doubt whether phrases used by the parties
properly mean that there is a further negotiation to be done—
in which case there is no contract—or merely that the agreement
which they have reached is to be reproduced in a formal
document—in which case there is a contract. In *Branca v.
Cobarro*[16] a written agreement for a lease of a mushroom farm,
declared to be "a provisional agreement until a fully legalised
agreement, drawn up by a solicitor and embodying all the
conditions herewith stated is signed," was thought by Denning J.
to be an agreement to agree but by the Court of Appeal to be an
immediately binding contract—that was the effect of the word
"provisional".

AGREEMENTS "SUBJECT TO . . . "

It is very common for agreements to be made, "subject to"
something or other. Agreements to buy land are often made
"subject to satisfactory survey," "subject to the purchaser
obtaining a satisfactory mortgage," or "subject to planning
permission being given." Commercial contracts are often made

---

14 *Pitt v. PHH Asset Management Ltd* [1993] 4 All E.R. 961, CA; S. & T. 100.
15 *Chillingworth v. Esche* [1924] 1 Ch. 97; S. & T. 102.
16 [1947] K.B. 854.

"subject to the opening of a credit by the purchaser" or "subject to the obtaining of a licence" by one or other of the parties. These all present a different problem from the "subject to contract" case because they do not contemplate any further agreeing between the parties. In each case, something must be done before the contract becomes operative, but that thing is not further agreement. There may be a binding contract provided that, on its true interpretation, the clause—

    (i)   is sufficiently precise and definite for a court to be able to say when it is satisfied; and

    (ii)   does not leave either party with a discretion whether to go on with the transaction.

Since the whole contract is subject to the matter in question, it cannot be enforced unless the court is able to say whether the condition has been satisfied. It is not like a meaningless term which the court can ignore and still find a complete contract. In *Nicolene Ltd v. Simmonds*[17] a contract for the sale of steel included the words, "We are in agreement that the usual conditions of acceptance apply." There were no "usual conditions of acceptance." The Court of Appeal treated this as a meaningless term in a contract, not a condition precedent to the existence or operation of the whole bargain. It was severable from the rest of the contract in that, if those words were struck out, a perfectly good contract for the sale of steel was left. In that respect the case was unlike *Scammel v. Ouston*[18] where the striking out of the meaningless words would have destroyed the substance of the intended bargain—*i.e.* some sort of hire-purchase contract.

If the meaning of the clause is that one of the parties has a complete discretion whether to go on with the transaction or not, that is incompatible with the existence of a contract, the whole essence of which is that the parties bind themselves. It is important to remember that any phrase must be read in its context so that the same phrase may have different meanings in two contracts. It has been held in contracts both for the sale of land and of ships that the phrase, "subject to satisfactory survey" meant that the buyer reserved to himself the absolute right to say whether the surveyor's report was satisfactory to him. It might be expressed in glowing terms but he was still at liberty to say he did not like it. There was therefore no contract. But in another

17 [1953] 1 QB 543, CA; S. & T. 102.
18 Above, p. 50.

case[19] it was held that very similar words meant that the buyer was under an obligation to have the property surveyed and to consider, bona fide, whether the survey was satisfactory or not.[20] This assumes that, in the last resort, the court is prepared to decide that the survey was satisfactory—*i.e.* that it would satisfy any reasonable person and that the buyer's expression of dissatisfaction was immaterial. Similarly, different interpretations have been put on the phrase, "subject to the purchaser obtaining a satisfactory mortgage".[21] Such differences may be explicable on the ground of the different contexts in which the words are used or it may be that the cases are simply irreconcilable. The principle, however, is plain enough. The problem is one of interpreting the words used and it is not surprising that judges should sometimes disagree as to the proper interpretation of words.

If the parties agree that the arbiter of whether the survey (or other matter) shall be some third party, that clause does not preclude the existence of a contract. The parties have completed their agreement in the matter and neither has a discretion. A building society may have agreed to give the buyer a mortgage, subject to satisfactory survey. If the buyer then agrees to buy "subject to the survey being satisfactory to the building society," the agreement is sufficiently precise and definite because the society either says that it is satisfied, in which case the contract is on, or it says that it is dissatisfied, in which case it is off; and neither party has a discretion, even if the building society does.

Where a clause of this nature is for the exclusive benefit of one party, he may waive it, whereupon the contract, if in other respects complete, will become immediately operative. A survey, for example, will usually be for the exclusive benefit of the buyer. In such a case, a buyer, subject to survey, may simply inform the seller that he is not going to bother with a survey. There may have been no contract up to that point, because the clause gave the buyer a discretion. If so, the contract came into existence the moment he waived the condition. Such a clause then leaves the buyer in the position of an offeree. Unlike the "subject to

---

19 *Graham and Scott (Southgate) Ltd v. Oxlade* [1950] 2 K.B. 257, CA (land); *Astra Trust Ltd v. Williams* [1969] 1 Lloyd's Rep. 81, Megaw J. (a yacht).

20 *Ee v. Kakar* (1979) 124 S.J. 327.

21 *Lee-Parker v. Izzet* [1971] 1 W.L.R. 1688, Goff J.; *Lee-Parker v. Izzet (No. 2)* [1972] 1 W.L.R. 775, Goulding J. In *Graham v. Pitkin* [1992] 2 All E.R. 235 at 237, PC Lord Templeman doubted Goulding J.'s holding that there was no contract, saying that "the purchaser, if he had the money, could always have declared that a mortgage of £10 from his brother-in-law was 'satisfactory'". But this seems to confirm the view that the purchaser has an absolute discretion to declare anything, or nothing, "satisfactory;" *i.e.* an absolute discretion incompatible with the existence of a contract.

contract" case, no further agreement is required.

Where the parties have reached complete agreement and neither has reserved any discretion not to proceed, the better view is that there is a contract even though some condition must be satisfied before its major terms become operative. The matter has been confused by the leading case of *Pym v. Campbell*.[22] The defendant had agreed in writing to buy a share of the plaintiff's invention. He then declined to do so. The agreement was quite unconditional but the defendant adduced evidence that when the parties met to inspect the invention he was prepared to buy it only if an engineer, Abernethie, approved of it; and Abernethie could not be found. As it would be troublesome to arrange another meeting, the defendant agreed to sign the document on the understanding that it would be the agreement if Abernethie approved of the invention. When Abernethie saw the invention, he did not approve of it. An important question in the case was whether, because of the parol evidence rule,[23] oral evidence was admissible to qualify the effect of the written agreement. The court held that it was admissible because it showed that in fact there was "never any agreement at all." This was an inaccurate way of describing the situation. The parties had done all the agreeing they intended to do and there was no disagreement between them. The agreement was perfect—but subject to a condition: that Abernethie give his approval. In such a case it seems clear that there is a contract though its major terms are not yet operative. Surely the seller was bound to give Abernethie the opportunity to inspect the invention—just as the seller, at a price to be fixed by X, is bound to allow X the necessary facilities to fix the price.[24] The seller would have been in breach of contract if he had sold the invention to another before Abernethie had an opportunity to inspect it; and the buyer could have waived the condition since it was clearly exclusively for his benefit.

Later cases confirm that these are principles. In *Marten v. Whale*[25] the plaintiff agreed to buy a plot of land from Thacker in consideration of Thacker agreeing to buy the plaintiff's car. The sale of the land, and therefore the whole bargain, was "subject to purchaser's solicitor's approval of title and restrictions." The car was delivered to Thacker before the ownership passed to him and he wrongfully sold it to the defendant. The question whether Thacker had given a good title depended on whether he was a person who had "agreed to buy" the car within section 25(2) of

---

22 (1856) 6 El. & Bl. 379; S. & T. 425.
23 Below, p. 124.
24 Above, p. 49.
25 [1917] 2 K.B. 480; S. & T. 427.

the Sale of Goods Act 1893 (section 25(1) of the 1979 Act). The Court of Appeal held that he was. The contract for the sale of the car was "subject to '[the plaintiff's] solicitor's approval of title and restrictions' to the land"; but this did not give the plaintiff a mere option. There was an implied term that he would appoint a solicitor and consult him in good faith and that the solicitor would give his honest opinion. Clearly there was a contract as soon as the documents were signed, even though the major terms of the contract were to become operative only if and when the solicitor gave his approval.

CHAPTER SIX

Identity of Offeror and Offeree

The cases to be considered in this chapter have given rise to difficulty and controversy for many years but the principle underlying them is simple enough. If A makes an offer to B, and only to B, B may accept that offer but no one else can. A purported acceptance by C is obviously inoperative. Equally obviously, there is no contract where A makes an offer to B and B addresses an acceptance to C. The two situations may be illustrated diagrammatically.

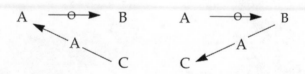

Where there have been negotiations it may often be a matter of chance whether A or B is the offeror but, in the context of this problem, it is not necessary to inquire. The result is the same in both cases; there is no contract.

It may then be vitally important to ascertain to whom A's offer was addressed. Was it addressed to B alone, or was C also an offeree? This question should be answered in accordance with the usual objective principles. An offer is made to the person or persons to whom it appears to be made. A secret reservation in the mind of the offeror, "I intended my offer only for B"—is irrelevant if the offer is so expressed that C reasonably thought it was addressed to him. The leading case of *Boulton v. Jones*[1] presents some difficulty in this regard. Jones sent an order for certain goods addressed to Brocklehurst at the latter's shop. On the same day, unknown to Jones, Brocklehurst had sold his business and stock-in-trade to his foreman, Boulton, who delivered the goods ordered. Jones consumed the goods, unaware that they had been delivered by Boulton and, when Boulton asked for the price, refused to pay. Boulton's action failed. This was held to be a case of C purporting to accept an offer which was addressed to B and to B alone. If the offer was properly regarded as addressed to Brocklehurst personally, and to him alone, this was obviously right; but might not Boulton, as a reasonable man, have thought that the offer was addressed to the owner of the business for the time being, and the fact that Jones wrongly thought his name was Brocklehurst was irrelevant? The court was persuaded that the offer was for Brocklehurst only because Jones had a running account with him and a "set-off" against him. That is, Brocklehurst was indebted to Jones and Jones intended to set off the amount of the debt against the price of the goods—and he could not do that against Boulton or anyone else. This may have been excellent evidence that Jones *intended* to deal with Brocklehurst personally, but it is not clear that it is relevant to the objective interpretation of the offer. If Boulton neither knew nor ought to have known of the set-off, it seems to be irrelevant. Arguably, then, he was entitled to suppose, as a reasonable man, that the offer made by Jones was an offer to the owner of the business, whoever he might be, and, if that were the case, there was a contract.

However dubious the application of the principle to the facts, the principle itself is clear enough: if A makes an offer to B, C cannot accept that offer. But B may accept the offer and make a valid contract even if A was making some quite important mistakes when he made the offer. Suppose for instance A supposes B to be a wealthy man, a baronet and the owner of a large mansion, a thoroughly creditworthy person. B is none of these things. Still, the offer is made to him and he can accept it. This is so even though B has dishonestly misled A about these attributes, for fraud makes a contract merely voidable, not void, *i.e.* there is a contract with all the effects of a perfect contract until A takes steps to rescind it. This drives us, inevitably, into making a distinction between A's mistake as to B's attributes and A's mistake as to identity—his confusing B with C. The distinction has been much criticised for, it is pointed out, identity is merely the sum of a person's attributes. It may be extremely difficult in

1 (1857) 2 H. & N. 564; S. & T. 165.

borderline cases to say whether a mistake is as to attribute or as to identity. But almost all legal distinctions run into these problems at the borders and this in no way invalidates the distinction.

VOID AND VOIDABLE CONTRACTS AND THE PASSING OF PROPERTY

In *Boulton v. Jones* there was no question of any fraud or dishonesty but that was an exceptional case. The problem usually arises in the following form. O, the owner of goods, encounters a rogue, R, who by fraud induces O to sell the goods. R gets possession of the goods but does not pay for them. He then re-sells and delivers the goods to a bona fide purchaser for value (a "BFP")—that is, a person who buys and pays for the goods in good faith, quite unaware of the dishonest way in which R has come by them. R then usually disappears from the scene. He cannot be identified or found, or he is sent to prison and, at all events, there is no money to be got out of him. O discovers that his property (as he believes) is in the possession of BFP who, having paid for it in good faith, is naturally unwilling to part with it. So O sues the BFP in the tort of conversion, claiming that the defendant is wrongly asserting title to his, O's, property. Is he? It depends. There is a well established principle (though one subject to many exceptions) that no one can pass on to another a better title to goods than he has himself: *nemo dat quod non habet*. So, if R had no title to the goods, he gave no title to BFP, the goods still belong to O and O's action will succeed. But, if R had a title to the goods, even a voidable one, he could pass this on and, as against the bona fide purchaser for value, the principle is that the title is no longer voidable. O has lost his right to avoid the contract and his action will fail.

The outcome of the action, *O v. BFP*, will then turn on whether there was a contract between O and R. If there was, it was at least voidable because of R's fraud but, if it was merely voidable, the ownership in the goods passed to R. R had a title to the goods, though a voidable one and, once the BFP had paid for the goods in good faith, the BFP had a title which was no longer voidable. Suppose then that O's offer to sell the goods was not made to R but to S, and R had purported to accept. Clearly that is not a contract (though it is often described as "a void contract") and, though R may get possession of the goods, he does not get ownership of them and consequently (*nemo dat quod non habet*) he can pass on no title to BFP. O's action will succeed. If, on the other hand, R's fraud merely misled O as to R's attributes so that O's offer was made to R, then, notwithstanding his fraud, R could accept it so as to create a voidable contract and acquire the ownership of the property delivered to him.

The leading case on the matter is *Cundy v. Lindsay*.[2] The rogue, Blenkarn, hired a room in 37 Wood Street, London, close to a well-known and reputable firm, Blenkiron & Sons, carrying on business at 123 Wood Street. Blenkarn wrote letters to the owner, Lindsay, ordering a large quantity of handkerchiefs and signing the letters, "A Blenkarn & Co.," but hoping that this would be read as "A Blenkiron & Co." It was indeed so read by a member of Lindsay's firm who knew of Blenkiron and Sons as a reputable firm. Consequently the handkerchiefs were despatched to "Messrs Blenkiron & Co., 37 Wood Street," where they were received by Blenkarn and re-sold by him to the BFP, Cundy. Blenkarn received the price from Cundy but, of course, he did not pay Lindsay. The fraud was discovered and Blenkarn was sent to prison. Lindsay sued Cundy for conversion of the handkerchiefs. Was this the case of an offer made by A (Lindsay) to B (Blenkiron & Sons) which was "accepted" by C (Blenkarn)? If so, Blenkarn got no title and Lindsay's action would succeed. Or was it a case of an offer made to C (Blenkarn) under a mistake as to C's attributes? If so, C got a voidable title to the goods and passed on a perfect title to the BFP, Cundy. The Queen's Bench Division took the latter view, holding that Lindsay intended to deal with the person carrying on business at 37 Wood Street— Blenkarn—and therefore there was a contract with him. But the Court of Appeal and the House of Lords held otherwise. Lindsay intended to deal with the well-known, reputable firm of Blenkiron & Sons, of whose existence they were well aware and not with Blenkarn, of whom they had never heard. This was surely the right answer. Blenkarn intended Lindsay to think they were dealing with Blenkiron and that is what they did think. They mistakenly believed that the letter came from Blenkiron and that Blenkiron's address was 37 Wood Street. Of course, it is literally true to say that they intended to carry on business with the person at 37 Wood Street (who in fact was Blenkarn) but only because they thought that person was Blenkiron. The address, in itself, was of no significance. Of course, the outcome was hard for Cundy. They had paid for the goods in good faith and now found themselves bound to pay the value to Lindsay. It was a case where the court had to decide which of two innocent persons should suffer because of the fraud of a third.

With *Cundy v. Lindsay* it is useful to contrast *King's Norton Metal Co. Ltd v. Edridge, Merrett & Co. Ltd*.[3] The rogue, Wallis,

2 (1878) 3 App.Cas. 459, HL; S. & T. 167–169.
3 (1897) 14 T.L.R. 98, CA; S. & T. 171.

wrote a letter to the owner, KN, on notepaper purporting to be that of Hallam & Co., Soho Hackle, Pin and Wire Works, Sheffield, with a representation of a large factory and statements that Hallam & Co. had depots at Belfast, Lille and Ghent. He ordered goods which were sent off to "Hallam & Co.'s" address. They were never paid for but were resold to the BFP, E.M. Again, O sued BFP and the question was whether there was a contract between O and R. It looks, at first sight, just like *Cundy v. Lindsay*, but there is a crucial difference. Blenkiron & Sons was a real, existing firm, known to Lindsay. "Hallam & Co." with its factory and depots, on the other hand seems merely to have been a figment of R's imagination. But O intended to deal with someone. Who? There was only one candidate—the writer of the letter, R. True, he had made some pretty fundamental misrepresentations—that he was carrying on business under the name of Hallam and Co., that he owned a large factory, etc.; but these were representations as to his attributes—he had not represented himself to O to be some other real, existing person. The court said "If it could have been shown that there was a separate entity called Hallam & Co. and another entity called Wallis, then the case might have come within *Cundy v. Lindsay*."

WHERE THE PARTIES ARE FACE TO FACE

In *Cundy v. Lindsay* where the contract was made through the post it was not too difficult for the courts to conclude that Lindsay intended to deal, not with Blenkarn, but with Blenkiron. When O and R are face to face it is less easy to conclude that O intended not to deal with R, the only person present, but with someone else. The problem is particularly difficult when R represents himself to be another existing person so that, like *Cundy v. Lindsay* and unlike *King's Norton v. Edridge*, there are two separate entities. It by no means follows that *Cundy v. Lindsay* will be applied. In a much discussed case, *Phillips v. Brooks*,[4] the rogue, North, went to a jeweller's shop and selected pearls at the price of £2,550 and a ring at £450. Up to that point, North had not mentioned his name so the jeweller was plainly dealing with the man in shop, whoever he might be. It has indeed been suggested that the contract was made at this point and the ownership in the goods passed to North before he had made any misrepresentation. More likely, however, the jeweller contemplated discussion of further terms, such as mode of payment and time of delivery. He would hardly be expecting the buyer to produce this large sum in cash. Even if there was a

4 [1919] 2 K.B. 243, S. & T. 173, Horridge J.

contract of sale, it was a contract for payment in cash and North immediately proposed a rescission of it. He produced a cheque book and wrote out a cheque for £3,000, saying that his name was Sir George Bullough and giving an address in St James's Square. The jeweller had heard of Sir George and he checked in a directory that the address was correct. On being asked if he would like to take the goods with him, North said that the jeweller had better have the cheque cleared first but he would like to take the ring as it was his wife's birthday the next day. North took the ring and promptly pledged it with the BFP, the defendants. The cheque, of course, was dishonoured and the plaintiff jeweller sued in conversion. His case was that he intended to sell to Sir George, not to North, but Horridge J. held that he intended to deal with the person present. There was a contract with North, though voidable for fraud, ownership passed to him and he gave a good title to the defendants. The jeweller was undoubtedly dealing with the man in the shop until he gave the false name and the judge's view was that what happened subsequently was not sufficient to displace that initial intention to sell to that person. He was misled as to his attributes—he believed the man in the shop to be called Sir George Bullough, to be a baronet, with an address in St James's Square, and to be an honest and creditworthy person; but he was still dealing with the man in front of him.

There are two subsequent Court of Appeal decisions with rather similar facts. In the first, *Ingram and Others v. Little*,[5] it was held that there was no contract with the rogue, but the second, *Lewis v. Averay*,[6] reached the same result as *Phillips v. Brooks*. It is doubtful if the cases can be reconciled. *Ingram v. Little* concerned three ladies selling a car. A rogue (who was never identified) calling himself Hutchinson offered to buy it for £717 which they were prepared to accept. They were undoubtedly dealing with the man in their drawing room at this point. But, when he offered a cheque, they said they would in no circumstances accept a cheque and the deal was off. This seems to be the only possible point of distinction from *Phillips v. Brooks*. Up to this point, the identity of the man present had been unimportant to the sellers because they were anticipating a cash sale and one man's cash was as good as another's. The rogue was now opening negotiations for a sale on credit, where identity was vitally important. He said he was P. G. M. Hutchinson of Stanstead House, Stanstead Road, Caterham. One of the ladies ascertained from a directory that there was such a person.

5 [1961] 1 Q.B. 31; S. & T. 175.
6 [1972] 1 Q.B. 198; S. & T. 182.

Eventually, they were persuaded to take a cheque and let him have the car. He went off with it and was never seen again but the car was found in the possession of the defendant, the BFP. Pearce L.J. posed the difficulty facing the court: "It is not easy to decide whether the vendor was selling to the man in her drawing-room (fraudulently misrepresented as being a man of substance with the attributes of the real Hutchinson) or to P. G. M. Hutchinson of Stanstead House (fraudulently mis-represented as being the man in her drawing-room)." The majority of the court were influenced by the fact that the trial judge had held that they intended to sell to the real Hutchinson, holding that they should not lightly interfere with the opinion of the trial judge, who had heard the witnesses, on a question of intention. Devlin L.J., dissenting, thought the trial judge was no better equipped than the Court of Appeal to answer this question. He held that the presumption that a person is intending to contract with the person to whom he is actually addressing words of contract is a very strong one and was not rebutted in this case.

The facts in the second case, *Lewis v. Averay*,[7] were very similar. The rogue represented that he was Richard Greene, the well-known actor, and so persuaded the seller to take a cheque for his car. A differently constituted Court of Appeal applied the presumption stated by Devlin L.J. Lord Denning thought that *Phillips v. Brooks* and *Ingram v. Little* were irreconcilable and that *Phillips v. Brooks* was right. This is probably the better view.

Devlin L.J. did however recognise that there is at least one way in which the presumption of dealing with the party present can be rebutted. That is where the rogue dishonestly claims to be acting as agent for another. There is no contract with that other because the rogue has no authority of any kind to act as his agent; and there is no contract with the rogue because the contract does not purport to be made with him. *Hardman v. Booth*[8] is an illustration of this. The plaintiffs went to the office of Gandell & Sons and encountered Edward Gandell, the rogue. He was not a member of the firm of Gandell and Sons and had no authority to act on their behalf, but he gave the plaintiffs an order in their name, intercepted the goods when they arrived and delivered them to the defendant, the BFP. The plaintiffs' action succeeded. There was never any suggestion that they were selling the goods to Edward Gandell personally, so there was no contract with him; and there was no contract with Gandell & Sons because Edward had no authority to bind them in any way.

This is not necessarily the only way in which the presumption

7 *ibid.*
8 (1863) 1 H. & C. 803.

is rebuttable. Suppose that R impersonates O's established customer S, so that from the start O believes that he is dealing with S. If the negotiation were conducted over the telephone, R imitating S's well-known voice to perfection, there would surely be no contract if identity was important. If he entered O's shop with an equally effective disguise, so as to be greeted, "Good morning Mr S," it is difficult to see that there is any difference in principle.

In *Shogun Finance Ltd v. Hudson*[9] R agreed with a dealer to buy a car on hire-purchase. He produced a stolen driving licence belonging to DP and forged DP's signature on the proposed hire-purchase agreement. The finance company, O, made a credit search in respect of DP which was satisfactory. The dealer accepted a 10 per cent deposit from R. The agreement transferred the ownership in the car from the dealer to O and purported to let it to the hirer named in the agreement, *i.e.,* DP. R sold the car to BFP. O sued BFP in conversion. A person who has possession of a car under a hire-purchase agreement (called "the debtor") is not the owner; but the Hire Purchase Act 1964, s. 27, provides that a BFP from the debtor nevertheless acquires a good title. In the opinion of the majority of the Court, R did not hold the car under a hire-purchase agreement and was not "the debtor", because O intended to deal, not with R, but with DP. BFP was liable in conversion. Sedley L.J., dissenting, held that the dealer was O's agent for certain purposes, including the ascertainment of the hirer's identity so that this was a face-to-face transaction with R. The majority agreed that if the dealer had been authorised by O *to make the hire-purchase agreement*, the face-to-face principle would have applied and the contract would have been made with R—but this was not the case. It is thought that the majority opinion is correct.

ESTOPPEL

In some circumstances, the BFP can invoke the doctrine of estoppel. If O has represented to him that R is the owner of the goods, or has power to dispose of them, when he knows, or ought to know, that BFP will act on that statement, and BFP does so by giving R value for the goods, O will be estopped from denying that R was the owner or had that power. The effect is that BFP gets a good title. In *Henderson v. Williams*[10] Grey & Co. owned a quantity of sugar lying in the defendant's warehouse. The rogue, Fletcher, by pretending to be the agent of Robinson, a

9 *The Times,* July 4, 2001.
10 [1895] 1 Q.B. 521.

well-known customer of Grey, fraudulently induced Grey to "sell" him the sugar. It seems clear that the ownership passed neither to Fletcher (because there was no intention to contract with him) nor to Robinson (because Fletcher was not his agent and he knew nothing of the transaction) so the sugar still belonged to Grey. But Grey advised the defendant that they had sold the sugar and that he was to hold it to Fletcher's order. Fletcher offered to sell the sugar to the plaintiff, the BFP, who, before accepting, asked the defendant whether the sugar was held to Fletcher's order. The defendant replied that it was and the plaintiff thereupon "bought" the sugar from Fletcher. Grey, having discovered the fraud, induced the defendant to detain the sugar and indemnified him for doing so. Thus, Grey were the real defendant. It was held that, even if there was no contract at all with Fletcher, Grey, having (through the defendant) "held out" Fletcher as having power to dispose of the goods, were estopped from setting up their title against the plaintiff who had acted on that representation.

There is, however, a vital difference between "holding out" the rogue to be the owner and enabling the rogue to hold himself out. In the latter case there is no estoppel. In *Cundy v. Lindsay*, Lindsay by putting the goods into Blenkarn's possession, enabled him to hold himself out as owner. As the possessor he was able to present every appearance of being the owner; but there was no question of an estoppel. Otherwise everyone who entrusted his goods to another would be estopped from asserting his title if that other dishonestly disposed of them to a BFP.

Proposals for reform

Under the present law, either the owner bears the whole loss or the BFP does so; and the outcome depends on the nature of a transaction (the "contract" between O and R) of which, by definition, the BFP knew nothing. Someone (or someone's insurer) has to bear the loss. Devlin L.J., in his dissenting judgment in *Ingram v. Little*[11] suggested that the law should be reformed, as it has been in other areas, to allow an apportionment between O and the BFP. The loss would be borne equally unless there was fault or imprudence on one side or the other. If there was, the party at fault would bear such greater proportion of the loss as the court found to be just. This suggestion was considered and rejected by the Law Reform Committee.[12] They foresaw great practical difficulties, particularly in cases where

11 [1961] 1 Q.B. 31; S. & T. 175 at 180.
12 Twelfth Report (Transfer of Title to Chattels), Cmnd. 2958 (1966); S. & T. 180.

there has been more than one BFP. Some goods, such as cars, pass from hand to hand very rapidly. It may be that R has sold to A who has sold to B who has sold to C, before O discovers the fraud. He finds the goods in the hands of C so it is C whom he sues in conversion. But in every contract of sale there is an implied undertaking by the seller that he has a right to sell the goods; so C will wish to join B in the action on the ground that, if he (C) is guilty of conversion of O's goods, it is because B is in breach of his contract that he had a right to sell the goods. If they belonged to O all the time, he did not. So he must indemnify C against any damages C has to pay O for conversion. And similarly B will wish to join in A. Sometimes the chain may be much longer. The Committee thought that the court would thus become involved in an inquiry into the degree of fault, if any, of each party in the chain, resulting in so much complexity and uncertainty as to render the proposal undesirable. The committee did recommend that, where goods are sold under a mistake as to the buyer's identity, the contract should, so far as third parties are concerned, be voidable and not void. The effect would be, of course, that the BFP would get a good title and *Cundy v. Lindsay* would be reversed. But this proposal has not been implemented.

CHAPTER SEVEN

Consideration

THE PRICE-TAG ON THE PROMISE

We have seen that an offer is not an offer to contract unless, expressly or impliedly, it asks for something in return. Acceptance consists in giving what is asked for, whether it be a promise or an act. That promise, or that act, is the consideration. An offer which asks for nothing in return is an offer to make a gift and is not enforceable.

It is for this reason that, in many of the seminal cases we find the court looking for a "request" in the offer. An instructive example is *Shadwell v. Shadwell*.[1]

An uncle wrote to his nephew:

> "I am glad to hear of your intended marriage with Ellen Nicholl and, as I promised to assist you at starting, I am happy to tell you that I will pay to you one hundred and fifty pounds yearly during my life, and until your income derived from your profession of a Chancery barrister shall amount to six hundred guineas . . .".

The nephew married Ellen, his income never reached 600 guineas and uncle paid 12 annual sums but died leaving five unpaid. The nephew sued uncle's personal representative for the unpaid instalments. One of the defences was that the marriage had been arranged before the alleged agreement, without any

1 (1860) 9 C.B.N.S. 159; S. & T. 229.

request from the testator, and that there was no consideration for uncle's promise to pay. Since an agreement in consideration of marriage was one of those contracts which the Statute of Frauds 1677 then required to be evidenced in writing, the consideration had to be found in uncle's letter or not at all. The word "request" appears repeatedly in the judgments of the majority, who decided in favour of the nephew, and of Byles J. who dissented. The majority, taking into account the relationship between uncle and nephew, held that the letter was an inducement to the nephew to marry and therefore a request to marry. Byles J. agreed that "Marriage of the plaintiff at the testator's express request would be, no doubt, an ample consideration; but marriage of the plaintiff without the testator's request is no consideration to the testator." The difference between the judges was not on the principles of the law of contract, but on the construction of the letter. Byles J. could find no request to marry in the letter and Salmon L.J. said (in 1969)[2] that he would, without hesitation, have decided the case in accordance with the views of Byles J. The majority seem to have taken a very strained view of the letter. Was not uncle simply offering a rather handsome wedding present? If the relatives and friends of an engaged couple promise them lavish wedding presents, this may indeed be an inducement to marry, but it would be surprising if they were held to have contracted to give the presents.

Suppose, however, that young Shadwell had told his uncle that he intended to break off his engagement to Ellen and uncle had written: "I am disappointed to hear that you are thinking of breaking off your engagement. Ellen is a splendid girl. If you marry her, I will pay you . . .". Clearly uncle would then have been asking for something in return for his promise and presumably Byles J. (subject to another difficulty to be discussed shortly) and Salmon L.J. would have taken a different view.

There is sometimes difficulty in distinguishing between a conditional offer to make a gift and an offer to contract. If the offer is to pay money (or give some other benefit) in a certain event, not being an act or promise by the offeree, that appears to be an offer to make a gift. The offeree is not asked to do anything. "If you should be so unlucky as to catch flu, I will pay you £100," is an offer of a conditional gift; but "If you will use the smoke ball three times daily for two weeks and then have the misfortune to catch flu . . ." is an offer of a contract, the use of the smoke ball being the consideration requested.

The problem is more difficult when the alleged condition is something to be done or, as the case may be, not done, by the offeree. In *Wyatt v. Kreglinger and Fernau*[3] the defendant firm wrote to their retiring employee, the plaintiff, who was not entitled to any pension, that they had decided to pay him a pension of £200 a year and that he was at liberty to enter into any business or employment, "except in the wool trade". After some years the defendants stopped the pension and the plaintiff sued. All the judges in the Court of Appeal agreed that, if this was a contract, it was illegal as being in restraint of trade; but Scrutton L.J. agreed with the trial judge that this was a voluntary gratuitous payment and that the words "except in the wool trade" were merely an intimation to Wyatt that, if he did enter the wool trade, the pension would stop. Slesser and Greer L.J. however thought that, but for the illegality, there would have been a good contract, the consideration being Wyatt's refraining from entering the wool trade.

A person who makes a gift may surely make it clear that, if the donee, behaves in a certain way, the gift will come to an end, without turning the gift into a binding contract. If a man promises to pay his widowed daughter-in-law £5,000 a year, he could surely withdraw the promise on finding himself in straitened circumstances, or on falling out with her, or because she has married a wealthy man. Suppose he limits his promise to pay the allowance by the addition of the words, "so long as you remain unmarried"? Is this merely the definition of the extent of a gratuitous promise or has it now become an offer to contract, the consideration being the lady's forbearance from marriage? It is thought that the former is the better view. Of course, it would be different if the man, distressed at hearing of the lady's intention to remarry, were to say, "Please do not remarry. I will pay you £5,000 a year so long as you remain unmarried". Then he would clearly be asking a price for his promise. So too, in *Wyatt v. Kreglinger*, if the employers had discovered, to their dismay, that their former employee was about to join their greatest rival and had offered him a pension to refrain from doing so.

Of course, there is no magic in the word "request". The question is one of substance. Was the promisor asking a price for his promise? Was his promise a free gift or was he "selling" it? Was it, in a word, a bargain?

"Gifts" of onerous property

A special case is that where O offers to give A certain property, the ownership of which involves obligations. O will get rid of

3 [1933] 1 K.B. 793, CA.

those obligations and A will undertake them. O offers to assign his leasehold property to A, or he offers to give him his shares on which calls are due. If A accepts, he will have to pay the rent or the calls when they are made. The value of property may greatly exceed the obligation but it seems that this is regarded as a contract, not a gift.[4] A's agreement to take the obligations which attach to the property off O's shoulders on to his own is consideration.

Benefit and detriment

It has been traditional to state that consideration must be a benefit to the promisor or a detriment to the promisee. Of course, it is almost always both. O asks for a "price" because it is a benefit he wants to receive; and the giving of the price is, almost inevitably, a detriment of some kind to A. Associated with the language of benefit and detriment is the notion that consideration must be of some economic value.

The practice of the courts, as distinct from what they say, shows that the language of benefit and detriment has long been out of date and has no substantial meaning at the present day. It is true, as we shall see, that there are some things which the law, for reasons of policy, regards as incapable of amounting to consideration, but, subject to that, *anything* that the promisor asks for in return for his promise is consideration. If O makes a promise to A in consideration of A's supplying him with three, quite useless, chocolate wrappers, which O will instantly throw away, there is a perfectly good contract provided that the promise was seriously intended. O has got what he asked for and that is a sufficient "benefit." A has parted with something he might have kept, he has done something which he did not have to do, and that is a sufficient detriment. It is immaterial that the wrappers are of no value and that A is glad to be rid of them. As for economic value, the judges have recognised (in a hypothetical but much quoted example) that O's promise to pay A £100 if A will walk to York can be a perfectly good contract; and no one has ever demonstrated what economic value there is in walking to York. Similarly with promises of a reward for not smoking[5] or by the father of an illegitimate child to pay the mother an allowance if she proves to him that the child is well looked after

---

4 *Cheale v. Kenward* (1858) 27 L.J.Ch. 784 (shares); *Price v. Jenkins* (1877) 5 Ch.D. 619; *Johnsey Estates Ltd v. Lewis & Manley Engineering Ltd* (1987) 54 P. & C.R. 296, CA.

5 *Hamer v. Sidway* (1881) 27 N.E. 256.

and happy.[6] The promisor may derive satisfaction and peace of mind from the fact that the promisee is not smoking or that the child is happy, but there is no economic value in it for him. It does not matter; he has got what he bargained for and that is consideration.

"Past consideration"

Since, to lead to a contract, an offer must ask for something in return, a promise to pay for services already rendered, or some other benefit already conferred, and which asks for nothing more, is not enforceable. A man brings up an orphan and spends large sums on his maintenance and education. On growing up and achieving success in life, the orphan promises to repay the money spent. The promise is not enforceable.[7] While you are away on holiday, the roof of your house is damaged by a storm. I do the essential repairs. On your return, you gratefully promise to reimburse me for my time and trouble. Your promise is of no effect in law. "Past consideration," it is said, "is no considera-tion". It is, of course, entirely different from the "executed consideration" which is found in unilateral contracts because, there, the act is done at the request of the promisor. The old case of *Lampleigh v. Brathwait*[8] distinguished an act done at the request of the promisor from "a mere voluntary courtesy".

A service may be requested without any express promise to pay for it but, if it is an ordinary commercial service, which everyone expects to pay for, a promise to pay a reasonable sum for it is necessarily implied. If I invite a passing window-cleaner to clean the windows of my house, saying nothing about payment, there is clearly a contract to pay a reasonable sum when the windows have been cleaned. In *Lampleigh v. Brathwait* B had killed a man and he asked L to get him a pardon from the king. At considerable trouble and expense, L obtained the pardon and B then promised to pay him £100 for his efforts. It was held that the promise was enforceable, because the service was rendered at B's request. This looks very like a past consideration, but *Lampleigh v. Brathwait* is an old case and has been restrictively interpreted. W must now take it that the request to L to obtain a pardon contained an implied promise to pay him for his trouble. Though it looks very different from the window-cleaner case, we must take it that it is the same in principle: B would have been liable to pay a reasonable sum,

6 *Ward v. Byham* [1956] 1 W.L.R. 496; S. & T. 228.
7 *Eastwood v. Kenyon* (1840) 11 Ad. & El. 438.
8 (1615) Hob. 105; S. & T. 204.

even if he had never made the promise. Where a service has been rendered which the parties, as reasonable men, must have intended should be paid for, but no price was stated and subsequently a promise is made to pay—

> " . . . that promise may be treated either as an admission which evidences or as a positive bargain which fixes the amount of that reasonable remuneration on the faith of which the service was originally rendered."[9]

When A has rendered the service, a reasonable sum is due. If O offers to pay a specified sum that is acceptable to A, that will be regarded as excellent evidence of what that reasonable sum is; but it only "evidences" and does not "fix". O, being sued for the amount he promised, may argue that his promise was an extravagant one, that the reasonable sum is, say, £100, and that his promise to pay £200 was made without any consideration for the additional £100. But, if there is a dispute about the reasonable price, O offers £100, A demands £300, and they finally agree on £200, that will be the "positive bargain which fixes" the amount of the reasonable remuneration. There is a new contract, each party giving consideration by abandoning his claim in favour of the intermediate sum. It is thus not strictly true to say, as the Privy Council did in a modern case—

> "An act done before the giving of a promise to make a payment or confer some other benefit can sometimes be consideration for the promise."[10]

The enforceable promise is either the implied promise which is made *before* the act is done; or the subsequent express promise, the consideration for which is the abandonment of his claim by the other party. *Lampleigh v. Brathwait*, as interpreted today, is not an exception to the rule that past consideration is no consideration.

There is one minor exception to that rule under the Bills of Exchange Act 1882. Section 27(1) provides that "Valuable consideration for a bill may be constituted by . . . (b) An antecedent debt or liability." So, if I owe you £100 and I give a cheque (a variety of bill of exchange) in payment, you may sue me on the cheque—as well as on the original debt. But it is a limited exception. If, owing you £100, I give you a cheque for

9 *Re Casey's Patents; Stewart v. Casey* [1892] 1 Ch. 104 at 115]–[116; S. & T. 205, 201.
10 *Pao On v. Lau Yiu Long* [1980] A.C. 614, S. & T. 233, PC.

£200, you can only recover £100 on the cheque. The promise to pay the other £100 is without consideration.[11] If I owe you £100 for work done and a third person, X, not acting as my agent, gives you his cheque in payment of my debt, you have no right of action against X if the cheque is dishonoured. X has received no consideration for the promise implied in the cheque.[12]

The adequacy of the consideration

It is always said that the court will not inquire into the adequacy of the consideration.[13] This is, in effect, the rule that if the promisor gets what he has asked for in return for his promise, that is sufficient consideration. The court is not concerned with the question whether he was making a good bargain or not— whether the satisfaction of having A walk to York was worth £100, whether the goods or services were worth the price that the promisor agreed to pay for them, etc. A leading case is the strange one of *Bainbridge v. Firmstone*.[14] The admitted facts were that the defendant said to the plaintiff (in effect) "If you will let me weigh your two valuable boilers, I promise you that I will return them to you in perfect condition". The plaintiff then allowed the defendant to weigh the boilers. The defendant left the boilers in pieces and the plaintiff had great trouble putting them together again. The plaintiff recovered damages for breach of contract. An argument that there was no consideration was rejected. It was not apparent what benefit the defendant derived from his strange request, but that was immaterial. He got what he wanted in return for his promise. The case has been criticised; but, given the facts admitted by the parties, it seems a perfectly clear case of a contract. A boiler-weighing fetishist must pay the price he promises to pay for the indulgence granted by a boiler-owner.

The consideration must be "sufficient"

Although the court will not inquire into the adequacy of the consideration, there are certain acts and promises which, for reasons of policy, are deemed to be of no value in the law and which are therefore an "insufficient" consideration. Hence the curious terminology—the consideration need not be adequate

11 *Thoni Gesellschaft v. RTP Eqpt.* [1979] 2 Lloyd's Rep. 282, CA.
12 *AEG (UK) Ltd v. Lewis, The Times*, December 29, 1992.
13 The adequacy of the consideration may be relevant in determining the extent of the other party's obligation; the less you pay, the less you may be entitled to expect—*cf* the *Photo Production case*, below, p. 173.
14 (1838) 1 P. & D. 2; S. & T. 208.

but it must be sufficient. A promise to do any act, or forbear from doing any act, which the promisor might lawfully do, is generally a sufficient consideration; but the law regards some promises as void and, if a promise is void, a nullity, it is not a sufficient consideration for a counter-promise. A wife's promise not to go to court to seek maintenance from her estranged husband was deemed to be void as contrary to public policy—the courts would not countenance the exclusion of their statutory jurisdiction to award maintenance—so it followed that her husband's promise to pay her money in consideration of her promise not to go to court was made without consideration and also void.[15] That particular case has now been altered by statute[16] but the principle of the common law, that a void promise is not consideration, is not affected.

A promise to forbear from suing, or actual forbearance from suing, is generally a sufficient consideration. If I claim £5,000 which I believe you owe me, and you promise me £2,500 if I will drop the claim, that is an offer to make a binding contract. It makes no difference whether I have started an action against you or not. My discontinuing, or not initiating, the action, or my promise to do so, is consideration for your promise to pay £2,500. In a sense, one of us may appear to be getting something for nothing. Either the action would have succeeded (in which case I have thrown away £2,500) or it would not (in which case you have thrown away £2,500); but the outcome of legal proceedings is rarely, if ever, absolutely certain and the reality is that I have abandoned my claim that you owe me £5,000 in consideration of your abandoning your claim that nothing is due. In *Cook v. Wright*[17] Commissioners responsible for executing a local Act wrongly believed the defendant to be liable to pay certain charges. He denied liability but, being threatened with legal proceedings, he agreed to pay a reduced sum in three instalments by promissory notes. Though it was now admitted he had never been liable to pay the charges, he was held liable on the notes which had been given in consideration of the Commissioners refraining from bringing the action which they thought to be a proper claim.

It is very important that such agreements should be binding because the great majority of legal disputes are settled by a

15 *Gaisberg v. Storr* [1950] 1 K.B. 107, CA.
16 The Matrimonial Causes Act 1973, s.34 confirms that the wife's promise is void but provides that the husband's promise shall not be void or unenforceable, unless there is some other reason why it should be. This appears to be an example of a promise (that of the husband) which, by statute, is enforceable although not under seal and without consideration. S. & T. 224.
17 (1861) 1 B. & S. 559; S. & T. 218.

compromise of this kind. This assumes, however, that my claim is brought in good faith. If I start, or threaten to start, legal proceedings against you, knowing that I have no cause of action, my forbearance to prosecute that claim which I know to be unfounded is not a sufficient consideration for any promise which you may make. You may in fact receive a substantial benefit in being saved the worry and expense of defending the action and, notwithstanding its invalidity, there is the possibility that the claim might have succeeded through perjury or error; but it would be contrary to policy to recognise that the abandonment of a claim, known by the claimant to be invalid, is of any value in the eyes of the law.[18]

Forbearance from doing what one has no right to do cannot be a sufficient consideration. If I, without any claim of right, constantly trespass on your land, your promise to pay me money if I refrain from doing so is made without consideration. If, on the other hand, you are irritated by my lawful use of the highway past your house and offer me money if I will go another way, my forbearance from exercising my liberty to use the highway is sufficient consideration. It does not follow, however, that refraining from doing what one may lawfully do is always sufficient consideration. If I know my neighbour is committing adultery, I have a perfect right to tell his wife; but the offer to him, "I will refrain from telling her if you will pay me £1,000", is clearly blackmail and therefore cannot be an offer of a valid contract. The borderline between a good contract and blackmail may be quite fine.[19]

The answer perhaps depends on whether the person has a legitimate commercial interest in doing that which he refrains from doing. If A has written his memoirs, which are true but contain information very damaging to B, there seems to be no reason why A should not make a contract with B that he will refrain from publishing if B will pay him the sum which he has been offered by a newspaper. Here A has something of commercial value, something he may lawfully sell and, if he can sell it to the newspaper, there is no reason why he should not sell it to B for what it is worth. But if he requests from B more than the commercial value of the memoirs, then he is taking advantage of B's predicament, probably committing blackmail

<hr/>

18 *Wade v. Simeon* (1846) 2 C.B. 548; S. & T. 217. However, in *Pitt v. PHH Asset Management Ltd* [1993] 4 All E.R. 961 at 966, Peter Gibson L.J. said that the plaintiff's refraining from seeking an injunction, although a claim which was bound to fail and had only "nuisance value," was a benefit to the defendant which amounted to an element in the consideration.
19 See S. & T. 215–220.

and therefore not making a good contract.[20] This, then is an exceptional type of case where the court will have regard to the value of the alleged consideration in determining whether it is sufficient.

Performance of a legal duty as consideration

The question here is whether A's doing, or promising to do, something that he is already under a legal obligation to do is a sufficient consideration, in a contract with B. There are three types of duty to consider.

(i)   A duty imposed by the general law.
(ii) A duty owed by A to B, arising out of an existing contract, or the judgment of a court, or otherwise.
(iii) A duty owed by A to C to do that thing for B—*i.e.* A has contracted with C to do it.

Duties imposed by law

It has generally been stated that the performance of, or the promise to perform, such a duty is not a sufficient consideration. A is only doing, or promising to do, what he is already bound to do, B is getting nothing more than that to which he is entitled under the general law, so he is receiving no consideration. So a promise to pay a fee to a witness who has been properly subpoenaed to attend a trial has been held to be made without consideration: *Collins v. Godefroy*.[21] The witness had a public duty to attend. But the authority for this rule is rather slight and it was consistently disputed by Lord Denning.[22] The leading case is *Glasbrook Bros Ltd v. Glamorgan County Council*,[23] but that is far from conclusive. The council, as the police authority, sued on a contract to pay for a police garrison supplied to a colliery to protect the "safety men" during a strike. The safety men were unwilling to go to work without police protection and, if they had not done so, the mine would have become flooded. The defence was that there was no consideration for the promise because the police were under a duty to protect persons and property. The action succeeded, but on the ground that the police were doing more than their public duty required. In the

---

20 Lord Denning seems to have taken an unduly generous view of such conduct in his Report on the Profumo affair, Cmnd. 2152, (1963) p. 35.
21 (1813) 1 B. & Ald. 950; S. & T. 216.
22 *Williams v. Williams* [1957] 1 W.L.R. 148, S. & T. 222; *Ward v. Byham* [1956] 1 W.L.R. 496; S. & T. 228.
23 [1925] A.C. 270; S. & T. 225.

judgment of the senior police officer, a garrison was unnecessary to preserve the peace; a mobile force would have been quite adequate. On the insistence of the colliery manager, he agreed to provide the garrison in return for the promise to pay for it. The decision as to what measures were necessary to preserve the peace was for the senior police officer on the spot and, provided it was made reasonably and in good faith, the court could not interfere with it. So the police had done more than they were obliged to do and were entitled to be paid for it. If, as two dissenting judges in the House of Lords held, the police had done no more than their duty, their action would presumably have failed; but this might have been put on grounds of public policy rather than on lack of consideration.

Not only is there little authority in favour of the rule, but there is some which is hard to reconcile with its existence. There are numerous cases in the law reports concerning offers of rewards for information leading to the conviction of felons and the validity of any resulting contracts to pay never seems to have been questioned.[24] Yet in *Sykes v. DPP.*[25] in 1961 it was decided that the concealment of, or failure to reveal, information about a felony known to have been committed, was an offence, known as misprision of felony. Citizens had a legal duty to reveal felonies known to them. A person giving information leading to the conviction of a felon was doing no more than the criminal law required him to do. One of the arguments advanced in *Sykes* was that the reward cases showed that there was no such crime as misprision of felony; if there were, actions for rewards would all have failed on the ground that the informer was doing no more than his legal duty. The House decided there was such a crime and did not deal with this argument. That leaves two possibilities: either the reward cases were all wrongly decided (which seems very unlikely); or there is no general rule that the performance of a public duty is incapable of being consideration. It should be added that felonies, and therefore the offence of misprision of felony, were abolished by the Criminal Law Act 1967, so the problem does not arise today; but that in no way affects the validity of the above argument.

In most cases it would make no difference if the court proceeded on the basis that the matter was one for public policy rather than consideration. If, when Lord Denning was on the bench, he had been faced with witnesses demanding payment for appearing in response to *subpoena* and police officers claiming money promised them in return for doing their plain duty, he

24 *cf. Williams v. Carwardine*, above, p. 24.
25 [1961] A.C. 528, HL.

would have given them short shrift on public policy grounds. But this approach gives the court more flexibility (and Lord Denning was always in favour of that), allowing for the opinion, perhaps, that there is nothing against public policy in rewards to encourage members of the public to betray felons, even if that was their duty.

Performance of a duty owed only to a third party

The law on this point is now settled. In deciding whether there is a contract between A and B, it is immaterial that the only consideration supplied by A is the performance, or the promise to perform, an obligation which he owes only to C. Here B clearly is getting something more than *he* is entitled to. A's failure to perform his obligation to C would be a breach of contract with C but it would not amount to any legal wrong against B. In *Shadwell v. Shadwell*, (considered above, p. 66) Byles J., as well as taking the good point that the uncle had made no request, took a bad one; that nephew was already engaged to Ellen Nicholl (then an enforceable contract) so, in marrying her, he was only doing what he was legally bound to do. But uncle had no right to demand that nephew should marry Ellen and so his doing so, at uncle's request, would have been sufficient consideration. Modern cases in the Privy Council have established the point beyond doubt. So, where a stevedore, at the request of the shipper of goods, removed the goods from a ship, this was consideration for a promise by the shipper, although the stevedore, in removing the goods, was only performing the contractual duty he owes to the shipowner.[26]

Some situations which formerly fell within this category may, since the coming into force of the Contracts (Rights of Third Parties) Act 1999 (below, p. 000), now fall into the next. If X contracts with Y to do something for the benefit of an identified person, Z, X's performance was, before the Act, generally the fulfilment of a duty owed only to Y. If the Act applies to the contract, the duty is now also owed to Z. If Z promises X remuneration to perform the contractual obligation, he is now promising to pay for something to which he is already legally entitled.

Performance of a duty owed to the promisor

This is much more controversial. The nineteenth-century

---

26 *New Zealand Shipping Co. Ltd v. A. M. Satterthwaite & Co. Ltd* [1975] A.C. 154; S. & T. 300, PC; *cf. Pao On v. Lau Yiu Long* [1980] A.C. 614; S. & T. 233, PC.

authorities, however, were clear. The performance by A, or his promise to perform, a duty which he already owed to B, was no consideration for a promise by B. Here B is getting nothing more than he is already entitled to. Where seamen had contracted to serve on a voyage at a specified rate and, in the course of the voyage, the captain promised to divide among them the wages of two seamen who had deserted, it was held that the promise was unenforceable. The seamen had sold the whole of their services for the voyage. In continuing to sail the ship after the desertion of their two colleagues, they were doing nothing more than they were already obliged to do: *Stilk v. Myrick*.[27] It was different where, in the course of a voyage, nearly half the crew deserted. The effect of this was to frustrate the contract of the remainder. Sailing the ship at little more than half strength was fundamentally different from the obligation that they had undertaken. They were free to make a new bargain; so the captain's promise to pay them additional wages was enforceable: *Hartley v. Ponsonby*.[28] It has been argued,[29] unconvincingly, that the true ground of decisions like *Stilk v. Myrick*[30] was public policy, the captain in those days being at the mercy of his crew on a long voyage. There is, however, no indication in the leading cases of any evidence of a demand, still less of a threat by members of the crew and, in the most authoritative report of *Stilk v. Myrick*, the public policy ground is doubted by Lord Ellenborough who put his decision plainly on the ground that the agreement was void for want of consideration.

The status of the principle of *Stilk v. Myrick* is in some doubt as a result of *Williams v. Roffey Bros.*[31] The defendants had contracted to re-furbish a block of flats and had sub-contracted the carpentry work to the plaintiff for a price of £20,000. The plaintiff had made a bad bargain. The price was, as the defendants acknowledged, unreasonably low and the plaintiff got into difficulties. The defendants were liable to a penalty if the work was not completed on time. In order to ensure that the plaintiff continued with the work and finished it on time, they offered him an additional £10,300. The plaintiff then substantially completed the work. The defendants declined to pay the additional sum and the plaintiff sued. It was held that he was entitled to recover the additional payment, although he had done

27 (1809) 2 Camp. 317; S. & T. 234.
28 (1857) 7 El. & Bl. 872.
29 Gilmore, *The Death of Contract*, 22–28.
30 That of Campbell referred to above. The other report is by Espinasse (6 Esp. 129) who was notoriously unreliable.
31 [1990] 2 W.L.R. 1153; S. & T. 236, CA. *cf. Atlas Express Ltd v. Kafco*, below, p. 251.

no more work than he had originally agreed to do. It was sufficient that the performance of the work amounted in practice to a benefit, or obviated a "disbenefit" (in the inelegant terminology of the court), to the promisor. All three judges asserted that their decision was compatible with *Stilk v. Myrick* but it is hard to see that this is so. Surely it was a great benefit (and the avoidance of a "disbenefit") to the master in that case to have the crew sail the ship home rather than abandon him and it in a foreign port. Indeed, there must be few cases in which it will not be a benefit to a contracting party to have the other party perform rather than default; and in any case where he has agreed to pay more to secure performance, it is self-evident that he regarded performance as a significant benefit.

Williams v. Roffey was followed and *Stilk v. Myrick* was again distinguished in *Anangel v. IHI*[32] where the plaintiffs' agreement to take delivery of a ship on the date on which they were already contractually bound to take it was held to be consideration for promises by defendants. Performance by the plaintiffs was seen by the defendants as a very substantial benefit because it would encourage other reluctant customers to take delivery in accordance with their contracts. This factor was regarded as significant in the same way as the existence of the penalty clause in *Williams v. Roffey*. Yet neither factor was an element in the price to be paid by the respective promisees, so it is hard to see how it could be regarded as consideration.

If these cases are rightly decided, *Stilk v. Myrick*, notwithstanding the lip-service paid to it, must be wrong. But the implications of that conclusion would be very far reaching; for the same principle which underlies *Stilk v. Myrick* is also the basis of the famous (or notorious) rule in *Pinnel's* case of 1602— which, remarkably, was not mentioned in *Williams v. Roffey*. The rule in *Pinnel's* case is—

> "that payment of a lesser sum on the day [that it is due] cannot be any satisfaction for the whole because it appears to the judges that by no possibility a lesser sum can be satisfaction to the plaintiff for a greater sum . . . ".[33]

The creditor is getting less than he is entitled to and that cannot be sufficient consideration for any promise he may have made to forgo the balance. Notwithstanding such a promise, he may sue for, and recover, the balance. But, if the debtor, in addition, offers or is requested to do, and does, anything that he is not bound to

---

32 [1990] 2 Lloyd's Rep. 526, Hirst J.
33 (1602) 5 Co. Rep. 117a.

do, that is consideration and the court will not inquire into its adequacy. So where the debtor offers to pay a day before the debt is due, if the creditor will accept half the sum due in full satisfaction, he is offering consideration. The creditor who accepts may be making a bad bargain in, say, forfeiting half his debt for the sake of getting payment a day earlier, but that is immaterial. Similarly, if the debt is payable at a particular place, payment at another place is a sufficient consideration if that is at the request and for the benefit of the creditor. A creditor's promise that he would not serve a bankruptcy notice if the whole debt was paid on the day due was held not binding (he was only getting what he was entitled to) although the debt was due in London and payment was made in Eastbourne. By paying in Eastbourne, the debtor was doing something he was not bound to do, but the evidence showed that it was entirely for the convenience of the debtor that the variation in mode of payment was made. It was a concession by the creditor; the debtor was getting, not giving, by paying in Eastbourne rather than in London.[34]

The court in *Pinnel's* case went on—

> "but the gift of a horse, hawk or robe, etc., in satisfaction is good for it shall be intended that a horse, hawk or robe, etc., might be more beneficial to the plaintiff than money, in respect of some circumstance, or otherwise the plaintiff would not have accepted it in satisfaction."

In giving the horse, hawk or robe the debtor is doing something which he is not obliged to do; and the court will not inquire into the adequacy of the consideration. In such a case, it is thought that the argument that the "change in mode of payment" is for the benefit of the debtor is not open. If I offer you my old car in full satisfaction of the debt of £10,000 which I owe you—"It's the best I can do—take it or leave it—but it is to be in full satisfaction"—and you take it, the debt is satisfied, however grudging and grumbling your acceptance.

The rule in *Pinnel's* case was confirmed by the House of Lords in *Foakes v. Beer*[35] in 1884. The House of Lords did not like the rule and it was only an *obiter dictum*, never applied, apparently, by the Court of Exchequer Chamber, let alone the House itself; but it had the authority of the great "Lord" Coke and had been accepted as law by the profession ever since, so it was the law. It is worth observing, however, that there is nothing very special

34 *Vanbergen v. St Edmund's Properties Ltd* [1933] 2 K.B. 223; S. & T. 250.
35 (1884) 9 App.Cas 605, S. & T. 245.

about the rule if it applies in cases like *Stilk v. Myrick*. It is simply an application of the same general principle.

In *Re Selectmove Ltd*[36] the Court of Appeal was confronted by the conflict between *Williams v. Roffey* and *Foakes v. Beer*. The alleged consideration was an agreement to pay to the Revenue income tax which was due in law. The court pointed out that if the principle of *Williams* was extended to an obligation to pay money, it would leave the principle of *Foakes* with no application. That was not possible. The court was bound to follow *Foakes*. This leaves us with an utterly illogical distinction: the performance of an obligation to render services may be good consideration, but the performance of an obligation to pay money may not. The law urgently requires the attention of the House of Lords or of Parliament.

In *Foakes v. Beer* the written but unsealed agreement recited that Beer had obtained judgment against Foakes for £2,090 19s in the High Court and that, at Foakes's request, Beer had agreed to give him time to pay. The agreement went on to provide that, in consideration of the debtor paying £500, receipt of which the creditor acknowledged, in part satisfaction of the debt, and on condition of his paying £150 on July 1, and January 1, every year until the whole of the sum of £2,090 19s should be paid, the creditor agreed not to take any proceedings on the judgment.

The debtor duly paid off the whole sum by instalments as agreed. But, by law, interest is payable on a judgment debt from the day on which it becomes due. Beer demanded the interest which had accrued, Foakes refused to pay, and Beer brought an action on the judgment—the very thing she had promised not to do—for the interest. But what consideration had Foakes given for that promise? The expressed consideration—the payment of £500—was only part of the larger sum already due and, even if the payment of the instalments were to be treated as part of the consideration, it only amounted to the fulfilment of an existing obligation. Foakes had not done or promised to do, anything that he was not already obliged to do and was held liable to pay the interest.

Before we shed too many tears over the plight of Foakes, it should be noted that Beer probably never intended to forgive him the interest anyway. The object of the agreement was probably only to give Foakes time to pay whatever was due, not to forgive him anything. Lords Watson and Fitzgerald indeed, held that this was the proper construction of the agreement and that Beer succeeded on that ground; but the majority thought that the operative part of the agreement could not be controlled by the recitals and they were unable to read into the operative part the words, "and interest thereon", that were not in fact there. So, if the agreement had been under seal, the majority (but not the minority) would have held that the action failed and that Beer, probably unwittingly, had forfeited her interest.[37]

Compositions with creditors

One of the matters that have worried the courts and the commentators is the validity of compositions with creditors. An insolvent person meets his creditors and they all agree to accept a dividend, a percentage of the debt due, in full satisfaction. Of course, the rule in *Pinnel's* case could be satisfied by the debtor offering each creditor some chattel of trivial value in addition to his dividend, thus giving consideration; but as Sir George Jessel M.R. caustically remarked, not every debtor had "a stock of canary birds, or tomtits, or rubbish of that kind to add to his dividend".[38] There is, however, no difficulty in finding consideration between the creditors. Each of them agrees to accept the dividend in full satisfaction, in consideration of every other creditor doing so; so that, if one creditor goes back on the agreement and, to the detriment of the rest, sues for the full amount due to him, that is a breach of contract with every other creditor. The debtor, though perhaps a party to the agreement, is not a party to the contract since he gave no consideration; but, if he is sued by one of the creditors, he might be able to join in other creditors and have the action stayed on the ground that it is brought in breach of contract with them. If, however, all the creditors who were parties to the composition unite to sue the debtor—as, for example, where he has unexpectedly come into money—it would seem that at common law he would have no answer to the action. Since, however, the composition apparently "purports to confer a benefit" on the debtor, he might now enforce it "in his own right" by virtue of the Contracts (Rights of Third Parties) Act 1999 (below, p. 111). This is so whether he is sued by one or all of the creditors, provided he has assented to the composition or relied on it.

A somewhat similar issue arises where a third party pays the creditor part of the debt in full satisfaction. If the creditor accepts the part payment, any action against the debtor will be a breach of contract with the third party. In *Hirachand Punamchand v.*

---

37 If it could have been clearly proved that the document did not truly represent the agreement between the parties, it might have been rectified: above, p. 17.
38 *Couldery v. Bartrum* (1881) 19 Ch.D. 394 at 400.

Temple[39] a variety of reasons were given why the creditor's action must fail. The debtor had given the creditor a promissory note for the sum due. The creditor sued on the note. Vaughan Williams L.J. thought that, when the creditor accepted the lesser sum, (i) the note ceased to be a negotiable instrument just as if the debtor's signature had been erased—a remarkable proposition from which he passed on with understandable haste to (ii), that the creditor now held the note on trust for the third party— in effect, that the third party had bought the equitable interest in it, and (iii) that the action was a fraud on the third party which the court could not aid, so the debt was gone. It may well be that this case is now also covered by the 1999 Act, giving the debtor a defence in his own right and avoiding these complexities; but if the trust solution is correct, the benefit to the debtor is qualified; for then the third party could sue on the note and might be justified in doing so if, for example, the debtor came into money and refused to refund to the third party the amount paid out for his benefit.

THE HIGH TREES CASE AND PROMISSORY ESTOPPEL

The rule in *Pinnel's* case as applied in *Foakes v. Beer* still undoubtedly represents the common law but there is some question as to how far it is modified by an equitable principle known as promissory estoppel. The starting point for this discussion must be the decision of Denning J. in *Central London Property Trust Ltd v. High Trees House*.[40] The plaintiffs granted the defendants a lease of a block of flats for 99 years from September 1937 at £2,500 a year. During the war the flats could not be fully let, so the defendants were in some difficulty about paying the rent. The plaintiffs agreed that the rent should be reduced, as from the commencement of the lease, to £1,250. The defendants paid the reduced rent to the beginning of 1945, when all the flats were let, and continued to pay it thereafter. A receiver was appointed for the plaintiffs and he claimed that arrears of £7,916 were due. To test the legal position, he brought an action to recover the difference between the reserved rent of £2,500 and the reduced rent of £1,250 for the two quarters ending September 29, and December 25, 1945.

Denning J. held that the agreement to reduce the rent was intended to apply only while the wartime conditions prevailed. It was clearly not intended to run for the full term of the lease. It

39 [1911] 2 K.B. 330; S. & T. 252, CA.
40 [1947] 1 K.B. 130; S. & T. 254, KBD.

had come to an end before the two quarters in question so the plaintiff was entitled to recover the amount claimed. Denning J. could have stopped there and, arguably, everything else he said was *obiter dictum*, but this would not really have answered the question that concerned the two companies. Denning J. was not the man to pass over such a wonderful opportunity, so he considered whether the wartime agreement was binding and decided that it was: the plaintiffs were estopped from claiming the balance of the rent. In so deciding, Denning J. had to overcome two obstacles, either of which would have been sufficiently formidable to deter any ordinary judge. The first was the decision of the House of Lords in *Jordan v. Money*[41] that estoppel applies only to representations of fact. That was brushed rather summarily aside on the ground that the law had not been standing still and, anyway, it was distinguishable because the promisor in that case did not intend to be legally bound—a fact not discoverable easily, if at all, from the report. The second obstacle, of course, was *Foakes v. Beer. High Trees* was a case of a lesser sum being accepted in satisfaction of a greater. That received even more summary treatment. The principle to be applied in the present case was an equitable principle that was not considered in *Foakes v. Beer*. The principle was that a promise, intended to be binding, intended to be acted on and in fact acted on, is binding in the sense that the courts will not allow the promisor to act inconsistently with it. It was immaterial that there was no consideration. Denning J. added, however, that the courts had not gone so far as to allow an action for damages for breach of such a promise.

THE CREDENTIALS OF THE HIGH TREES CASE

Denning J. relied on a series of decisions which, he says, were a natural result of the fusion of law and equity in 1873–1875. The most important of these cases is that of the House of Lords in *Hughes v. Metropolitan Railway Co.*[42] A landlord gave his tenant six months' notice to repair the premises, the lease being forfeitable if the tenant failed to comply. During the six months, the parties entered into negotiations for the sale of the lease to the landlord and, with the landlord's concurrence, no repairs were done while the negotiations were in progress. The negotiations failed. On the expiry of six months from the original notice, the landlord claimed to treat the lease as forfeit. The House held that the tenant was entitled to relief in equity

41 (1854) 5 H.L.C. 185; S. & T. 257.
42 (1877) 2 App.Cas. 439; S. & T. 259.

against forfeiture; the six months allowed for repair should run from the date of the failure of the negotiations. This was a case, then, where A said, in effect, to B, "You need not fulfil your contractual duty to repair the premises within six months of the notice I have given you"; and then, when B took him at his word and did not carry out the repairs, declared that B had broken his contract and that he was terminating it. It seems a very elementary principle of justice that a party who has agreed to the non-performance of contract should not be allowed to treat that non-performance as a breach of contract. Since he has consented to it, no wrong is done to him—he has "waived" his right to performance. There would be an exact analogy in a case like *High Trees* if the landlord, having accepted half-rent for, say, one year, were to say to the tenant, "You have broken your contract by failing to pay the whole rent and I forfeit the lease".

Most of the cases relied on in support of the *High Trees* decision are waivers of this kind. For example, in *Panoutsos v. Raymond Hadley*,[43] a case frequently cited by Lord Denning, B, a buyer of goods, had a duty to open a confirmed credit. He opened an unconfirmed credit. A, the seller, led B to suppose that he was content with an unconfirmed credit. Then, without prior warning, A terminated the contract on the ground of B's breach in failing to open a confirmed credit. It was held that he could not do so—but he could insist that B open a confirmed credit within a reasonable time. If B did not do so, he would then be in breach of contract.

The principle of these cases is this: that if A tells B, by words or conduct, that B need not perform a contractual obligation owed by B to A, and B takes A at his word and does not perform that obligation, A cannot treat the non-performance as a breach of contract, entitling him to damages or to terminate the contract.

The *High Trees* case was quite different. The landlord did not claim that the tenant had broken the contract—he was not asking for damages or claiming to be entitled to terminate the lease. He was saying only that the tenant must perform the contract by paying the stipulated rent. *Hughes* does not say that he cannot do this. The landlord could require performance of the contractual obligation to repair in the future. There could be no question of the obligation to repair being enforced retrospectively; it is impossible to comply with an obligation to do something by a specified date when that date has passed. But there was no such impossibility in the obligation to pay the full rent in *High Trees*. *Foakes v. Beer* says that the creditor may enforce the obligation retrospectively. There is no material difference between the

43 [1917] 2 K.B. 473, CA.

interest on the judgment debt which had accrued from day to day in *Foakes v. Beer*, and the rent payable under the lease which accrued from time to time in *High Trees*. Both were obligations which had arisen, but had been waived, before the plaintiff made the claim in issue.

Foakes v. Beer (1884) was, of course, decided after the fusion of law and equity and indeed after *Hughes v. Metropolitan Railway* (1877). *Hughes* was not cited in *Foakes* although Lords Selborne and Blackburn were in both cases. This is not surprising. The principle was not applicable. *Hughes* certainly tends to show that the non-payment of rent in *High Trees* was not a breach of contract, but it says nothing on the question whether the tenant could be required to perform his contract. *High Trees* was then a new and radical departure.

The effect of *High Trees*

Assuming for the moment that the *High Trees* principle now represents the law, what is its effect? A number of questions arise.

(i) Does it create a cause of action?   In *Combe v. Combe*[44] Denning L.J. confirmed what he had said in *High Trees*: " . . . the principle never stands alone as giving a cause of action in itself" and "it can never do away with the necessity of consideration when that is an essential part of the cause of action." Birkett L.J. said that the doctrine can be used as a shield but not a sword. A husband had promised to pay his wife £100 a year after their divorce. Byrne J. had held that this was a promise, intended to be binding, intended to be acted on and in fact acted on as required by *High Trees* and that the wife could sue on it. That was wrong. The promise to pay was not binding unless there was consideration for it. But the "sword and shield" metaphor is misleading. Estoppel, of whatever kind, may be part of the armoury of the plaintiff no less than of the defendant. In itself, it is neither a cause of action nor a defence, but it may enable a party to establish the conditions necessary for either. In *Robertson v. Minister of Pensions*[45] the War Office wrote to the plaintiff, "Your disability has been accepted as attributable to military service." On the faith of that assurance, he took no steps to obtain an independent medical opinion, as otherwise he would have done. Subsequently a pensions appeal tribunal decided that his injury was not due to war service. Denning J., following the *High Trees*

44 [1951] 2 K.B. 215; S. & T. 260.
45 [1949] 1 K.B. 227.

case, held that the Crown was estopped from denying that the injury was due to war service. Arguably, this was an ordinary estoppel, being a representation of fact. Whatever its nature, it enabled the plaintiff to make out his cause of action which was based, not on any promise, but on his statutory right to a pension. It is possible that there is an exception to the rule that estoppel does not in itself found a cause of action in the case of proprietary estoppel, to be considered below.

(ii) Does it suspend or extinguish rights? There has been much controversy about this, but the answer seems reasonably clear. As regards existing obligations, it is extinctive, as regards future obligations, it is suspensory. Both these points emerge in the *Tool Metal* case.[46] Tool Metal had licensed Tungsten to deal in certain metals, for which Tool Metal owned the patents, in consideration of Tungsten paying a royalty of 10 per cent up to a certain amount and, thereafter, 30 per cent. During the war, Tool Metal agreed to waive their right to 30 per cent and to accept a flat rate of 10 per cent. After the war a dispute arose. Tool Metal claimed the waived 20 per cent in respect of material which had been used since June 1, 1945. In these respects, then, it was exactly like the *High Trees* case, except that the wartime agreement had not terminated. It was held by the Court of Appeal, following *Hughes v. Metropolitan Railway*,[47] that the claim failed. So, clearly, the existing "rights" under the contract were extinguished—the extra 20 per cent was lost for ever. But the contract to pay 30 per cent was still in existence (though waived) and the House of Lords held, on the assumption that the waiver was, as the Court of Appeal had held, binding, that Tool Metal could resume their rights to the 30 per cent for the future, by giving reasonable notice that the waiver was at an end. Their future rights under the contract were only suspended until they had given proper notice that they wished to resume them. It seems to follow from this decision that if, in *High Trees* during the war years when the agreement was operative, the landlord had given notice that, from a reasonable time in the future, say three months, he wanted the full rent, he would have been entitled to it; but that, for the past, the balance of the rent was lost for ever. His "rights" for the past were extinguished, his "rights" for the future merely suspended.

46 *Tool Metal Manufacturing Co. Ltd v. Tungsten Electric Co. Ltd* [1955] 1 W.L.R. 761; S. & T. 269.
47 The court did not refer to *High Trees*; yet as submitted above, *Hughes* has nothing to say on this issue, while *High Trees* is directly in point.

(iii) Does *High Trees,* in effect, "overrule" *Pinnel's* case and *Foakes v. Beer?* Of course, a judge of first instance has no power to overrule those cases in the strict sense but, if the effect of his judgment, as subsequently applied, destroys their effect, the result is the same. The answer to the question must, however, be in the negative. Lord Denning himself has recognised that *Foakes v. Beer* still represents the common law and that the *High Trees* doctrine only operates (like other equitable doctrines) as a supplement or corrective to the common law, when it would otherwise do injustice. The *High Trees* principle is applicable only when it is equitable to apply it. In *D. & C. Builders v. Rees*[48] the defendants owed the plaintiffs £746. Payment was well overdue and the plaintiffs were in desperate need of money. The defendant offered £300, insisting that it was to be in full satisfaction of the debt. Because of their financial plight, the plaintiffs reluctantly accepted, saying, "We have no choice." Later they sued for the balance. The Court of Appeal held, following *Foakes v. Beer,* that they were entitled to recover. "The creditor", said Lord Denning, "is barred from his legal rights only when it would be *inequitable* for him to insist on them." In this case it was not inequitable because the creditor had agreed to take a lesser sum only because of undue pressure by the debtor who was guilty of intimidation by threatening to break his contract to pay the full amount. So *Foakes v. Beer* still represents the common law, and *High Trees* applies to qualify it only when it is fair that it should do so. If Lord Denning had been in *Foakes v. Beer* it may be that he would have been happy to concur in the result on the ground that Beer did not intend to forgive the interest anyway and that it was therefore not inequitable for her to insist on her statutory right to it.

The status of *High Trees*

Although the *High Trees* case has provoked an enormous amount of discussion, the occasions for the application of the principle seem to have been very few. In *High Trees* itself, the principle was not applied because Denning J. held that plaintiff's claim to recover the balance of the rent succeeded. In *Combe v. Combe,* Denning L.J. remarked on the excellence of the doctrine but agreed that it did not apply in the circumstances of that case. In *D. & C. Builders v. Rees,* while again commending the virtues of the doctrine, Lord Denning held that it was inapplicable and *Foakes v. Beer* ruled. In other cases where Lord Denning has given the doctrine an airing, the case could have been decided, or was

48 [1966] 2 Q.B. 617; S. & T. 271, CA.

decided by other judges, on some other well-established principle: common law estoppel in *Robertson v. Minister of Pensions*[49] and *Lyle-Meller v. Lewis*[50] and a variation of the contract in *Alan v. El Nasr*,[51] and in *Brikom Investments Ltd v. Carr & Others*.[52] The only decision squarely on the point seems to be that of the Court of Appeal in the first action in the *Tool Metal* case. The decision of the House of Lords was in a second action in which the parties were estopped[53] by the decision in the first from denying that the principle operated. The House made it very clear that they were not deciding whether the first Court of Appeal was right or wrong. Given that a promissory estoppel was in operation, the only question for them was whether a sufficient notice had been given to bring it to an end. They decided only that, *if* there is a doctrine of promissory estoppel which operates in these circumstances, its operation may be terminated by reasonable notice and, in the circumstances, reasonable notice had been given.

The problem of reconciling *Foakes v. Beer* with the *High Trees* principle and its application by the Court of Appeal in the *Tool Metal* case remains. Denning J. apparently took the view that they were irreconcilable, *Foakes v. Beer* having been decided *per incuriam*, through overlooking a principle of equity. The irreconcilability may be accepted, the opinion that all the Law Lords forgot about equity—especially when two of them had been involved in the leading case five years before—is harder to swallow.

PROPRIETARY ESTOPPEL

This arises where A purports to give, but does not effectively convey, or promises to give, land, or an interest in land, to B, knowing that B will expend money or otherwise act to his detriment in reliance on the supposed or promised gift. When B does so act, this gives him an "equity" to require A to complete the gift. In *Dillwyn v. Llewellyn*[54] a father, wishing his son to reside near him, signed a memorandum "presenting [a freehold estate] to my son for the purpose of furnishing him with a dwelling-house." The son took possession and expended a large sum in building a house and generally improving the property.

49 Above, p. 86.
50 [1956] 1 W.L.R. 29.
51 [1972] 2 Q.B. 189.
52 [1979] Q.B. 467.
53 Estoppel by record (the record of the court)—an entirely different variety of estoppel from those discussed in this book.
54 (1862) 4 De G. F. & J. 517, CA in Chancery.

The father never conveyed the estate and, after his death, the son, claiming to be the equitable owner in fee simple, sued for and obtained an order that the trustees convey the estate to him. Lord Westbury L.C. said that "the subsequent expenditure by the son with the approbation of the father supplied a valuable consideration, originally wanting." The case might therefore be explained simply as one of unilateral contract, the element of request being implicit in the father's wish that his son live near him. Later cases such as *Inwards v. Baker*[55] are not readily explicable on this ground. The conveyance of proprietary interests does not however, depend on the existence of consideration. A gift is complete when the property is delivered to the donee and, *ex hypothesi*, no consideration is given. Perhaps the explanation of the proprietary estoppel cases is that the action in reliance on the promise created the equity in the nature of a constructive trust and the plaintiff sues in reliance on his proprietary interest. This seems to have been, in effect, the view of the County Court judge in *Pascoe v. Turner*[56] where a man's promise to give his mistress his house and everything in it was held binding on him because, in reliance on the promise, she had spent money on decoration, improvements and repair. The judge thought the beneficial interest had passed to the mistress by virtue of the estoppel, but the Court of Appeal treated the case as one of a promise which had to be carried out—a promise which was better than a contract because it was enforceable even though there was no writing. Section 40 of the Law of Property Act 1925 then provided that no action should be brought upon any contract for the sale or other disposition of land or any interest in land; and this surely meant that oral promises to dispose of land should not be enforceable. To call the promise "an equity" or "an estoppel" so that the section was not applicable seems to be an evasion of the statute. The same considerations apply now, when the Law of Property (Miscellaneous Provisions) Act 1989 provides that such contracts can only be made in writing.

In *Crabb v. Arun District Council*[57] Lord Denning said: "There are estoppels and estoppels. Some do give rise to a cause of action. Some do not. In the species of estoppel called proprietary estoppel, it does give rise to a cause of action."

The Council had led Crabb to believe "that he had, or would be granted, a right of access" at a certain point, and he took detrimental action in reliance on that assurance. If the assurance

55 [1965] 2 Q.B. 29, CA.
56 [1979] 1 W.L.R. 431.
57 [1976] Ch. 179, S. & T. 263.

was that he *had* the right—*i.e.* it had already been granted to him—it was a case of estoppel under established principles; but, if it was a case of "would be granted", it was a promise which might be expected to be unenforceable in the absence of consideration or of the appropriate writing. Though the language of the court is ambiguous, Lord Denning's conclusion was that Crabb "has a right of access . . . and a right of way . . . I would declare that he has an easement accordingly." This was not to say that there was a promise which had to be performed, but that a proprietary interest had been granted.

THE FUTURE OF CONSIDERATION

Some lawyers have suggested that the decision in *Williams v. Roffey* undermines the doctrine of consideration. This is not so. Even if the decision were regarded as overruling *Stilk v. Myrick* and were to lead to the overruling of *Pinnel*'s case and *Foakes v. Beer*, the essence of that doctrine would remain intact. A person who agrees to pay an increased price in order to induce another to fulfil his contractual duty, or to take a lesser sum in full satisfaction in order to induce his debtor to pay something, is making a bargain. He asks for something in return for his promise to pay more, or not to sue for the balance, as the case may be, and gets what he asks for. To hold him bound, far from impairing the basic rule that bargains are binding, would be to abolish an exception to that rule. Lord Blackburn recognised this in *Foakes v. Beer* but was dissuaded by his brethren from dissenting on that ground.

The bargain would not always be enforceable. The outcome would depend on whether the party surrendering his contractual rights did so under economic duress, which is discussed below, Chapter 21. So the result in *D. & C. Builders v. Rees*[58] would be unaffected as would that in *Atlas Express Ltd v. Kafco Ltd*.[59] Further inquiry into the facts of *High Trees*—irrelevant, while the rule in *Foakes v. Beer* prevails—might reveal a bargain ("We shall have to go into liquidation and be unable to pay you anything unless you can reduce the rent") which would be enforceable as a contract, unless it involved duress. The actual result in *Foakes v. Beer* might be unaffected because there probably was no bargain, no intention to release any existing rights. Economic duress, which would assume greater importance is a doctrine of uncertain extent—but so is the *High Trees* doctrine which, to some extent it would replace.

58 Above, p. 88.
59 Below, p. 251.

All this is somewhat speculative until the courts face the fact that *Williams v. Roffey* is irreconcilable with *Stilk v. Myrick* and therefore with *Foakes v. Beer*.

CHAPTER EIGHT

Privity of Contract

There are two principal questions to be considered in this chapter. (i) May a person who is not a party to a contract acquire rights under it? (ii) Can a contract impose duties on a person who is not a party to it? Subject to some exceptions, the common law answered both questions in the negative.

ACQUISITION OF RIGHTS BY THIRD PARTIES

If A, for consideration supplied by B, promises to do something for the benefit of C, C acquires no rights at common law. If A fails to carry out his promise, he commits a breach of contract with B; but B might be able to recover only nominal damages because he has suffered no loss. C, generally, has no remedy at common law. The Contracts (Rights of Third Parties) Act 1999 now creates a major exception to that rule. Before we come to that Act, it is necessary to consider the common law which is still important because (a) the Act does not apply to some classes of contract, and (b) the parties can always exclude its operation if they wish, when the common law will continue to apply.

It is usually said that there are two principles involved here. The first (Case 1), commonly called privity of contract, is that only a promisee can enforce the promise. A promises B, for consideration supplied by B, that he will do something for the benefit of C. Because C is not a promisee, he has no right to enforce the promise.

The second principle (Case 2) is that "consideration must move from the promisee." A promises B *and* C for consideration supplied by B, that he will do something for the benefit of C. C is a promisee but no consideration "moved" from him, so he cannot enforce the promise.

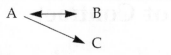

C is no better off in the second case than the first. Since it is immaterial whether he is a promisee or not, it is clear that the crucial principle is the second one. Indeed, the first can scarcely be said to be a principle at all, since the operation of the second leaves no room for any independent application of the first. The rule of privity of contract is really no more than an application of the doctrine of consideration, which is why it is considered at this point. The leading cases bear out this theory. One that has been particularly influential is that of the Court of Queen's Bench in *Tweddle v. Atkinson*.[1] After the plaintiff's marriage, his father (B) made a contract with the bride's father (A) by which each of them undertook to pay a sum of money to the plaintiff (C). It was a contract made by A and B for the benefit of C. C was not a promisee and he gave no consideration. B paid C as agreed, but A did not. This was, of course, a breach of contract with B. Although the agreement provided that C should have "full power to sue" for the sums promised, C's action against A's executor failed. It failed, not because he was not a promisee, but because he was, as Wightman J. put it, "a stranger to the consideration". The judges appear to have thought it self-evident that one from whom no consideration moved should have no right to sue. "It would be a monstrous proposition", said Crompton J., "to say that a person was a party to the contract for the purpose of suing upon it for his own advantage and not a party to it for the purpose of being sued." Why did not B sue? Possibly because B had suffered no loss (apart from losing the satisfaction of seeing a benefit accrue to his son) and so would

1 (1861) 1 B. & S. 393; S. & T. 283.

have received only nominal damages; but we shall return to this point.

Of even greater importance is the decision of the House of Lords in *Dunlop Pneumatic Tyre Co. Ltd v. Selfridge*.[2] Dunlop sold their tyres to a wholesaler, Dew. In order to maintain the prices of their tyres, they included a term in their contract of sale requiring Dew to obtain from any trade customers to whom he resold the tyres an undertaking in writing that, in consideration of being allowed a discount off the list prices of the tyres, they would observe the list prices on any further resale to a consumer and would pay Dunlop £5 for every tyre sold in breach of that agreement. Dew sold a tyre to Selfridge and duly obtained the undertaking in favour of Dunlop from Selfridge. Selfridge sold the tyre in breach of this agreement and Dunlop sued for the £5.

DUNLOP◄─►DEW◄─►SELFRIDGE ◄─►CONSUMER

| ACTION ▲

The action failed because Dunlop gave no consideration to Selfridge for the latter's promises to observe the list price and to pay Dunlop £5 if they failed to do so. It seems clear that Dew were acting as agents for Dunlop in exacting from Selfridge the undertaking in Dunlop's favour. A promise made to, and received by, one's agent to receive it is as good as a promise made to oneself—but no better. So this might be regarded fairly as a case where the promise was made to C (Dunlop), as well as to B (Dew); but that did not avail C. Five of the six judges in the House of Lords were prepared to accept that Dew might have been acting as Dunlop's agents in obtaining Selfridge's promise; but Dunlop gave Selfridge no consideration for that promise— and that was fatal.

It was argued that Dunlop gave consideration to Selfridge by allowing them to buy the tyres at a discount—below list price; but their lordships had no difficulty in exposing the fallacy in that argument. The tyres belonged to Dew and any reduction in the price charged to Selfridge came out of Dew's pocket, not Dunlop's.

The question in *Dunlop v. Selfridge* could not arise in that form today because resale price maintenance agreements of that kind have been outlawed since the Resale Prices Act 1956, now replaced by the Competition Act 1998; but this in no way impairs

2 [1915] A.C. 847; S. & T. 283.

the authority of the case on the principles of the common law involved.

IS THE RULE THAT CONSIDERATION MUST MOVE FROM THE PROMISEE A MYTH?

It has now to be noted that it has been strenuously argued in recent years that, where there are joint promisees, one of them may sue even if the consideration was supplied exclusively by the other: if the promise is made to B *and* C, C may sue although only B supplied consideration. This theory has the support of the *dicta* of four out of five judges of the High Court of Australia in *Coulls v. Bagot's Executor and Trustee Co. Ltd.*,[3] distinguished academics[4] and, most important, the Law Commission. If they are right, the rule that consideration must move from the promisee is a myth; but that is hard to believe. We return to this question when considering the 1999 Act.

CONTRACT NOT AVAILABLE TO THIRD PARTY AS A DEFENCE

Dunlop v. Selfridge and *Tweddle v. Atkinson* concerned the question whether C can sue A on a promise made by A in a contract with B. The question may also arise whether C can rely on that contract by way of defence when he is sued by A. The answer is generally the same. C, having given no consideration to A, cannot rely on A's promise by way of defence any more than he can use it to found a claim. Since there is no contract between A and C, any right of action A may have against C must be in tort. A duty of care may be imposed by the law of tort on C in relation to goods or other property of A. If C, in breach of that duty of care, damages that property, A may sue him in the tort of negligence. If, in pursuance of the contract between A and B, A delivers goods to B who entrusts them to C, C owes a duty to A to take reasonable care not to cause damage to the goods. Similarly, where B, in pursuance of his contract to do certain work on A's premises, employs C as a sub-contractor, C owes A a duty of care in respect of the premises. C's duty of care in these examples is imposed by the general law. The question is, can the existence of that duty, or the effect of a breach of it, be affected by the contract between A and B?

---

3 (1967) 119 C.L.R. 460.
4 Atiyah, *Consideration in Contracts, A Fundamental Restatement.* 41–42, Treitel, *Law of Contract* (10th ed.), p. 536 *Contra,* Coote "Consideration and Joint Promisees" [1978] C.L.J. 300.

One modern case holds that the duty may be negatived. In *Norwich City Council v. Harvey and others,*[5] A employed contractors, B, to extend a swimming pool. The contract, by clause 20, provided that the risk of damage by fire should be on A and required A to maintain adequate insurance. B sub-contracted roofing work to C2. The sub-contract referred to clause 20 of the main contract and stated that it would apply. C2's employee, C1, negligently set fire to the building. A's action against C1 and C2 failed on the ground that the defendants owed no duty of care to A. The justice of the result is obvious. Presumably A fulfilled their obligation to insure and were compensated by their insurers. In that case, the action was brought for the benefit of the insurers. C2, reasonably relying on clause 20, may have thought it quite unnecessary to insure and in that case it may have been disastrous if they had been held liable. The workman, C1, could not have been expected to know of the existence of clause 20; but he might reasonably have supposed that his employer would have taken adequate precautions regarding insurance. It is easier to be satisfied of the justice of the result than of the legal principles or of how it is to be distinguished from the leading case, *Scruttons Ltd v. Midland Silicones Ltd,*[6] which holds that, at common law, C cannot "take advantage" of a contract between A and B by way of defence, any more than he can sue on it. *Scruttons* was cited in argument in the *Norwich* case but not mentioned in the judgment. *Scruttons* was a case about a contract for the carriage of goods by sea and, for the proper understanding of such a case, some special rules have to be explained. When a person (the shipper) sends goods, he receives a written document, a bill of lading, signed on behalf of the shipowner (or carrier), acknowledging receipt of the goods and undertaking to deliver them at the end of the voyage, subject to the conditions contained in the bill. There is some debate as to whether the bill is the contract of carriage or only evidence of its terms; but that is not material for present purposes. The shipper delivers the bill of lading to the consignee and this enables the consignee to get possession of the goods at the end of the voyage. Not only does the delivery of the bill transfer the ownership in the goods from shipper to consignee, it also transfers the contractual relationship with the carrier from shipper to consignee. The Bills of Lading Act 1855 (now replaced by the Carriage of Goods by Sea Act 1992), section 1 provides that the consignee to whom the property passes "shall have transferred to and vested in him all rights of suit, and be subject to the same

5 [1989] 1 W.L.R. 828; S. & T. 309, CA.
6 [1962] A.C. 446; S. & T. 293, HL.

liabilities in respect of such goods as if the contract contained in the bill of lading had been made with himself." The consignee steps into the shipper's contractual shoes so that, in the cases, the one is equated with the other. The cases involve a second contract—one made by the carrier with a firm of stevedores to load or unload the goods on to or from the ship. The position may be represented as follows.

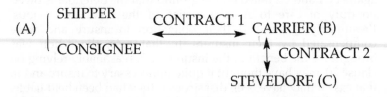

In *Scruttons* the contract between the shipper and the carrier (contract 1) included a clause, limiting the liability of the carrier to $500. The contract between the carrier and the stevedore (contract 2) also contained a clause limiting the liability of the stevedore to $500. The stevedore negligently dropped the shipper's goods, causing damage to the amount of £593. The stevedore owed a duty of care to the owners of the goods he was handling, so the shipper sued him in the tort of negligence. The stevedore argued that his liability should be limited to $500 but his difficulty is readily apparent. There were two contracts limiting liability but, on the face of it, no contract between shipper and stevedore. The stevedore was held liable for the full amount. The stevedore relied on contract I, but the answer was that he was not a party to that contract. He had not been asked for, and had not given, any consideration to the shipper. Even Lord Denning, who dissented, agreed that the stevedore could not rely on contract 1, but he, unlike the rest of the House, would have held that the stevedore was entitled to rely on that contract if it had stated clearly that the exclusion clause applied for the protection of the stevedore as well as the carrier. It did not; and, for the majority, in the absence of consideration moving from stevedore to shipper, it would have made no difference if it had.[7]

Lord Denning invoked a different principle, on which the majority had nothing to say. The stevedore could rely on contract 2. The carrier is a bailee of the shipper's goods and it is a special feature of the law of bailment that the bailor is bound by any contract which he has expressly or impliedly authorised the

---

7 Because the stevedore was not indentified in contract 1, either individually or as a member of a class, he could not, as we shall see, now rely on the 1999 Act; but, if he had been thus identified, he could do so.

bailee to make in relation to the goods. The shipper of goods may be presumed to know that the carrier will have to make contracts with stevedores for the loading and unloading of the goods, so he is bound by the terms of any exclusion clause in such a contract.

This argument was not mentioned by the majority, but Lord Denning reiterated it in *Morris v. Martin*[8] and it now has powerful support, having been applied by the Privy Council in *The Pioneer Container* and approved in *The Mahkutai*.[9] In *The Pioneer Container* the plaintiffs (A) contracted with carriers (B) for the carriage of A's goods from Taiwan to Hong Kong by bills of lading which provided that B was entitled to sub-contract "on any terms" the whole or any part of the carriage. B sub-contracted the carriage to the defendants (C) on bills of lading which provided that the contract was governed by Chinese law and any dispute was to be determined in Taiwan ("the exclusive jurisdiction clause"). The ship sank and the question was whether A could sue C in Hong Kong. It was accepted that there was no contract between A and C but the Hong Kong Court of Appeal held that A was bound by the exclusive jurisdiction clause. The Privy Council, applying the principle stated by Lord Denning in *Morris v. Martin*, dismissed A's appeal. C became a bailee of the goods for reward and both A and B had concurrently the rights of a bailor against C. The obligation owed by C to A (as well as to B) was that of a bailee for reward, (A bailee for reward (consideration) owes a higher obligation than a gratuitous bailee) although the reward was payable not by A but by B. It would be inconsistent to impose on the bailee two different standards of care in respect of the goods entrusted to him. Arguably, then, the failure of the majority in *Scruttons* to consider the law of bailment means that that case was decided *per incuriam*. But decisions of the Privy Council are not binding on English courts and *Scruttons*, pending any reconsideration by the House of Lords, remains the law.

In the meantime, other decisions of the Privy Council have avoided the effect of *Scruttons* by taking a rather strained view of the facts.

In *The Eurymedon*[10] the facts were very similar to those in *Scruttons* with the important exception that the bill of lading stated that the exemptions contained in it should extend to

8 *Morris v. C. W. Martin & Sons Ltd* [1966] 1 QB 716; S. & T. 306, CA.
9 *The Pioneer Container* [1994] 2 A.C. 324; S. & T. 307, PC; *The Mahkutai* [1996] 3 All E.R. 502, PC.
10 *New Zealand Shipping Co. Ltd v. A. M. Satterthwaite & Co. Ltd, The Eurymedon* [1975] A.C. 154, PC; S. & T. 300.

protect agents of the carrier including independent contractors—
like stevedores.[11] That would certainly have been enough for
Lord Denning but not, it seems for the other judges in
Scruttons—but none of them was in *The Eurymedon*—for there
remained the vital question of consideration. The Privy Council
overcame this difficulty by finding that the shipper was, in effect,
saying to the stevedore, through the shipper's agent, the carrier,
"If you will load (or unload) my goods, I undertake that your
liability will be limited . . . ". If this really happened, the matter
is quite straightforward. There was now a third contract between
shipper and stevedore. When sued, the stevedore relied on that
contract. He was a party and had supplied consideration by
doing the act requested, loading or unloading the ship. The
difficulty, of course, is to see that it did happen. Viscount
Dilhorne and Lord Simon of Glaisdale, dissenting, were unable
to find that it did. The clause in the bill of lading was not an offer
to the stevedores but an agreement between the shipper and the
carrier and there was in fact no request to the stevedore or any
action by him in reliance on the promise. This seems to be the
true view of the facts but it is a minority view and it is the fiction
which prevails. *The Eurymedon* was followed by the Privy
Council in *The New York Star*[12] and, though these decisions are
not technically binding on English courts, it is likely that they
will be followed. They were "explained" in *The Mahkutai* on the
basis that a *bilateral* agreement between the stevedores and the
shippers, entered into through the agency of the shipowners,
may, though initially unsupported by consideration, become
enforceable by consideration supplied by the stevedores performing their duties. The Privy Council indicated that the time
may come when the courts take "the final, and perhaps
inevitable step in this development and recognise in these cases
a fully fledged exception to the doctrine of privity of contract".[13]
This would be better than indulging the fictions relied on by the
majority in the *Eurymedon*. It should be noticed that they do not
create any exceptions to the doctrine of privity or the rule that
consideration must move from the promisee. The stevedore is
protected because he is held, however artificially, to be a party to
a contract and to have given consideration.

11 If this sufficiently identified the stevedore company as a member of a class, it
   could now rely on the 1999 Act, enjoying the double protection of contracts 1
   and 3.
12 *Port Jackson Stevedoring Pty Ltd v. Salmond & Spraggon Pty. (Australia) Ltd, The
   New York Star* [1981] 1 W.L.R. 138.
13 [1996] 3 All E.R. 512.

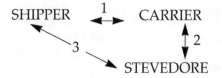

In the *Norwich* case (above, p. 97) the contract between A and B established the defence to C which failed in *Scruttons* and did so without resort to the artificial device of the third contract on which C succeeded in *The Eurymedon*. Why? One possible answer is that the *Norwich* case was wrongly decided; but it was so obviously just that a court might be reluctant so to hold. A possible distinction is that, in the shipping cases, there was no question of the contract between A and B *negativing* C's duty of care, for, if the relevant clauses affected C's liability at all, they merely limited it—*i.e.* they assumed that C *did* owe a duty of care to A and was, indeed, in breach of it. It would however be a strange law which allowed the contract to which C is not a party to negative his liability altogether, but not to limit it. The analogy of a principle governing the interpretation of exclusion clauses would suggest the opposite result (below, p. 169).

WHERE CONSIDERATION MOVES FROM BOTH B AND C

Although A's dealing is exclusively with B, it may be that, in reality, the consideration moves from both B and C; and in that case B and C are both contracting parties. Where B deposits money in a bank account in the names of B and C, the consideration is given by both and either may sue the bank for failure to return the deposit or to pay the agreed amount of interest.[14] It is immaterial that the money deposited belongs to B alone, or, indeed to C alone. Who owns the money is simply not the bank's business.

C is also a contracting party where, though A expects B to supply the consideration, C will be bound to supply it if B does not. A wife, who was poisoned by a meal in a restaurant, successfully sued the restaurateur for breach of contract in supplying unfit food, although her husband had paid the bill.[15] Although, in 1938, the restaurateur was no doubt looking to the husband for payment, the source of the money was no more his

14 *cf. McEvoy v. Belfast Banking Corporation* [1935] A.C. 24, HL; S. & T. 281.
15 *Lockett v. Charles* [1938] 4 All E.R. 170 (K.B.D.). *cf. Olley v. Marlborough Court* [1949] 1 KB 532, CA, where a wife's action against a hotel succeeded although the husband booked the accommodation and paid the bill.

business than the ownership of the deposit was that of the bank manager; and, if the husband had left without paying, it may confidently be expected that he would have looked to the wife for payment. If she was undertaking only a contingent liability, that would be sufficient consideration.

ENFORCEMENT OF THE CONTRACT BY A CONTRACTOR FOR THE BENEFIT OF A THIRD PARTY

When A and B have made a contract under which A, for consideration supplied by B, has made some promise for the benefit of C, and A withholds that benefit, he commits a breach of contract with B. What can B do to enforce the contract? There are three possibilities.

  (i)   B might obtain a decree of specific performance against A and so compel him to confer the benefit on C.
 (ii)   B might sue A for damages for breach of his contract to confer the benefit on C.
(iii)   Where A is taking action against C in breach of his contract with B, B might seek an injunction to restrain him from doing so.

Each of these possibilities will be considered in turn.

Specific performance

If the contract between A and B belongs to that limited class of contracts for which specific performance is available, B may, if he chooses, sue A and obtain an order from the court, requiring A to perform the contract in favour of C. Once the order has been obtained, by the Rules of the Supreme Court,[16] C is able to enforce it himself. The leading case is *Beswick v. Beswick*.[17] Peter Beswick (B), entered into a contract with his nephew (A) under which he assigned to A his business of coal merchant in consideration of A employing him as a consultant for the rest of his life and paying an annuity to B's widow, C, after his death. After B's death, A declined to pay the annuity to C. C sued as the administratrix of her husband's, B's, estate and obtained a decree of specific performance. Ignoring (as the courts did) the element of personal service (the "consultancy"), the contract was one which was specifically enforceable by either A or B during B's

16 RSC, Ord. 45, r.9(1).
17 [1968] A.C. 58, S. & T. 312, HL.

lifetime and it continued to be specifically enforceable after his death. As B's administratrix, C stood in his shoes for legal purposes, and was able to exercise all his legal rights. It was thus a case where the legal personalities of B and C were combined in the one person, C.

It is important to notice the limitations of the decision. It applies only where the contract between A and B is of a kind which is specifically enforceable. If it had been a true contract for personal services it would not have been specifically enforceable and the action must have failed. If B, a famous painter, contracts with A to paint his portrait in consideration of A's undertaking to pay an annuity to B's widow, C, she will not, even as the deceased B's personal representative, be able to obtain specific performance. A could not have obtained such a decree during B's lifetime, therefore, the remedy being "mutual", B could not; and C could be in no better position that B himself.

Beswick v. Beswick does not provide any remedy for C personally. From the widow's point of view, it was a happy accident that she was her late husband's personal representative and so able to enforce his rights. If he had appointed an executor who had declined to sue for C's benefit, it seems that she would have had no redress. If (as was not the case) B had died insolvent and his creditors were pressing for payment, it may be that it would have been the duty of B's personal representative to compromise the contract with A—"I will release you from your obligation to pay the annuity to C in return for £1,000"—thus providing more money to meet the legitimate claims of B's creditors. After all, B, during his lifetime, could have rescinded the contract by agreement with A, so his personal representative should have been able—and it may even have been his duty—to do so after B's death. C had no personal right to recover the annuity. But she would now be able to enforce the contract in her own right under the 1999 Act.

Recovery of damages

This is more problematic. There is no doubt, of course, that A by failing to confer the promised benefit on C, has broken his contract with B. It follows that B is entitled to damages. The question is, how much and for whose benefit? One view is that B is entitled only to nominal damages because he, B, has suffered no loss. In *West v. Houghton*[18] the lessor of shooting rights (B) sought damages for breach of a covenant by the lessee (A) to keep down the rabbits so that no appreciable damage would be

18 (1879) 4 C.P.D. 197, DC.

done on the estate. Damage had been done by the rabbits, to the detriment of C, the tenant of the land. A had committed a breach of his contract with B; but the Divisional Court took the view that B had suffered no loss and so was entitled only to nominal damages. It would have been different if B had been under a duty to C to keep the rabbits down and that fact had been brought to the attention of A before he entered into the covenant. In *Beswick v. Beswick* the question of damages was considered. In the Court of Appeal Lord Denning was adamant that A could not escape from his obligation "by such a shifty means" as an allegation that B had suffered only nominal damages: B should be able to recover the money which should have been paid to C, for C's benefit. But this is doubtful. In the House of Lords Lord Pearce, agreeing with Windeyer J. in the Australian case of *Coulls v. Bagot's Executor*,[19] thought that the damages which B would suffer on A's failure to pay a promised £500 to C would not be merely nominal; they might be less or more than £500. Notice that, unlike Lord Denning, he was talking about the damages that B (not C) would suffer. It is difficult to see what the basis of assessment would be. Is it the loss of satisfaction which B would have derived from the benefit to C? That is not the kind of loss for which contractual damages are usually awarded, and it would be difficult to estimate realistically. Or is it the value of the consideration which B has given to A in return for A's promise to benefit C? As a result of this breach, that has become a wasted expenditure and damages are sometimes recoverable for wasted expenditure. There is no certain answer to these questions, but in *Woodar Investments Development Ltd v. Wimpey Construction U.K. Ltd*[20] the House of Lords made clear its opinion that B cannot recover the loss sustained by C. B had agreed to sell land to A in consideration of A paying £750,000 to B and £150,000 to C. The Court of Appeal held that, on a breach of contract by A, B was entitled to recover by way of damages not only their own loss but also that of C. As it turned out, the House of Lords held that there had been no breach of contract by A; but, if there had been, B would not have been entitled to recover damages for the loss sustained by C. Whether they could recover any more than nominal damages was, thought Lord Wilberforce, "a question of great doubt and difficulty." It still awaits resolution.

---

19 (1967) 40 A.L.J.R. 471 at 486.
20 [1980] 1 W.L.R. 277, HL; S. & T. 319 and 570.

Exceptions to any rule that B cannot recover for damage sustained by C

If there is a rule that, where A has failed to perform a contract to benefit C and B has suffered no loss B can recover only nominal damages (which some eminent authorities doubt), the common law recognises some exceptions to it.

Where B and C each has an insurable interest in goods and B takes out a policy with A covering the insurable interests of both, B may sue on the policy for C's loss (for which he must account to C) as well as his own loss.[21] B contracted to carry two lorry-loads of cigarettes belonging to C and to insure them comprehensively. Without any fault on B's part, the cigarettes were stolen. A argued that the policy covered only such liability as B might incur to C, and B, not being at fault, had incurred none; but it was held that B could recover the full value of the goods for which he must account to C.

Where, in a commercial contract, the parties, A and B, contemplate that the proprietary interest in goods might be transferred from B to C after the contract has been entered into and, subsequently, A's breach causes loss or damage to goods now belonging to C, B may recover the loss sustained by C.[22]

Where A contracts with B to erect buildings on C's land and the work is defective, B, who has suffered no loss, may recover damages for the loss sustained by C.[23]; but that principle was excluded where A had executed a deed in favour of C giving C a direct remedy for A's failure to exercise reasonable care.[24]

Some eminent judges, however, would base these decisions on a broader ground: they are not exceptions but examples of a general principle that B, far from being limited to nominal damages, is entitled to compensation for loss of his bargain—his own loss not that of C. In *Linden Gardens* Lord Griffiths put the case of a husband (B) who contracts with a builder (A) to repair the roof of the matrimonial home, which is owned by B's wife. When the repair is botched B has suffered financial loss "because he has to spend money to give him the benefit of the bargain which the defendant had promised but failed to deliver". This theory would cover, not only the case where performance was defective, but also that where A fails to perform at all and B has to pay a higher price to second builder. Lords Goff and Millett, differing from the majority, favoured this broader ground in

21 *A Tomlinson (Hauliers) Ltd. v. Hepburn* [1966] A.C. 451.
22 *The Albazero* [1977] A.C. 774, H.L.
23 *Linden Gardens Trust Ltd. v. Lenesta Sludge Disposals Ltd.* [1994] 1 A.C. 85.
24 *Panatown Ltd. v. Alflred McAlpine Construction Ltd.* [2000] 4 All E.R. 97, HL.

Panatown. Lord Clyde, on the other hand thought that, while a breach of contract may cause a loss, it is not itself a loss in any meaningful sense. Moreover, since B is recovering damages for his own loss, he would be under no obligation to use the damages for the benefit of C. Lord Goff puts the case of a philanthropist (B) who undertakes to renovate the village hall, owned by trustees, at his own expense. He contracts with a builder (A) who does defective work. B recovers damages. In Lord Goff's opinion, he could not keep the damages for himself, leaving the hall in its defective state. It would be implicit in the licence to renovate the hall that, if the work was begun, he would take reasonable steps to procure its satisfactory completion. This controversy is unresolved. The advent of the Contract (Rights of Third Parties) Act 1999 reduces its importance.

B's damages affected by effect on C

Sometimes, however, it may be proper to consider the effect on C of the breach of contract in determining the amount of the loss sustained by B. In *Jackson v. Horizon Holidays*[25] the plaintiff (B) entered into a contract with the defendants (A) for a holiday for himself and his family (C). It was a disaster. Reversing the trial judge, the Court of Appeal held that the damages should include the distress to the plaintiff's wife and two small children, as well as to himself. Lord Denning took the view that he was recovering damages on their behalf: but in *Woodar v. Wimpey*, the House of Lords, while agreeing with the amount of damages awarded, considered that they were damages for loss sustained by the husband, B. Lord Russell said, "[B] had bought and paid for a high class family holiday; he did not get it, and therefore he was entitled to substantial damages for the failure to supply *him* [Lord Russell's italics] with one."

Injunction to restrain breach

If A, for consideration supplied by B, has undertaken that, in certain circumstances, he will not sue C and, those circumstances having arisen, proceeds to do so, B may be able to obtain an injunction to restrain A from breaking his contract. In *Gore v. Van Der Lann*[26] Liverpool Corporation, (B), gave Gore, a "retirement pensioner" (A), a "free pass" for their buses in consideration, *inter alia*, of A agreeing that neither the corporation nor its servants or agents should be liable to A for any injury, however

---

25 [1975] 1 W.L.R. 1468, CA; S. & T. 317.
26 [1967] 2 Q.B. 31.

caused. A was injured by (she alleged) the negligence of Van Der Lann, (C), a bus conductor employed by the corporation. She sued him. The corporation applied for a stay of the action on the ground that, by bringing the action, the plaintiff, A, was defrauding them. The corporation failed on the ground that the grant of the pass was a contract for the conveyance of a passenger in a public service vehicle and section 151 of the Road Traffic Act 1960 (now the Public Passenger Vehicles Act 1981, s.29) renders void any term in such a contract which purports to exclude liability for bodily injury. A was therefore not acting in breach of her contract with B in bringing the action against C. Willmer L.J. gave two additional reasons why the action failed. (i) Though A had agreed with B that C should not be liable, there was no express promise by A not to sue C. (ii) That, since it had not been proved that B was liable to indemnify C against any damages C might have to pay A, B had no sufficient interest entitling them to relief. This, however, was *obiter*, and in *Snelling v. John G. Snelling Ltd*[27] Ormrod J. decided in favour of B though there was no express promise by A. Three brothers A, B1 and B2 who had each loaned money to the company, Snelling Ltd. (C) contracted that, if any one of them resigned his directorship of the company, he would forfeit the money owed to him by the company and the remaining directors would use the money to pay off a loan made to the company by a finance company. A resigned and, in breach of that contract, sued JGS Ltd for repayment of his loan. Ormrod J. held B1 and B2 were entitled to a declaration that A was bound by the agreement; that C, not being a party to the agreement, was not entitled to rely on it; but that a declaration should be granted that A was not entitled to call upon C to repay the loan and A's action against C was dismissed. Ormrod J. said that, notwithstanding *Gore's* case, it was not essential that A should have expressly promised not to sue C. It is sufficient that such a promise is a necessary implication. Surely that is right. There is no material difference between A's agreeing, as in *Gore's* case, that C is "not to be liable" to A and A's agreeing not to sue C. Once again, it will be noted that C has no personal right to rely on the contract between A and B; he is dependent on the willingness of B to intervene to protect him from action by A.[28]

---

27 [1973] 1 Q.B. 87.
28 Comparison may however be made with *Hirachand Punamchand v. Temple*, above, pp. 82–83, where C, the debtor, was able to invoke the contract between A, the creditor, and B, on the ground, *inter alia*, that A's action was a fraud on B, although there was no intervention by B.

THE THIRD PARTY'S RIGHT TO RECEIVE AND TO RETAIN A BENEFIT

Although C has no right to recover the benefit which A and B have contracted to bestow on him, once he has received it, the benefit belongs to him. B, by giving consideration to A, has paid for the benefit, so it is a gift to C; but once a gift is completely constituted, it cannot be undone by the donor.

Moreover, where the contract between A and B is that A shall confer a benefit on C, B has no right to prevent A from carrying out the contract and conferring the benefit. He may, of course, invite A to rescind the contract and, if A agrees to do so, C will not receive the benefit and he has no redress. But if A declines to rescind and insists on performing, any attempt by B to prevent A from carrying out the contract by conferring the benefit will be a breach of contract by B and perhaps a tort or even a crime.

These principles are stated in *Re Schebsmann*.[29] B, on his retirement from a company, A, entered into a contract with A by which A agreed to pay a sum of money to B by annual instalments and, if B died during the period of repayment, to make the payments to his widow, C. B died insolvent before all the instalments were paid. His trustee in bankruptcy, who inherited all B's legal rights, claimed a declaration that the money payable by A belonged to B's estate and should therefore be available for B's creditors. The action failed. A was entitled to perform the contract and pay C. During his lifetime, B could have rescinded the contract by agreement with A but he had no right unilaterally to terminate or change it; and his trustee could be in no better position. The court rejected an argument that, because B had supplied the consideration for it, C held the money on a resulting trust for B's estate. The contract was that the money should be paid by A to C for her own benefit and, if the court had prevented that from happening, it would have been assisting in a breach of contract.

PRIVITY AND TRUSTS OF CONTRACTUAL OBLIGATIONS

If A transfers property to B who agrees to hold it on trust for C, C acquires an equitable interest in the property. C has given no consideration, but he has acquired enforceable rights. This is because he is not merely the beneficiary of a promise but has acquired a proprietary interest in the property. In equity, the gift to him is complete. His rights are not dependent on someone

29 [1944] Ch. 83, CA.

doing what they have promised to do; they exist because of something done. The A-B-C situation is quite similar to that discussed in this chapter in relation to contracts. If only we could say that B was a trustee for C, C would have acquired enforceable rights and what are seen as deficiencies in the law would be overcome. However, in order to have a trust, we have to find some property which B holds on trust and in which C has an equitable interest. This is not impossible, for the contractual right which B has against A is a "thing in action", intangible property. If B holds the contractual right on trust for C, then B, as trustee, is bound to exercise that contractual right for C's benefit and to hold any property which accrues from it on trust for C. C, as the equitable owner, may insist on his doing so.

The courts, have, in the past, utilised the trust device in this way. For example, in *Walford's* case,[30] A, a shipowner, entered into a contract to charter a ship to B and undertook to pay a commission to a broker, C. C was not a party to the contract. It was held that C was entitled to recover the commission from A. B had contracted as trustee for C and held on trust the contractual obligation owed by A to pay money to C. As trustee, B could have sued for the agreed sum. There would have been no question of his being limited to nominal damages because he would not have been claiming for any loss *he* had suffered. He would have been getting in the trust property. As C could have required B to take this action, it was held that C could proceed personally and recover the commission directly from A.

This then appears to be a readily available solution to what otherwise might be manifest injustice: but, in effect, the remedy has been discarded by the courts since the decision of the Privy Council in *Vandepitte's* case[31] when Lord Wright stated that "the intention to constitute a trust must be affirmatively proved." This is likely to be difficult because rarely will there be, in truth, any such intention. Frequently there will be formidable reasons for saying that no trust was intended. Prominent among these is the fact that, if A and B have set up a trust for C, they have put it out of their power to rescind or vary their contract, for C now has vested equitable rights of which they cannot deprive him without his consent. As, in most cases, it is highly improbable that A and B intended to put it out of their power to rescind or vary their contract, it follows that they did *not* intend to set up a trust. In *Re Schebsmann*,[32] for example, where an argument that

30 *Les Affréteurs Réunis Société Anonyme v. Leopold Walford (London) Ltd* [1919] A.C. 801, HL.
31 *Vandepitte v. Preferred Accident Insurance Corporation of New York* [1933] A.C. 70.
32 Above, p. 108.

there was a trust for C was rejected, B might have wished, during his lifetime, to vary the arrangement if his wife, C, had gone off with another man. Unless he intended to put it out of his power to do so, he did not intend to create a trust in favour of C. This point strongly influenced the court in its decision that there was no trust.

If the exact facts of *Walford's* case were to recur today, C could probably invoke the 1999 Act but, whether that is so or not, he could rely on his right as a beneficiary under a trust; so the utility of the trust concept in this area cannot be said to be entirely defunct. But it appears unlikely that it will be applied to any new situations unless there really is affirmative evidence that B was contracting as trustee for C. If he declared to B that he was so contracting, then no doubt a trust would arise on the conclusion of the contract.

SOME EXCEPTIONS

Some cases which are often treated as if they were exceptions to the rule of privity of contract are not true exceptions. *The Eurymedon* and *The New York Star* (above, pp. 99–100) do not create exceptions because the courts found, however deviously and improbably, that there was a separate contract between the shipper and the stevedore. Nor do the cases on collateral contracts, such as *Shanklin v. Detel Products* (below, p. 126). In all these cases, C is found to be a contracting party, not the beneficiary of a contract between A and B. Trust cases, such as *Walford's* case, may be regarded as true exceptions.

Another is the rule in the *Elder Dempster* case[33] that, in a contract of carriage between the shipper of goods, A, and the charterer of a ship, B, a clause in the bill of lading providing that "the shipowners" should not be liable for any damage is effective to protect not only B (who is a "shipowner" for this purpose) but also the shipowner, C, who chartered the ship to B. Lord Denning attempted to use this decision to undermine the whole doctrine of privity of contract but, in *Scruttons* case, the House rejected this opinion, Lord Reid concluding that the case was "an anomalous and unexplained exception to the general principle that a stranger cannot rely for his protection on provisions in a contract to which he is not a party." Other judges condemned the decision as "a judicial nightmare" and "heavily comatosed, if not long interred", but it appears now to have been rehabilitated and is regarded as properly decided on the ground that the shippers impliedly agreed that the goods were received

33 *Elder Dempster & Co. Ltd v. Paterson, Zochonis & Co. Ltd* [1924] A.C. 522, HL.

by the shipowners as bailees subject to the exceptions and limitations in the bill of lading.[34]

Statute has created numerous exceptions to the doctrine of privity, but this is not the place to consider these.[35]

THE CONTRACTS (RIGHTS OF THIRD PARTIES) ACT 1999

It is now time to consider the effect of the 1999 Act on the rule that consideration must move from the promisee, and any separate doctrine of privity that may exist. The Act came into force on November 11, 1999, and applies to contracts made on or after May 11, 2000, and any contracts made between those dates which expressly provide that it should apply.

The Law Commission, in their report *Privity of Contract: Contracts for the Benefit of Third Parties* (Law Com. No. 242, 1996) intended the Act to apply only to Case 1 (above, pp. 93–94). Clause 8 of their draft Bill expressly excluded Case 2 but the clause was not included in the Bill introduced in Parliament nor does any such provision appear in the Act. The Commission acknowledged that it would be absurd if C were better off if he was not a promisee than if he was, but they proposed to exclude the promisee for two reasons: (i) They assumed that the *dicta* in *Coulls v. Bagot's Executors* (above, p. 96) are correct so he had a right at common law of which he should not be deprived; it was a more secure right than he would obtain under the Act because he would not have to satisfy the statutory test of enforceability. (ii) The rules of joint creditors, which are different from the new rules regarding third parties, should continue to apply.

The 1999 Act is, according to its preamble, "An Act to make provision for the enforcement of contractual terms by third parties". This is ambiguous. Does it mean third parties *to the contract*? Or third parties *to the promise*? If the former, C, in both Case 1 and Case 2 (above, p. 93) is a third party. If the latter, C is "a third party" in Case 1, but not in Case 2.

It is now a question of the construction of the Act. A third party is (s. 1 (1)): "a person who is not a party to a contract". Is C in Case 2 "a party to a contract"? If he is, (as the Law Commission thought) he cannot rely on the Act but must invoke his common law rights. If he is not, he may rely on the Act. Pending the resolution of the problem, C, when he is a promisee, might be well advised to make his claim in the alternative.

---

34 *The Pioneer Container* [1994] 2 A.C. 324; S. & T. 307, PC; *The Mahkutai* [1996] 3 All E.R. 502, PC; S. T. 304.

35 For some examples, see S. & T. 327–329.

The third party's right

Section 1 provides that a person who is not a party to a contract:

" ... may in his own right enforce a term of the contract, if

    (a)   the contract expressly provides that he may, or
    (b)   the term purports to confer a benefit on him."

But this does not apply if, on a proper construction of the contract, it appears that the parties did not intend the term to be enforceable by C. The Law Commission thought that section 1(1) created a rebuttable presumption in favour of C. Presumably the test of intention is objective but it must be the intention of both parties. C must be *expressly* identified in the contract by name, or as a member of a class, or as answering a particular description. Thus the Act would have been of no assistance to C, the stevedore in *Scruttons' case*,[36] but it might have assisted C in *The Eurymedon*, had he not been, in the view of the majority, a party to the contract supplying consideration. C need not, however, be in existence when the contract is made. An unborn child or a company not yet formed may acquire rights when he is born, or it comes into existence.

It is clear that, on the facts of *Tweddle v. Atkinson*, C (who was expressly identified and was not a party to the contract) would today be able to recover the specified sum from A; and, but for the Competition Act 1998, Dunlop (if not "a party to a contract") would be able to recover £5 from Selfridge under the Act. When the section applies, C has all the remedies that a party to the contract would have. The term enforceable by C is intended to include implied terms. Suppose that B contracts to buy furniture from A Ltd as a wedding present for C, informing A that it is a present and instructing A to deliver the goods to C. If the furniture proves defective, C, in the opinion of the Law Commission, can sue A for breach of the implied term (Sale of Goods Act 1979, s. 14) that the goods will be of satisfactory quality. But if B does not advise A that the furniture is a gift until after the contract has been concluded, it would seem that C has no remedy.

Rescission or variation

If, immediately after making the contract for the benefit of C, A and B agree to rescind or vary it in any way, they may do so; but

36 Above, p. 97.

they lose this right when:

(i) C communicates his assent to the promisor (A); or
(ii) A is aware that C has relied on the term; or
(iii) A can reasonably be expected to have foreseen that C would rely on the term and C has in fact relied on it: s. 2(1).

Once one of these events has occurred, C's right may not be revoked without his consent, unless there is an express term in the contract allowing revocation. If A and B wish to obtain C's consent to rescind or vary the contract but C's whereabouts cannot reasonably be ascertained, or he is mentally incapable of giving his consent, they may apply to a court or arbitral tribunal which may dispense with C's consent: s. 2 (4). Similarly where they satisfy the court or arbitral tribunal that it cannot reasonably be ascertained whether C has in fact relied on the term: s. 2 (5).

Defences available to A

It may be that if B had sued A for breach of his contract to benefit C, A would have been able to rely on some matter by way of defence or set-off. B may, *e.g.* have induced the contract by misrepresentation; or he may be indebted to A in respect of some related transaction. If C sues A in reliance on the Act, the defence or set-off that would have been available to A in an action against him by B is available against C: s. 3 (2). In addition, the contract may expressly provide that a defence or set-off that would have been available against B shall be available against C: s. 3 (3). Again, it may be that if C had been a party to the contract, A would have had a defence or set-off or counterclaim to an action brought by C. C might, *e.g.* have induced A to contract with B by a misrepresentation. If C, not being a party to the contract, sues A under the Act, such a defence, set-off or counterclaim is available to A: s. 3 (4).

Enforcement of the contract by B

B's common law right to enforce A's promise to benefit C is expressly preserved: s. 4. But A is protected from double liability. Where B has recovered from A a sum representing the loss caused to C by A's breach, or B's expense in making good to C the default of A, then, in proceedings brought by C, the court "shall reduce any award to [C] to such extent as it thinks appropriate to take account of the sum recovered by [B]": s. 5. A should not have to pay twice for the same damage.

Exceptions

Section 6 of the Act provides that section 1 confers no rights on a third party to (i) a contract on a bill of exchange, promissory note or cheque; (ii) a contract binding on a company and its members under s. 14 of the Companies Act 1985 (the contracts implied in the memorandum and articles of association); terms in contracts of employment; contracts for the carriage of goods by sea, or by road, rail or air which are subject to the appropriate international transport convention, with the important exception that a person may avail himself of an exclusion or limitation of liability in a contract.

IMPOSITION OF BURDENS ON THIRD PARTIES

It would be surprising if a contract between A and B could impose an obligation on C and the general principle is that it cannot do so. Of course, if B is C's agent to enter into the contract with A, C does incur obligations as well as acquiring rights, but then he is a contracting party. A true exception, however, may be that relied on by Lord Denning in *Scruttons'* case—that a bailor of goods is bound by contracts made by the bailee in relation to the goods, to which the bailor has impliedly consented. There, it will be recalled, Lord Denning held that C, the shipper of goods (the bailor) was bound by the contract entered into by B, the carrier (the bailee), with the stevedore, A, limiting the stevedore's liability. Another case in which Lord Denning saw scope for the application of this principle is *Morris v. C. W. Martin & Sons Ltd*[37] C (the bailor) sent a mink stole to B, (the bailee) to be cleaned. B, acting as principal and not as agent for C, made a contract with A for the cleaning of the stole. A lost it and C sued him in tort. A relied on a clause in his contract with B, which he claimed excluded his liability to C. The Court of Appeal held that it did not do so, Lord Denning on the ground only that the clause was not clearly expressed to exclude liability to C. If it had been clearly expressed, he thought it would have been effective, notwithstanding the fact that it was in a contract between A and B to which C was not a party. Salmon L.J. was strongly attracted by this view. Lord Denning said:

> "Suppose the owner of a car lets it out on hire, and the hirer sends it for repair, and the repairer holds it for a lien. The owner is bound by the lien because he impliedly consented

---

37 [1966] 1 Q.B. 716; S. & T. 306.

to the repairs being done, since they were reasonably incidental to the use of the car: see *Argus v. Tappenden* [1964] 2 Q.B. 815."

It may be argued, however, that this is a case going beyond simple contract because the repairer's lien is in the nature of a proprietary interest (sometimes called "a special property") in the car. This is another of Lord Denning's theories about which there is some degree of uncertainty.

A person who acquires property may find himself bound by obligations, contractual in origin, which are incidental to the property. Covenants in a lease are binding, not only on the original parties, but also on their successors in title. Covenants restricting the use of land are binding in equity, not only on the original covenantor, but also on subsequent purchasers of the land with notice of the covenant, provided that the covenantee has retained other land for the benefit of which the covenant was taken.[38] In *Taddy v. Sterious*[39] Swinfen Eady J. declined to apply a similar principle to a chattel—a packet of cigarettes with a notice stating that it was sold on the express condition that retailers would not sell it below stipulated prices—adding that "acceptance of the goods will be deemed to be a contract between the purchaser and Taddy & Co. that he will observe these stipulations." The defendants, who had purchased through a wholesaler with notice of the conditions, were not bound by them.

A case in which C may, in a sense be bound by the terms of a contract between A and B is that, where, knowing of the contract between A and B, he has entered into another contract, the performance of which will cause a breach of the contract between A and B. C may be restrained by injunction from enforcing his contractual rights so as to cause such a breach. It is a tort to procure a breach of contract between two other parties, so C is restrained from committing a tort. Knowing that B has granted A a right of first refusal over certain land, C enters into a contract to buy the land from B.[40] He may be restrained from enforcing the contract. Similarly, where C has acquired a proprietary interest, he may be restrained from exercising it in such a way as to cause a breach of a contract between A and B of which he was aware when he acquired the proprietary interest. Knowing that B has chartered his ship to A, C buys the ship from

38 *Tulk v. Moxhay* (1848) 2 Ph. 74.
39 [1904] 1 Ch. 354.
40 *Manchester Ship Canal Co. v. Manchester Racecourse Co.* [1901] 2 Ch. 37.

B. He may be restrained by injunction from using the ship inconsistently with A's rights.[41]

---

41 *Lord Strathcona Steamship Co. Ltd v. Dominion Coal Co.* [1926] A.C. 108, PC. *cf. Swiss Bank Corporation v. Lloyds Bank Ltd* [1979] 2 All E.R. 853; S. & T. 324, Browne-Wilkinson J., reversed on other grounds, by the Court of Appeal and House of Lords, [1982] A.C. 854.

CHAPTER NINE

Intention to Create Legal Relations

DOMESTIC TRANSACTIONS [1]

"I will entertain the sewing club to supper next Wednesday if you will do so the following week." "I agree." All the elements of a bargain, offer, acceptance and consideration are present here; but it is extremely improbable that this is a binding contract. In the unlikely event of the matter coming before a court at all, it would almost certainly be held that it was not a contract because there was no intention to create legal relations. And so it is said that an intention to create legal relations is an essential and distinct element in the formation of a contract.

In ordinary business matters, however, such an intention is presumed. The ordinary shopper in the high street does not have a conscious intention to create legal relations as he makes his various purchases, but he is undoubtedly entering into a series of contracts for the sale of goods. If he is poisoned by the fish purchased from the local fishmonger, he will have his action on the terms implied into the contract by section 14 of the Sale of Goods Act 1979 that the fish is of satisfactory quality and reasonably fit for eating. The truthful shopper might admit under cross-examination that it had never crossed his mind that, when he bought fish, he was making a contract; but that would not matter in the least. The matter would be judged objectively.

In a purely domestic or social transaction (like the arrangements for the sewing club) the objective test might lead to the conclusion that there was no intention to create legal relations. In the leading case of *Balfour v. Balfour*,[1] an agreement by a man who was returning to his employment abroad and leaving his wife in England that he would pay her a monthly allowance was held not to be binding, even if the wife was giving consideration by accepting this sum in lieu of the husband's obligation to maintain her. The court, reversing Sargant J., held that the agreement was not intended by the parties to have legal consequences. The parties had not said this, it was the court's inference from the circumstances. Certainly, there are many domestic arrangements where it would be wholly inappropriate for the courts to intervene—for example, the arrangements between spouses for meeting housekeeping expenses—but *Balfour v. Balfour* was closer to the borderline and spouses may, and often do, evince an intention to create legal relations in respect of property. The presumption that legal relations are not intended does not apply where spouses are not living in amity but are separated or about to separate.[2] The importance of the action to be taken by one party in reliance on the promise of the other may persuade the court that the promise must have been intended to be legally binding. An agreement to share a house was held to be a contract when, as both parties knew, it was necessary for one of them to take the drastic and irrevocable step of disposing of his own residence in order to adopt the arrangement.[3] An arrangement between A, A's granddaughter and A's lodger to enter a Sunday newspaper fashion competition in A's name, each party filling in one line, created a contract.[4] The arrangement whereby a number of employees go to work in a vehicle belonging to one of them, the others agreeing to share the costs, has caused difficulty in the courts and much must depend on the circumstances of the particular arrangement.[5] This is not an area in which any precise rules can be elucidated.

COMMERCIAL TRANSACTIONS

In a commercial transaction, there is a strong presumption that legal relations are intended but it is not irrebuttable. In *Esso Petroleum Ltd v. Commissioners of Customs and Excise*[6] Esso displayed posters offering one "World Cup Coin" with every four gallons of petrol. Pennycuick J., and the majority of the

1 [1919] 2 KB 571, CA; S. & T. 187.
2 *Merritt v. Merritt* [1970] 1 W.L.R. 1211.
3 *Parker v. Clark* [1960] 1 W.L.R. 286, Devlin J.
4 *Simpkins v. Pays* [1955] 1 W.L.R. 975, Sellers J.
5 See *Coward v. Motor Insurer's Bureau* [1963] 1 QB 259; S. & T. 189; *Albert v. Motor Insurers' Bureau* [1971] 3 W.L.R. 291.
6 [1976] 1 W.L.R. 1; S. & T. 195.

House of Lords, held that this resulted in a contract to supply the coins; but the Court of Appeal thought it was an offer of free gifts and, in the House, Viscount Dilhorne and Lord Russell, dissenting, agreed, saying that there was no intention to enter into legal relations. It was, of course, extremely improbable that anyone would ever have sued on a contract to supply one of these coins of minute intrinsic value, but that did not deter the majority from holding that there was a binding contract. The question was one of great financial importance because the liability of Esso to pay purchase tax depended on whether there was a sale of the coins. Viscount Dilhorne thought the offer of a "free" coin was not properly regarded as a business matter but Lord Simon stressed that the advertising was for commercial advantage and that the transaction took place in a setting of business relations.

Even in a commercial transaction the parties may expressly exclude any intention to enter into legal relations. In *Rose and Frank Co. v. Crompton Bros.*[7] the parties entered into an agency arrangement for the sale of tissues—clearly a commercial transaction—and provided that the agreement was not written as a formal or legal agreement" and that it should not be subject to legal jurisdiction in the law courts . . . ". It was held that the arrangement was not a binding contract; but the "honourable pledge clause", as it was called, applied only to the arrangement it was expressed to apply to; and subsequent orders given and accepted, without any such clause, constituted binding contracts. The presumption that legal relations were intended came into effect again.

A modern development is the use by business men of "letters of comfort." These appear usually to take the form of encouragement, falling short of a guarantee, to a lender to advance money to a third party. They are frequently, and perhaps deliberately, phrased in equivocal and ambiguous language. In *Kleinwort Benson Ltd v. Malaysia Mining Corporation Bhd*[8] the plaintiffs agreed to make a loan of £10m to Metals Ltd, a wholly owned subsidiary of the defendants. The defendants had declined to guarantee repayment by Metals but offered instead a letter of comfort in which they stated that it was their "policy to ensure" that Metals was at all times in a position to meet its liabilities. Hirst J. held that, in a commercial banking transaction, this amounted to an undertaking, a contract; but the Court of Appeal contrasted the wording of paragraph 3 with paragraph 2 which said, "We confirm . . ." and held the defendants were at

7 [1925] A.C. 445; S. & T. 191.
8 [1989] 1 All E.R. 785; S. & T. 193.

liberty to change their "policy" at any time. That was what the document meant and the very serious consequences of the repudiation by the defendants of their moral responsibility was not a matter for the court.

There is a rule of public policy that an agreement purporting to oust the jurisdiction of the courts is "illegal" and void. How is this to be reconciled with *Rose and Frank's* case? The answer seems to be that any attempt to set up another contract-enforcing authority to the exclusion of the courts is void, but there is nothing contrary to the public policy in an agreement that the transaction shall not be enforceable at all, by anyone. As Scrutton L.J. said, the parties may "exclude all idea of settling disputes by any outside intervention . . .".[9] But, to avoid the public policy ban, it is probably necessary that the agreement, like that in *Rose and Frank* should not be enforceable, even by the private sanctions of an association with which the defaulting party has contracted.[10]

---

9 [1923] 2 K.B. 261.
10 *Baker v. Jones* [1954] 1 W.L.R. 1005.

CHAPTER TEN

Representations and Terms

The question to be considered in this chapter is the extent of the contractual obligations undertaken by the parties. During the course of the negotiations statements about the proposed contract will frequently be made by one or both of the parties. These statements may or may not form part of the contract. Even if they are not terms of the contract they may affect its enforceability. The first question, however, is whether a statement has become a term of the contract or not.

It is convenient to consider oral and written contracts separately. If the contract is an oral one it is likely that its terms are to be found in the negotiations. For example, the offer and acceptance in a contract for the sale of a car may consist simply of, "I offer you £1,000 for the car"; "I accept." But the buyer may have received various assurances from the seller in the course of the negotiations—that it is a 1999 model, that the seller has owned it since it was new, that the mileage on the odometer is correct. Such assurances will, as the seller as a reasonable man must know, have contributed to the buyer's decision to make his offer and been present to his mind when he did so. Was the buyer, as a reasonable man, entitled to believe that the seller was promising him that the car was a 1999 model, that he was giving an undertaking to that effect? If the answer to that question is, yes, then this is a term in the contract and, if it is broken (the car is in fact a 1998 model), the buyer can recover damages.

It has always been said by the courts that whether a statement is a term of the contract depends on whether the parties intended it to be a term; but the test of intention is objective. In applying the objective test, the court will take into account all the relevant circumstances in the particular case but there are some matters which will commonly be influential.

THE RELATIVE MEANS OF KNOWLEDGE OF THE PARTIES

A.L. Smith M.R. was once rebuked by Lord Moulton for asserting in respect of a representation made prior to a contract of sale,

> "In determining whether it is so intended [sc., to be a term], a decisive test is whether the vendor assumes to assert a fact of which the buyer is ignorant or merely states an opinion or judgment upon a matter of which the vendor has no special knowledge, and on which the buyer may be expected also to have an opinion and to exercise his judgment."[1]

Because all the circumstances must be taken into account it is dangerous to state as a general proposition that any one is "decisive"; but this particular factor is highly significant and may indeed often be decisive. Where both parties have the same means of knowledge and they are aware of this, it is improbable that a statement by either of them will have the status of a term because the one will not be relying on the other, but on his own means of knowledge, in entering into the contract. In *Oscar Chess Ltd v. Williams*[2] the seller of a car stated that it was a 1948 model. In fact it was a 1939 model and therefore worth significantly less. This looks like a term at first sight; but the buyer was in the motor trade and the seller was a layman; and the seller was, as the buyer knew, simply repeating what he had read in the car's registration book. This had, at some stage, been forged to mis-state the year of the car's manufacture and it showed five changes of ownership between 1948 and 1954. The book was produced to the buyer. It was obvious to any reasonable buyer that the seller had no actual knowledge of when the car was first registered, indeed that he knew no more about this than the buyer. On the contrary, being in the trade, the buyer was in a much better position than the seller to check and find out the true date of manufacture of the car. The buyer was not entitled to believe that the seller was promising that the car was a 1948 car and undertaking responsibility for that fact. On the other hand, when a car dealer, having been instructed to find a "well-vetted"

---

1 *De Lassalle v. Guildford* [1901] 2 KB 215 at 221, criticised in *Heilbut, Symons & Co. v. Buckleton* [1913] A.C. 30; S. & T. 372, 374.
2 [1957] 1 W.L.R. 370; S. & T. 378.

Bentley car, tendered a car which, he said, had done only 20,000 miles since being fitted with a replacement engine and gear box, it was held that there was a term in the contract to that effect. The buyer was entitled, as a reasonable man, to suppose that the seller, being a person in the trade, knew what he was talking about and was promising him that the car was as described.[3]

Even where a party has done no more than express an opinion, his superior knowledge or means of knowledge may lead the court to infer that he was impliedly promising that he had reasonable grounds for the opinion expressed. In *Esso Petroleum Co. Ltd v. Mardon*[4] Esso's experienced representative persuaded Mardon to enter into a tenancy of a new petrol filling station by telling him that Esso estimated that the throughput of petrol would reach 200,000 gallons in the third year of operation. Even with good management, the site was not good enough to achieve anything like that throughput. There was clearly no promise by Esso that the throughput would reach the estimated figure—it was only an opinion—but there was an implied promise that the forecast was made with reasonable care and skill. That promise being broken, Mardon was entitled to damages.

RELIANCE AT THE TIME OF CONTRACTING

If A is reasonably relying on B's statement at the time of contracting, and B knows, or ought to know, that A is, or may be, so relying, the statement is probably a term of the contract. The smaller the interval between the statement and the time of contracting, the more likely it is that A is relying on the statement and that B is aware of it; but this is only a matter of evidence, not law. Where the owner of a horse said to a potential buyer who was examining it, "You need not look for anything: the horse is perfectly sound. If there was anything the matter with the horse I would tell you" and the buyer thereupon terminated the examination and, three weeks later, bought the horse, it was held that there was a warranty that the horse was sound: *Schawel v. Reade*.[5] In *Hopkins v. Tanqueray*,[6] a case where the material facts were, except in one respect, identical, a different result was reached. The difference was that in *Hopkins v. Tanqueray* both parties knew at the time of the conversation that the horse was to be sold by auction at Tattersalls on the day after the conversation

---

3 *Bentley (Dick) Productions Ltd and Another v. Smith (Harold) (Motors) Ltd* [1965] 1
   W.L.R. 623; S. & T. 385.
4 [1976] Q.B. 801; S. & T. 376.
5 [1913] 2 Ir.Rep, 81, HL.
6 (1854) 15 C.B. 130.

and it was at that sale that the plaintiff bought the horse. The well-known course of business at Tattersalls was that sales were without a warranty. The basis of the decision seems to be that, since both parties must be taken to have known of this, they could not have intended a warranty since they could not have supposed that this bidder would be in a better position than other bidders at the sale, who would have no warranty. The court expressed doubts about the legality of such a warranty, but the decision is that it was not intended. Clearly, the fact that the conversation took place the day before, and not on the day of, the sale, was not material. No doubt the buyer was in fact relying on what he had been told; but he had no right to take it to be a binding promise because he had no right to suppose that he was being promised more than other bidders.

WRITTEN CONTRACTS

The position with regard to written contracts is different because when the parties have formally recorded the whole of their agreement in writing that document, prima facie, is the contract, the whole contract; and the courts have long asserted that they will not admit evidence to add to, vary or contradict the written agreement—the "parol evidence rule." The rule is so riddled with exceptions that it has little substance left; but it does mean that a statement made in the course of negotiations, which would have been a term had the negotiations concluded with an oral agreement, cannot be held to be a term in that agreement when it is reduced to writing and the term finds no place in it. To take the example, given above, of the car. Suppose that the parties had entered into a formal written contract of sale which said nothing about the mileage covered by the car. It is now impossible to say that this is an express term of the contract, which it would have been if the contract had been concluded orally. It may take effect as a misrepresentation, a matter which is considered, below, p. 135; but, before we come to that, the possibility must be considered that it may be given contractual effect in another way.

COLLATERAL CONTRACTS

If A, a tenant, has declined to sign the lease until B, the landlord, gives him an assurance that the drains are in good order, and the lease says nothing about the drains, B may nevertheless be held to have contracted that this is so. This is what happened in *De Lassalle v. Guildford*[7] where the court held that, in addition to the

7 [1901] 2 K.B. 215, CA.

contract contained in the lease, there was a "collateral contract". In consideration of A's signing the lease, B was promising that the drains were in good order. Two contracts came into existence at the same moment, the bilateral contract contained in the lease and the unilateral contract just described. In such a case, this "collateral" contract obviously achieves a fair result and implements the true intention of the parties. Nor, if the facts are as described, is it in any sense a fiction. There was a real bargain.

The courts were discouraged from finding such contracts by the speech of Lord Moulton in *Heilbut Symons & Co. v. Buckleton.*[8] Lord Moulton recognised that a contract collateral to the main contract has an independent existence and the full character and status of a contract, but thought that such contracts must, from their very nature, be rare. The more natural way of adding to the terms of the main contract was by an additional term and contracts adding to or varying the main contract were "viewed with suspicion by the law." Though Lord Moulton's remarks are frequently quoted with great respect, they are usually also distinguished. The device of the collateral contract has proved too useful to be lightly brushed aside.[9] In *Heilbut v. Buckleton* itself, the contract was a written contract to take shares in a new company. The action was for breach of a warranty that the company was "a rubber company," a matter as to which the written contract was silent. It was alleged that the collateral promise was given in a telephone conversation; but the evidence did not establish that the plaintiff was seeking an assurance that the company was "a rubber company." What he wanted to know was whether the company was "all right"—a sound company, likely to make good profits. Had he said, "I am not interested unless you can assure me that it is a rubber company," and got that assurance he may well have succeeded in his action; but the defendants' representative might have declined to give any such assurance. On the true facts, it was not made clear to him that such an assurance was being required, nor, probably, was it.

The inhibiting effect of Lord Moulton's strictures seems, in practice, to have been slight. Where the seller of a car assured a buyer, hesitating to sign the written agreement, "If you buy the Hillman 10, we will guarantee that it is in good condition," it was held that signing the agreement was consideration for the guarantee and, when the car turned out to be "a mass of second-hand and dilapidated ironmongery," the buyer had a remedy

---

8 [1913] A.C. 30; S. & T. 372, HL.
9 For a case in which its utility seems to have been overlooked, see *W. v. Essex County Council* [1998] 3 All E.R. 111, C.A.; S. & T. 391–393.

although the written contract contained far-reaching exclusion clauses.[10] Again, the justice of the solution is obvious. Most remarkable of the cases is *City and Westminster Properties v. Mudd*[11] because here the collateral contract seemed directly to contradict the express written contract, thus making a great hole in the parol evidence rule. The contract was a lease which contained a covenant not to use the premises for purposes other than trade purposes. Under an earlier lease, the defendant had been in the habit (contrary to the lease) of sleeping on the premises, and he declined to sign the new lease unless the plaintiffs agreed to his sleeping there. They were unwilling to include a clause to that effect in the lease because it might have attracted the operation of the Rent Restriction Acts; but they assured him orally that he could sleep there. Later the plaintiffs brought an action for forfeiture of the lease, relying on the fact that the defendant was sleeping there, in breach of the covenant to use the premises for trade purposes only. The action failed. Harman J. held that there was a clear contract not to enforce the covenant, the consideration being the execution by the tenant of the lease in the form put before him. So we have two simultaneous contracts, one saying that the tenant may use the premises for trade purposes only, the other saying that he may sleep there. It is difficult not to conclude that this was a flat contradiction of the express terms of a written contract; yet, once again, the justice of the result, effectuating, as it did, the true intention of the parties, seems apparent.

The same principle applies where A makes a promise to B in consideration of B's entering into a contract, or making some arrangement, with C. When B does so, he concludes a unilateral contract with A and can sue A on his promise. In *Shanklin Pier Ltd v. Detel Products Ltd*,[12] the defendants (A) told the plaintiffs (B) that if B would specify (as they were entitled to) that their contractors (C) should use A's paint on the pier, they could assure B that the paint would last seven years. B did as A asked, C bought A's paint and it lasted about three months. Although the contract of sale was between A and C, B were able to sue A on the collateral contract; B had given the consideration that was required for A's promise that the paint was good for seven years by specifying that C should use that paint.

The principle was sometimes applied before the Sale of Goods Act 1979,[13] and is still capable of application, to the common

---

10 *Webster v. Higgin* [1948] 2 All E.R. 127, CA.
11 [1959] Ch. 129; S. & T. 390.
12 [1951] 2 K.B. 854, McNair J., S. & T. 392.
13 See section 14(3).

situation in which a dealer (A) induces his customer (B) to enter into a credit-sale or hire-purchase contract, not with A, but with a finance company (C), by representations as to the quality of the goods. The representation was held to be a promise by A given to B in consideration of B's entering into the contract with C. "It's a good little bus", said the car-dealer in *Andrews v. Hopkinson*,[14] "I would stake my life on it". The plaintiff was thus induced to enter into a contract of hire-purchase with C; and, on the car proving to be unroadworthy, B was able to sue A on the promise.

A remarkable application of the principle is found in *Wells (Merstham) Ltd v. Buckland Sand and Silica Ltd*.[15] B, a chrysanthemum grower, visited A, a sand merchant. B was looking for sand suitable for growing chrysanthemums. A said that their BW sand would be suitable and produced an analysis showing a low iron oxide content, which would have been suitable. Subsequently, B entered into a contract with C to buy from C BW sand which C purchased from A. Had B bought the sand directly from A there would clearly have been a contractual undertaking by A that the sand was suitable for the purpose. It was not, and B's chrysanthemums died. Edmund Davies J. held, nevertheless, that B had given consideration to A for A's promise by buying the sand from C. This goes further than the other cases in that there was no evidence that A requested B to enter into the contract with C or even contemplated the possibility that he might do so. Edmund Davies J. held that it was sufficient that (i) A's promise was one that B might reasonably regard as being contractual in nature and (ii) that B had bought the sand in reliance on that promise.

Although section 2 of the Law of Property (Miscellaneous Provisions) Act 1989 requires that, in a contract for the sale of land, all the terms expressly agreed by the parties must be incorporated in one document, or where the contracts are exchanged in each, it has been held, following *De Lassalle v. Guildford*, that a letter by the vendor offering a warranty as to the title to the land in order to induce the purchaser to exchange, amounts to a collateral contract when the offer is accepted by the exchange of contracts: *Record v. Bell*.[16]

---

14 [1957] 1 Q.B. 289, McNair J.
15 [1965] 2 Q.B. 170; Edmund Davies J.; S. & T. 393.
16 [1991] 4 All E.R. 471, Ch.Div. (Judge Baker).

CHAPTER ELEVEN

Implied Terms

In the last chapter, the question was whether words used by one of the parties amounted to a term in the contract. In the present chapter, the question is whether a term should be imported into the contract although it was never expressed in words. Should the term be implied? The reader has already encountered cases where this was done. The actual words used by the parties, even when these are set down in a formal written contract, do not always—indeed, they hardly ever—represent the full extent of the agreement. The parties may omit mention of some matter for the very reason that it is so obvious that "it goes without saying", A agrees to sell his car to B at a price to be fixed by C. We have seen[1] that if either party prevents C from fixing the price, he is liable in damages to the other. A did not expressly promise B that he would allow C to have access to the car in order to estimate its value. He is nevertheless in breach of contract if he refuses access to C. The contract simply cannot work if C cannot examine the car, and it must be taken that both parties intended their contract to work. The reasonable seller would, no doubt, be surprised if he was asked to make such a promise in express terms.

The court will then find that the contract includes such implied terms as are necessary to make it work—to give it "business efficacy", in the traditional terminology of the law. The theory is that the court is not making a contract for the parties but is implementing their intentions because this is something that

1 Above, p. 48.

they, as reasonable, men, *must* have intended. As MacKinnon L.J. put it,[2]

"Prima facie that which in any contract is left to be implied and need not be expressed is something so obvious that it goes without saying; so that, if, while the parties were making their bargain, an officious bystander were to suggest some express provision for it in their agreement, they would testily suppress him with a common 'Oh, of course!'"

The test is a strict one—at least as expressed by the courts. Lord Denning's opinion that the court should imply terms when it is *reasonable* to do so has been rejected. It must be not merely reasonable but *necessary*. So where a firm of solicitors made an unconditional offer of articles to a student, not drawing his attention to their standard terms, including a term that the offer was subject to the student's having passed (or be awaiting the results of) the Solicitor's Final Examination, it was held that no term to that effect should be implied. It was not necessary; it could not be said that the contract would make no sense without it, nor that it was so obvious that it was unnecessary to make it explicit. This was not something that "goes without saying".[3] In *Errington v. Errington*[4] it will be recalled that Lord Denning, applying the orthodox test, held that it was necessary to import a term into the father's offer that he would not revoke it, once the children had embarked on performance; but the House of Lords could detect no such necessity in *Luxor v. Cooper*.[5] The offer was an attractive one, which a reasonable business man might well have been happy to act on, without any such term. The express terms did not lack business efficacy.

The business efficacy principle is sometimes called the doctrine of *The Moorcock*,[6] after the leading case. A shipowner contracted with a wharfinger to moor his ship at the wharfinger's jetty on the Thames. Both parties knew that the ship would settle on the river bed at low water. When it did so, the centre of the vessel settled on a hard ridge beneath mud and sustained damage. The shipowner recovered damages in contract for breach of an implied term that the wharfinger had taken reasonable care to find out whether the berth was safe. If he

---

2 In *Shirlaw v. Southern Foundaries Ltd* [1939] 2 K.B. 206; S. & T. 401. Scrutton L.J. earlier had expressed the idea in much the same way in *Reigate v. Union Manufacturing Co.* [1918] 1 K.B. 592 at 605; S. & T. 400.
3 *Stubbes v. Trower* [1987] I.R.L.R. 321.
4 Above, p. 27.
5 Above, p. 26.
6 (1889) 14 P.D. 64; S. & T. 398.

had taken such care, he would have found out that it was unsafe and, it must be presumed, would not have invited ships to tie up there. In determining whether a term should be implied, the relative knowledge or means of knowledge of the parties is of no less importance than in determining whether an express statement is intended to be a contractual term.[7] A crucial fact here was that "with regard to the safety of the ground outside the jetty the shipowner could know nothing at all, and the jetty owner might with reasonable care know everything." The reasonable shipowner was entitled to suppose that the wharfinger had at least taken reasonable care to find out whether the berth was safe before inviting ships to moor there—otherwise the shipowner was simply "buying an opportunity of danger". The term was necessary to give the contract business efficacy. Note that the court went no further than was necessary to give the plaintiff redress. It did not hold that the wharfinger impliedly promised that the berth *was* safe, nor even that he had taken reasonable steps to make it safe. The berth outside the jetty was under the control of the river authority, not the wharfinger, and court indicated an unwillingness to imply a promise to do something (make the berth safe) which it was not within the alleged promisor's power to do.

CUSTOMARY TERMS

The *Moorcock* doctrine enables the court to imply a term because of the special facts of the particular case. Terms may also be implied because they are "customary" in a particular trade or profession, or in certain types of contract in a particular locality. Once again, the theory is that the court is implementing the intention of the parties, on the assumption that they intended to contract with reference to the known usages of the trade, profession or locality to which both parties belong. The court must, of course, be satisfied that there is such a custom as is alleged, but once it is so satisfied, the term will be imported unless there is something to show that the parties did not intend it to apply. An express exclusion of the custom will obviously be effective as will any express term which is inconsistent with the alleged implied term. In *Hutton v. Warren*[8] the tenant of a farm, on quitting in accordance with notice given by the landlord, was held entitled to a fair allowance for the seeds and labour which he had expended on the arable land and of which the landlord would now reap the benefit. There was nothing in the terms of

7 See *Oscar Chess v. Williams,* above, p. 122.
8 (1836) 1 M. & W. 466; S. & T. 396.

the lease to entitle the tenant to the allowance but it was proved
that there was a custom of the country to that effect and there
was nothing in the express terms of the contract which was
inconsistent with the existence of the customary term.

TERMS IMPLIED IN CONTRACTS OF COMMON OCCURRENCE

These terms are similar in principle to customary terms but they
are not confined to any particular trade, profession or locality.
Over the years the courts have established that some terms are so
generally implicit in contracts of a particular type that it can be
asserted that those terms will be implied unless the parties have,
in some way, indicated an intention that they should not apply.
The most conspicuous example is the contract for sale of goods.
The seller of goods will hardly ever say—"And I have a right to
sell these goods, you know". If he did, indeed, the buyer's
suspicions might well be aroused. It surely is something that
goes without saying; and so it became established that this term
would always be implied in a contract for the sale of goods
unless there was something to indicate that it should not apply.
For example, the seller might have found the goods and, being
unable to discover the true owner, decided to sell them. The
goods would remain the true owner's property and so the seller
had no right to sell them. The seller and buyer would both be
guilty of the tort of conversion and might find themselves liable
to pay damages if the owner ever turned up. In the meantime,
the finder has a better title to the goods than anyone other than
the true owner. Provided he made clear to the buyer that he was
a finder, and was only transferring such title as he had, no
promise that he had an absolute right to sell the goods could be
implied.[9]

Many other such terms were implied into contracts for the sale
of goods at common law and in 1893 the law was codified in the
Sale of Goods Act of that year. The Act was re-enacted with some
amendments in 1979. The general principle of the Act remains
that the terms will be implied unless there is something which
indicates that the parties intended otherwise, but, as we shall see,
it is now provided, in the interests of consumer protection, that
certain terms may not be excluded.[10] There are many other types
of contract of common occurrence where terms will be implied,
either by virtue of the common law or a statute, codifying,
modifying or adding to the common law terms.

9 Sale of Goods Act 1979, s.12(1) and (3); S. & T. 411–412.
10 Below, p. 175.

This is an area in which the common law is developing. In *Malik v. Bank of Credit and Commerce International S.A. (in liqidation)*[11] the House of Lords affirmed that, in a contract of employment, there is an implied term that the employer will not, without reasonable cause, conduct itself in a manner likely to destroy or seriously damage the relationship of trust and confidence between itself and its employee. BCCI broke this term by carrying on a massive and notorious fraud resulting in the collapse of company and the redundancy of the employee who was entitled to damages for any disadvantage incurred in the employment market through his association with BCCI.

The development of the common law may be influenced by statute. So a statute requiring an employer to provide his employee with a written statement of the terms of his employment, including a note of how to apply for redress of grievances, led to the finding that it is an implied term that the employer will provide an opportunity for the prompt and reasonable redress of employees' grievances.[12] On the other hand, in the important case of *Johnson v. Unisys Ltd.*[13] it was held that legislation precluded the court from implying a term that it might otherwise have considered necessary. An employer exercised its express contractual right to dismiss the claimant, J, with four–weeks notice, but did so unfairly. J contended that there was an implied term that the employer would not exercise its right except for good cause and after giving him the opportunity to show that there was no such cause. It was held that the statutory introduction of elaborate machinery for compensation for unfair dismissal precluded the court from implying that term. J's claim for damages for breach of contract, far in excess of the statutory compensation he received, failed.

There is no sharp dividing line between the various categories of implied terms; they are, as Lord Wilberforce said in the leading case of *Liverpool City Council v. Irwin*,[14] shades "on a continuous spectrum". The contracts in that case were tenancy agreements for flats in a tower block. The agreement imposed obligations on the tenant but said nothing whatever about the obligations of the landlord Council. The conditions of the block deteriorated seriously because of the activities of vandals and the behaviour of some of the tenants. The defendants refused to pay rent and, in the ensuing litigation, one of the questions was whether the Council was in breach of contract. Any breach must

---

11 [1998] A.C. 20; S. & T. 407.
12 *Goold (W.A.) (Pearmak) Ltd. v. McConnell* [1995] I.R.L.R. 516 (Morison J.).
13 [2001] 2 All E.R. 801, H.L., Lord Steyn dissenting.
14 [1977] A.C. 239; S. & T. 402.

be a breach of an implied term, since the Council had not expressly undertaken any obligations. It was held that there was an implied promise by the Council to take reasonable care to keep the block in reasonable repair and usability, but they had satisfied that obligation and so were not in breach of contract. Lord Salmon said that unless there was an obligation on the Council "at least to use reasonable care to keep the lifts working properly and the staircase lit, the whole transaction becomes inefficacious, futile and absurd." He asked, "Can a pregnant woman be expected to walk up fifteen . . . storeys in the pitch dark to reach her home?". The court would imply such a term as was necessary, no more and no less; and so, as in the *Moorcock*, the court would not imply an absolute obligation to keep in repair, only an obligation to use reasonable care to do so.

It looks an obvious case for the application of the *Moorcock* principle—a contract that is "futile, inefficacious and absurd" plainly lacks business efficacy—yet the House thought it an inappropriate case for the application of that principle. It was pointed out that the Court of Appeal found themselves faced with five alternative formulations of a business efficacy term and so rejected them all. But, if it was necessary to imply the one term which the House found to be implicit, alternative and different formulations were irrelevant.

The *Moorcock* principle is concerned with the particular contract. In the *Liverpool* case, however, the House looked to the *kind* of contract—*i.e.* leases of flats in high-rise blocks generally. This approach, it appears to have thought, enabled it to take into account a wider range of considerations; yet the considerations actually taken into account by the House all seem to have been aspects of this particular case, as well, no doubt, as of many similar tenancies. The effect, however is to lay down a rule that the term is to be imported into tenancies of this type generally, in the absence of a contrary intention. Yet the difference, if it exists at all, is marginal. Did not *The Moorcock* establish a rule for a class of contract—contracts for the berthing of ships at wharves where the river bed is owned by a third party?

EXCLUSION OF TERMS USUALLY IMPLIED

The general principle is that any term which would otherwise be implied must give way to an inconsistent express term. So in *Walford's* case[15] an express term in the contract that the broker's commission should be payable "on signing this charter"

---

15 Above, p. 109.

excluded a custom in the shipping trade that the commission was payable only in respect of hire duly earned under the charterparty. The express term showed beyond doubt that the parties did not intend the customary term to apply. This principle seems to have been misunderstood in *Lynch v. Thorne*.[16]

The plaintiff agreed to buy from the defendant, a builder, a plot of land with a partially erected house on it. The defendant agreed to complete the house in accordance with the specification he produced. This provided that the walls were to be nine-inch brick walls. The house was built precisely in accordance with the specification, with sound materials and good workmanship. Unfortunately, it turned out to be unfit for human habitation because rain penetrated the walls. Now there is generally no implied term on the sale of land (including houses and other buildings) that it is fit for any particular purpose; but in a contract to build a house, or to complete a partially built house, a term is implied at common law that the house, when completed, will be reasonably fit for habitation. The plaintiff relied on this term. The court accepted, for the purposes of the case, that such a term is usually implied but it must "yield to the express letter of the bargain".

In order to build a house on that site that would keep the rain out, the builder would have had to depart from the express letter of the bargain—to break his contract. Nine-inch brick walls would, inevitably, let in the rain. In order to build a habitable house, the builder would have had to erect cavity walls. Thus the court held that the alleged implied term was inconsistent with the express contract and could not be imported. But was not the buyer, as a reasonable man, entitled to suppose that the builder was promising him *both* (i) that he would build the house in accordance with the specification which he produced *and* (ii) that the house, when so built, would be habitable? In fact, it was impossible to fulfil both promises but the buyer certainly did not know that, nor presumably, did the builder. The "inconsistency" is entirely different from that in *Walford's* case. No sane man could possibly suppose that the shipowner was promising to pay the commission on the signing of the charter and promising to pay it only after the ship had sailed on the voyage.

In fact, there is clear authority that *Lynch v. Thorne* applied the inconsistency principle incorrectly. In *Harbutt's Plasticine Ltd v. Wayne Tank and Pump Co. Ltd*[17] the defendants contracted to supply to the plaintiffs machinery in accordance with a specification prepared by the defendants. The defendants carried

16 [1956] 1 All E.R. 744; S. & T. 416, CA.
17 [1970] 1 Q.B. 447, CA.

out the work in accordance with the specification, using "durapipe" as the specification required. Durapipe proved to be unsuitable and the results were disastrous. The factory was burnt down. The court held that the defendants promised both (i) to do the work according to a particular specification and, (ii), impliedly, that the work so done would be reasonably fit for its purpose. It was impossible to fulfil both promises—to satisfy the second the defendants would have had to use stainless steel pipes, which would have been a breach of the first—yet the court, rightly, had no difficulty in finding that both promises were made. Similarly, a contract for the sale of a Bugatti car, "fully equipped and finished to standard specification as per the car inspected", was held to be breached although the car delivered complied exactly with the specification. There was an implied term that it would be reasonably fit for the purpose for which the buyer had told the seller he wanted it—touring purposes. It was impossible to supply a car that both complied with the specification and was fit for touring purposes; but it was not impossible to promise to do so; and the court rightly found that this was what the seller had done.[18]

---

18 *Baldry v. Marshall* [1925] 1 K.B. 260, CA.

CHAPTER TWELVE

Conditions, Warranties and Innominate Terms

Not all promises in a contract have the same importance. They all have to be performed, of course, and if any one of them is not, the party in breach is liable to pay damages. But some breaches of contract entitle the injured party to put an end to the contract as well as to claim damages and it is in connection with the right to terminate the contract on breach that the nature of the term becomes important. For many years writers on the law of contract assumed that there were only two classes of contractual promise. Every promise was either a condition or a warranty. If it was a condition, any breach of it entitled the injured party to terminate the contract as well as to damages. Hence the name, "condition"—A's liability to perform is conditional on B's fulfilling his promise. A warranty, on the other hand, entitled the injured party to damages only. He was not entitled to terminate the contract. His liability to perform his part of the contract continued unimpaired. Whether a party had a right to terminate the contract depended on the nature of the term broken, and the nature of the term was, of course, determined in the light of the state of affairs when the contract was made. The nature of the breach was immaterial.

The exposure of the innominate term

This, at least, was the theory. In practice the court seems often to have had regard to the effect of the breach in deciding whether the injured party could treat the contract as at an end. Stock examples of a warranty and a condition used for many years in the text books were the cases of *Bettini v. Gye*[1] and *Poussard v. Spiers*.[2] The plaintiff in each case was a singer who, because of illness, was unable to be present on the day on which his presence was first required. In each case, the defendant purported to terminate the contract and the plaintiff sued for damages. Bettini was required by his contract to be present six days before the first performance for rehearsals and he arrived three days late. His engagement was to sing in theatres, halls and drawing rooms from March 30 to July 13, 1875. His failure to arrive on time clearly did not prevent the contract from being substantially carried out. If the engagement had been a very short one, it might have been different. It was held that his failure to arrive on time did not go to the root of the matter and the defendant was not entitled to dismiss him.

Poussard was taken ill five days before the first performance. Her illness appeared to be a serious one of uncertain duration. It was held that the defendant was justified in terminating her contract and engaging another artiste. Bettini was considered by the writers to have committed a breach of warranty and Poussard a breach of condition. In neither case, however, did the court scrutinise the contract at the time it was made and identify a term as a condition or a warranty. It looked at the effect of the failure to perform in the circumstances existing at the time of the failure. Thus, if a temporary substitute for Poussard could have been obtained on reasonable terms, the defendant would not have been justified in dismissing her. Because no such substitute was available, the plaintiff's "breach" went to the root of the matter. The term in issue in each case seems to have been the same—the promise to be available on a certain day. The difference between them was in the nature and effect of the breach.[3]

The courts have now recognised that the classification of promises into conditions and warranties is not exhaustive. There is a third class of term, a breach of which may or may not entitle the injured party to put an end to the contract. It depends on the nature and effect of the breach. The term is of such a kind that some breaches of it may have only a slight effect on the subsequent performance of the contract, whereas other breaches will render the contract substantially incapable of performance.

---

1 (1876) 1 Q.B.D. 183.
2 (1876) 1 Q.B.D. 351.
3 In any event, it is doubtful if there was a true breach by the singer in either case. The contract in *Poussard* was frustrated and thus at an end; and a failure to perform through illness is surely excused, even if it does not amount to a frustrating event. Below, p. 199.

If the breach is of the former type, the injured party has his remedy in damages but remains bound to perform his side of the contract. If it is of the latter type, he is entitled to damages and to put an end to the contract. Such terms, being a recent discovery of the courts, have no accepted name and in this book are called "innominate terms." Sometimes the courts and writers refer to them as "intermediate terms," because they lie between a condition—any breach of which entitles the injured party to end the contract—and a warranty—no breach of which entitles him to do so.

The leading case recognising the existence of the innominate term is the *Hong Kong Fir* case.[4] The contract was the charter of a ship, the Hong Kong Fir, for a period of 24 months. The term in issue was the shipowner's express promise that the ship was seaworthy—"she being in every way fitted for ordinary cargo service." Previous authorities showed that such a term was broken by the slightest failure to be so fit. A wooden vessel was unfit if a nail was missing from one of the timbers, or if proper medical supplies, or two anchors, were not on board at the time of sailing. It seemed to the court to be contrary to common sense that a party should be entitled to put an end to a large contract because of such trivial and easily remediable breaches. On the other hand, there might be other grave breaches of the same term which should obviously entitle the charterer to decline to proceed. Suppose that the bottom of the ship is so rotten that it is likely to fall out as soon as the ship puts to sea. So it is a matter of looking at the particular breach which has occurred and estimating its effect on the further performance of the contract. If the defaulter is still able to do substantially what he has promised to do, then the injured party has no right to put an end to the contract; but if the breach would deprive him of substantially the whole benefit he expected to receive from the contract then he may refuse to proceed.

In the *Hong Kong Fir* the unseaworthiness consisted in the defective state of the ship's engines and the inefficiency of the engine room staff which resulted in five weeks delay and a further 15 weeks to do repairs; but at the end of that period, the charter party still had 20 months to run. The breach thus did not, in the opinion of the court, deprive the charterers of substantially the whole benefit that it was the intention of the parties that they should obtain. They were not entitled to terminate the charter.

---

4 *Hong Kong Fir Shipping Co. Ltd v. Kawasaki Kisen Kaisha Ltd* [1962] 2 Q.B. 26; S. & T. 435.

THE SURVIVAL OF CONDITIONS AND WARRANTIES

One view is that the law ought to treat all terms like innominate terms—that the right to terminate the contract for breach ought always to depend on the nature and effect of the breach. It is clear that this is not the law and that conditions and warranties continue to exist. It is established law that certain classes of term have the status of conditions—unless, in a particular case, the parties have made it clear that the term is not to have that status. This is so in respect of many terms which bear the same characteristic as the shipowner's promise that the vessel is seaworthy—*i.e.* some breaches of the term may be extremely trivial, others extremely serious. When Chalmers drafted the Sale of Goods Act 1893, he assumed that every term must be either a condition or a warranty and categorised the implied terms in a contract for the sale of goods accordingly. Section 13 of the 1979 Act, as amended, provides that, in a contract for the sale of goods by description, there is an implied term that the goods will correspond with the description; and that the term is a condition. The description may be a very detailed specification. A failure to comply with specification in some respect, however trivial, is a breach of condition which, until 1994, entitled any buyer to reject the goods. Now a new section, 15A, provides that, where the buyer is not a consumer and "the breach is so slight that it would be unreasonable for him to reject [the goods]," it is not to be treated as a breach of condition but may be treated as if it were a breach of warranty. It follows that a consumer may reject goods which do not comply with the contract description, even though it is quite unreasonable to do so. Section 15A applies to terms implied by sections 14 and 15 (quality and fitness and sale by sample) as well as section 13. These terms, though described as conditions, are, in non-consumer contracts, in effect now innominate terms.

In commercial contracts, case law established that many stipulations as to time are conditions. Obviously breach of such a stipulation may vary greatly in its effect—the seller's tendering of goods one day late may be vastly different from his tendering them one month late—but both breaches are breaches of the same term and, if it is a condition, either breach entitles the buyer to put an end to the contract. It has sometimes been said by high authority that a condition is a term, any breach of which may fairly be considered by the other party to be a substantial failure to perform the contract at all; but this clearly needs qualification. If a term is of such a nature that any breach of it will have that effect, then it can hardly fail to be a condition; but the examples already given show that some recognised conditions do not have that characteristic. As Blackburn J. said, "Parties may think some matter, apparently of very little importance, essential; and if they sufficiently express an intention to make the literal fulfilment of such a thing a condition precedent, it will be one."[5] This principle is not confined to expressed intention, it may be inferred from commercial custom and precedent, as in stipulations as to time in mercantile contracts. In *Bunge Corporation New York v. Tradax Export SA, Panama*[6] a contract for the sale of goods required the buyers to give the sellers at least 15 consecutive days notice of probable readiness of the vessel to be loaded. The buyer gave only 13 days' notice and the seller repudiated the contract. It was held that he was entitled to do so. The term was a condition and it was not necessary to consider what the effect of the particular breach might be.

Whether a term has the status of a condition is a question of the construction of the contract. The fact that it is called "a condition" is not conclusive. In *Schuler (L.) A.G. v. Wickman Machine Tool Sales Ltd*[7] a contract granting W sole selling rights of presses manufactured by S provided that "It shall be a condition of this agreement" that W should send its representative to visit the six largest UK motor manufacturers at least once in each week. No other term in the 20 clauses of the agreement used the word "condition". Yet it was held, Lord Wilberforce dissenting, that the term was not a condition and S was not entitled to put an end to the contract on the particular breaches which had occurred. This conclusion was reached by looking at the contract as a whole; but the decision was much influenced by the opinion that it was wholly unreasonable that S should be able to put an end to the whole contract merely because, in one week, W failed to send its representative to one manufacturer. The majority were not prepared to put such a construction on the contract unless they had to; but Lord Wilberforce thought that this was to make an assumption, that he was not prepared to make, "that both parties to this contract adopted a standard of easygoing tolerance rather than one of aggressive, insistent punctuality and efficiency."

NO EVALUATION OF TERMS IN UNILATERAL CONTRACTS

The question does not arise in connection with unilateral

5 *Bettini v. Gye* (1876) 1 Q.B.D. 183 at 187.
6 [1981] 1 W.L.R. 711, HL; S. & T. 439.
7 [1974] A.C. 235; S. & T. 431, HL.

contracts, since, by definition, there is a promise on one side only. Either the offeree does the act requested, in which case the promisor must perform his promise, or he does not, in which case there is no contract. Similarly where the offer to enter into a bilateral contract requires the offeree, if he wishes to accept, to perform some defined act—which will usually be to give notice of acceptance within some defined period, or a reasonable time. A failure to do so within the stipulated period is not, of course, a breach of contract because the offeree is not bound to accept. In *United Dominion Trust (Commercial) Ltd v. Eagle Aircraft Services Ltd*[8] Eagle Aircraft wished to sell an aircraft to Orion Airways. The transaction was financed by Eagle selling the aircraft to a finance company, UDT, which then let it on hire-purchase to Orion. UDT agreed to buy the aircraft only on condition that Eagle agreed to buy it back again if Orion defaulted on their payments and UDT then called on Eagle to do so. The agreement required UDT to notify Eagle of any default by Orion within seven days of its occurrence. Orion defaulted, but UDT (i) did not notify Eagle within seven days and (ii) did not call upon Eagle to re-purchase within a reasonable time. Widgery J. held that these were two breaches of contract by UDT but that they did not go to the root of the contract and therefore did not allow Eagle to repudiate their obligation to re-purchase. The Court of Appeal thought this might be right regarding (i), but it was unnecessary to decide. The failure to call upon Eagle to re-purchase within a reasonable time, however, was not a breach of contract at all—there was no obligation on UDT to do so but simply a failure to accept within the time implicitly stipulated in Eagle's offer. It was immaterial whether this failure was great or small. The offer had come to an end before the purported acceptance, and that was that.

CONDITIONS AND "ENTIRE CONTRACTS"

Where the contract is bilateral but stipulates for one entire piece of work to be done by one party, the complete performance of that work is a condition of the liability of the other—unless the parties have stipulated otherwise. Suppose A says to O, "If you will *undertake* to walk to York, I promise to pay you £100, for doing so". O gives the undertaking, but fails to walk to York. He is in breach of contract. Suppose he gave up within 100 yards of the city boundary. It was only a little failure, but that will make no difference. He can recover nothing because complete

8 [1968] 1 W.L.R. 74, CA.

performance of his obligation will be regarded as a condition of A's liability.

This was, in effect, what happened in the leading case of *Cutter v. Powell*.[9] The defendant, the master of a ship, gave Cutter a note promising to pay him 30 guineas, "provided he proceeds, continues and does his duty as second mate in the said ship from [Kingston, Jamaica] to the port of Liverpool." The ship sailed on August 2 and Cutter served as second mate until September 20 when he died before the ship reached Liverpool. It seems clear that this was a bilateral contract—Cutter, no doubt, had a contractual obligation to do his duty as second mate—and Cutter was not guilty of any breach of contract. The contract was frustrated by his death. His widow's claim to recover 30 guineas failed because the condition precedent to his right to recover payment—doing his duty to Liverpool—had not been fulfilled. Furthermore, the widow's argument, that she was entitled to recover a proportionable part of the wages on a *quantum meruit* for work done, also failed. The action of a *quantum meruit* (to recover so much as the claimant had earned) depended on an implied contract, and a contract could not be implied if it contradicted the express contract. Cutter, in the court's opinion had contracted to receive 30 guineas if the whole voyage were performed and nothing if it was not. In reaching this conclusion, the court was much influenced by the fact that 30 guineas was very high pay—the voyage normally lasted two months and the usual rate of pay was £4 per month. Since the contract was frustrated by Cutter's death, it would be necessary to consider the effect of the Frustrated Contracts Act 1943 if a similar case arose today.[10]

The same principles were applied in *Appleby v. Myers*[11] to a contract to instal machinery in the defendant's premises. The bulk of the work was done when, without the fault of either party, the premises were burnt down and machinery destroyed. Blackburn J. stated that "there is nothing to render it either illegal or absurd in the workman to agree to complete the whole, and to be paid when the whole is complete and not till then; and we think that the plaintiffs in the present case had entered into such a contract." It is the same where the plaintiff does complete the job—but the work done is substantially different from that required by the contract. Where repairers undertook to do specified repairs to the defendant's ship, *Liddesdale*, and completed the job, doing good work which added value to the

9 (1795) 6 T.R. 320; S. & T. 446.
10 Below, p. 208.
11 (1867) L.R. 2 C.P. 651; S. & T. 438.

ship, they could recover nothing because the work done, as the plaintiffs admitted, was not the stipulated work. They had, for example, used iron girders where the contract required steel. It was irrelevant that the work was as good as, or indeed better than, the work contracted for—it was not what the defendants had contracted to pay for.[12]

It is different where the defendant has an option to accept or reject the incomplete or different performance. If he then accepts it, the court will infer a new contract to pay what it is worth. This contract is not inconsistent with the first contract because it is made later in time—there is no difficulty in holding that both contracts have been made. The application of the principle to contracts for the sale of goods is neatly summed up in the Sale of Goods Act 1979, s.30(1):

> "Where the seller delivers to the buyer a quantity of goods less than he contracted to sell, the buyer may reject them, but if the buyer accepts the goods so delivered he must pay for them at the contract rate."

Delivery of 143 bottles, instead of the gross contracted for, entitled a buyer to reject. If he is a "consumer" it still does. A consumer may reject, however unreasonable it is for him to do so. But, where the buyer is not a consumer, section 30(2)(a) (inserted by the Sale and Supply of Goods Act 1994), provides that a non-consumer may not reject if the shortfall is so slight that it would be unreasonable for him to do so. Similarly where the excess is slight (*e.g.* 145 bottles).

In *Cutter v. Powell* and *Appleby v. Myers* the defendant had no option to accept or reject the incomplete work. Similarly in *The Liddesdale* the Privy Council took the view that the shipowner's acceptance of the ship did not found a contract to pay for the work that had been done. Short of abandoning his ship, the shipowner had no option but to accept it with the iron girders and any other extra-contractual work.

The entire contracts rule works harshly in these cases. It is impossible not to feel sympathy with the plaintiffs in *Cutter v. Powell* and *Appleby v. Myers*; but these were cases of frustrated contracts and there is now the Frustrated Contracts Act 1943, one of the objects of which is to do justice in this sort of case. To what extent it does so is considered below, p. 209. But there are other cases where the plaintiff failed to render entire performance because of some event not amounting to frustration but still due

---

12 *Forman & Co. Proprietary Ltd v. The Ship "Liddesdale"* [1900] A.C. 190, PC; S. & T. 452.

to misfortune rather than his fault. Here the 1943 Act will not help.

In *Sumpter v. Hedges*[13] the plaintiff had entered into an entire contract to erect buildings for £565. When he had done work to the value of £333 he ran into financial difficulties and had to abandon the work. He had received part of the price but his action to recover the balance of the value of the work he had done failed. A personal financial failure, though rendering performance impossible in fact, is not a frustrating event. The defendant in fact completed the work, using materials left by the plaintiff on the site. He was held liable to pay for the materials, because he certainly had an option to use them or not; but he was not liable to pay anything in respect of the work done, on a *quantum meruit*, because the court found he had no option to accept or reject an unfinished building on his land. It was there, a fixture; and he was not bound to leave it in an incomplete state, constituting a nuisance on his land.

Because of the harsh effects of the rule, courts might be expected to be slow to construe a contract as entire where it is possible to regard it as severable into distinct parts. But *Bolton v. Mahadeva*[14] shows that the rule is still a live one. The plaintiff contracted to instal a combined heating and domestic hot-water system for £560. The installation was defective, providing inadequate heat and emitting fumes. The deficiencies were assessed at £174, but the contractor had refused to rectify them and it was held that he could recover nothing.

SUBSTANTIAL PERFORMANCE

There is one principle which may mitigate the defaulter's liability. It is the doctrine of substantial performance. If the performance falls short of the standard required by the contract only in some relatively trivial respect, that failure may be treated like a breach of warranty—the defaulter may recover the price for the entire work, but the defendant may counterclaim for the loss he has suffered by reason of the defective performance. In *Bolton v. Mahadeva* the court declined to apply this principle because the defect in performance was not a trivial one but went to the root of the contract. But in *Hoenig v. Isaacs*[15] the Court of Appeal declined to interfere with an official referee's finding that a contract to decorate and fit out a one-roomed flat had been substantially performed when the work had been completed but

13 [1898] 1 Q.B. 673; S. & T. 449.
14 [1972] 1 W.L.R. 1009, CA.
15 [1952] 2 All E.R. 176; S. & T. 452.

with defects which would cost £56 to rectify, the contract price for the whole being £750. The case was a borderline one and, if the official referee's decision had gone the other way, it is likely that it would have been upheld. The fact that the whole job was done (though defectively) was material. The court thought that if the second mate in *Cutter v. Powell* had completed the voyage, his widow would not have failed to recover the sum agreed in the note merely because he had committed some minor breach of contract in the course of the voyage. In that case, the master's remedy would have been a counterclaim for damages for that breach. But, as *Bolton v. Mahadeva* shows, the plaintiff will not necessarily succeed on the ground that he has done the whole job if the performance is defective. The question then, it seems, is whether the breach goes to the root of the matter.

The plight of the party who has failed to complete, or substantially complete, performance of an entire contract for some reason other than frustration has been considered by the Law Commission. They recommended that he should be entitled to recover from the other party to the contract a sum representing the value of what he has done under the contract to that person who has had the benefit of it, whether he is a party to the contract or not. The court would have no discretion to reduce or disallow the claim on the ground of the conduct of the party in breach; but the sum awarded would not exceed the proportion of the work done to that promised. The party not in breach would be able to counterclaim for damages and the normal rules relating to remoteness and mitigation would apply.[16]

---

16 Law Com. No. 121 (1983), "Pecuniary Restitution on Breach of Contract". The Report has not yet been implemented.

CHAPTER THIRTEEN

Misrepresentation

A statement made by A to B before they enter into a contract may induce B to do so and yet not become part of the contract. During negotiations for the sale of a house, A tells B that the drains are in good order. In due course, B signs a formal, written contract to buy the house for £50,000. The contract says nothing about the drains. In fact, they are in a bad state and B would not have entered into that contract had he known the truth. If, of course, B can prove that he made it clear that he was not going to sign the contract, or exchange the signed contracts, unless he had an assurance from A about the drains, and that assurance was given, there is a collateral contract[1] which, once proved, is as good as if it were written down in the main contract. But B may be unable to prove that all that happened and yet he may have relied on the truth of A's statement when he entered into the contract. In that case, he has no remedy for breach of contract, because there has been none, but he may have a remedy for misrepresentation. In order to ascertain the nature and extent of his remedies, it is necessary to look at certain rules of common law, of equity and of statute—the Misrepresentation Act 1967.

COMMON LAW AND EQUITY

The common law distinguishes between fraudulent and innocent misrepresentations. A misrepresentation is fraudulent if the maker knows that it is false or he is reckless whether it is true or

1 Above, p. 124.

false. He is reckless if he is aware that he does not know whether the statement is true or false—and yet he makes it. Thinking to himself, "I really have no idea whether the drains are in good order or not", A asserts that they are in good order. That is a fraudulent misrepresentation if the drains are not in fact in good order. If, on the other hand, the representor believes what he says to be true, he is making an innocent misrepresentation, even though he *ought* to have known that it was false. He is an honest man, even if a negligent one. In short, a misrepresentation is innocent if the maker believes it to be true; and it is fraudulent if he does not believe it to be true.

The significance of the distinction is that if a representee acted on a fraudulent misrepresentation (*e.g.* by entering into a contract with the representor) and incurred a detriment, this amounted to a tort known as deceit. The representee could sue in tort for damages and, if he had entered into a contract with the representor, he could rescind it. But if the misrepresentation was innocent, no action in deceit would lie. The common law afforded the representee no remedy at all until, in 1963, the House of Lords decided in *Hedley Byrne & Co. v. Heller & Partners*[2] that, in certain limited circumstances an action would lie in tort for merely negligent misrepresentation. The duty of care, on which such an action is founded, is however confined to cases where there is a "special relationship" between the parties—normally "a business or professional transaction whose nature makes clear the gravity of the inquiry and the importance and influence attached to the answer." For details of the law relating to deceit and negligent misrepresentation, the reader is referred to works on tort; but where misrepresentation has led to a contract, the common law remedies in damages, as will appear, are, since the Misrepresentation Act 1967, of slight practical importance.

EQUITY

The function of equity was to supplement the common law when it proved inadequate and this it did in connection with innocent misrepresentation. Equity did not afford any remedy in damages, but it allowed the representee to rescind the contract—to have the whole transaction set aside and both parties restored to the position they were in before the contract was entered into. The equity of the matter was that a person should not be allowed to retain a benefit obtained by a statement which, it is now admitted or proved, was false. It is morally

2 [1964] A.C. 465; S. & T. 345.

wrong of the representor to seek to retain that which he had obtained by a falsehood, albeit an innocent one; and equity does not allow him to do so.

The essence of the matter is that the representee must have entered into the contract in reliance on the truth of the false statement. If he was unaware that it had been made, or he was aware of it but did not believe it to be true, or attached no importance to it whatever, he has no redress, even in equity. If a company prospectus, with a view to enhancing the attractiveness of the company, states, falsely, as it turns out, that Mr X has agreed to be a director, a person who buys shares without reading the prospectus, or who reads it and knows the statement is false, or is wholly uninfluenced by it because he has no idea who Mr X is, may not rescind the contract. There was a misrepresentation, but it was not an operative one.

If the representee does enter into the contract in reliance on the misrepresentation, it is no answer to his claim to rescission that, if he had taken reasonable care, he would have known that it was false. In *Redgrave v. Hurd*[3] the defendant agreed to buy the plaintiff's house. This contract was associated with an agreement that the defendant would join the plaintiff's practice as a solicitor, as a partner. The plaintiff had represented that the practice was bringing in £300–£400 a year. He produced papers which, if carefully read, showed that the practice was practically worthless. The defendant did not read the papers and contracted to buy the house in reliance on the truth of the plaintiff's representation as to the value of the practice. On discovering the truth, he declined to complete and the plaintiff's action for specific performance failed. The defendant had in fact relied on the misrepresentation, and it was immaterial that a prudent buyer would have discovered the truth.

The representation must be a statement of fact, not merely of opinion. This must be decided objectively: would a reasonable person have supposed that the representor was asserting a fact, or merely expressing an opinion? In *Bisset v. Wilkinson*[4] a seller of land in New Zealand said that the place, if properly worked, would carry 2,000 sheep. This proved to be wrong; but the buyer knew that the land had never been used for sheep farming so that the seller's statement could not be other than a matter of opinion and he was not justified in treating it as anything more. It was not a ground for rescinding the contract. In that case, the seller had no special information. In an insurance contract a statement of belief does not import a representation that there

3 (1881) 20 Ch.D. 1; S. & T. 333, CA.
4 [1927] A.C. 177, PC; S. & T. 336.

are reasonable grounds for the belief.[5] E's statement that, "to the best of his knowledge and belief", his parents' valuables were worth £4,000 was a gross under-estimate but it did not entitle the insurer to repudiate liability. E relied simply on his father's statement of the value; his representatiion was made in good faith and was therefore true[6]—he *did* believe the valuables were worth only £4,000. In other circumstances, a statement of opinion might imply that the maker has reasonable grounds on which to base his opinion and that he has exercised reasonable care and skill in doing so—which are implied statements of fact. An implied mis-statement is just as effective as an express one, if it is relied on.

Mere silence, however, is generally not misrepresentation. In *Smith v. Hughes*,[7] it will be recalled, it was held that "the passive acquiescence of the seller in the self-deception of the buyer will not entitle the latter to avoid the contract." That is a very strong case, because it is assumed that seller knows that the buyer is making a mistake of fact about the seller's goods and does not undeceive him. In *Turner v. Green*[8] the plaintiff, having heard the result of a case, negotiated a settlement with the defendant, being aware that he had not heard the result of that case and would not have entered into that agreement if he had known of it. It was held that, while this was not the sort of conduct to be expected of solicitors, "a shabby trick", it did not invalidate the agreement. Cases of this kind may now have to be re-considered in the light of *Solle v. Butcher*[9] and its successors but they have not been overruled and must, in the meantime, be taken to represent the law.

One case in which the representor comes under a duty to speak is that where he makes a true statement which, because of a change of circumstances, becomes untrue before the contract is entered into. The crucial moment is that at which the representee enters into the contract and, when that moment arrives, the representation is false. If the representor has not undeceived him, the representative may rescind for misrepresentation. If the representor knows that the statement is now false and that the representee is acting in reliance on its truth, he may be guilty of the tort of deceit. In *With v. O'Flanagan*[10] a doctor, in January 1934, represented to the plaintiff, a potential purchaser of his practice, that it was worth £2,000 a year. This was true; but, by

---

5 *Economides v. Commercial Union* [1997] 3 All E.R. 636; S. & T. 337.
6 Marine Insurance Act 1906, s. 20 (5).
7 (1871) L.R. 6 QB 597; S. & T. 124, above, p. 16.
8 [1895] 2 Ch. 205, Ch.D.
9 [1950] 1 KB 671; S. & T. 513, below, p. 193.
10 [1936] Ch. 575, CA.

the time the contract was entered into in May 1934, it had become untrue. The practice had fallen away and was bringing in not more than £5 a week. The representation was to be treated as continuing until the contract was signed. The plaintiff had entered into the contract in reliance on it and was entitled to rescission. Presumably the converse applies, and a statement, false when made but true when the representee acts on it by entering into a contract, is not an operative misrepresentation.

It is instructive to consider *Wales v. Wadham*[11] where the court seems to have failed properly to apply the principle of *With v. O'Flanagan*. In an agreement made in contemplation of divorce on the breakdown of their marriage, Wales agreed to pay his wife £13,000 out of his share of the proceeds of the sale of the matrimonial home if she would not make any further claim for maintenance. She had stated on several occasions that she would never remarry but, by the time the agreement was signed, she had decided to marry Wadham. She did not reveal her intention to Wales because she did not wish Wadham to become involved in the divorce proceedings. Wales sought rescission of the agreement on the ground that he would never have entered into it had he known of his wife's intention to remarry—the agreement was intended to commute his liability for periodical payments, a liability which, in the event, he would never have had. Tudor Evans J. distinguished *With v. O'Flanagan* on the ground that there was no representation of fact in the present case.

> "A statement of intention is not a representation of existing fact, unless the person making it does not honestly hold the intention he is expressing, in which case there is a misrepresentation of fact in relation to the state of that person's mind."

This is surely wrong.

A statement of intention is a representation of existing fact— the present state of that person's mind—whether the speaker holds the intention or not. If he does not hold it, the statement is a misrepresentation; if he does hold it, it is no less a representation, but it is a true one. In that case the statement, "I will never remarry" truly represented the wife's state of mind—a fact—when it was made and it became untrue before the husband signed the agreement in reliance on it. The case proceeded on a false premise.

---

11 [1977] 1 W.L.R. 199; S. & T. 341.

CONTRACTS REQUIRING THE UTMOST GOOD FAITH

There are certain classes of contracts, which are said to require *uberrima fides*, the utmost good faith, where there is a duty to disclose material facts. The most common and important of these is the contract of insurance. In the case of marine insurance the principles have been codified in the Marine Insurance Act 1906 and, as it has been held that these are the principles which apply to insurance contracts generally, they cannot be better stated than in the words of that Act. Section 18 provides:

(1) The assured must disclose to the insurer, before the contract is concluded, every material circumstance which is known to the assured, and the assured is deemed to know every circumstance which, in the ordinary course of business, ought to be known by him. If the assured fails to make such disclosure, the insurer may avoid the contract.

(2) Every circumstance is material which would influence the judgment of a prudent insurer in fixing the premium, or determining whether he will take the risk.

It was decided in the *Pan Atlantic* case[12] that a circumstance is material if a prudent insurer would consider it in deciding whether to accept the risk and, if so, on what terms, even though, after consideration, the circumstance would not affect his decision on either of these matters. But it was also there held that section 18 (above) is subject to an implied qualification, applicable to non-marine as well as marine insurance: a non-disclosure, like a material misrepresentation, does not entitle the insurer to avoid the policy unless it in fact induced the making of the contract, *i.e.* he would not have made *that* contract if the disclosure had been made. So the insured must disclose facts which a prudent insurer *might* think material; but his failure to do so will have no effect unless the particular insurer *would* have so considered it.

In *Lambert v. Co-operative Insurance Society Ltd*[13] a woman, renewing an insurance policy covering her own and her husband's jewellery, did not disclose that he had recently been convicted of conspiracy to steal and theft and sentenced to 15 months' imprisonment. It was held that the insurance company

12 *Pan Atlantic Insurance Co. Ltd v. Pine Top Insurance Co. Ltd* [1994] 3 All E.R. 581, HL, Lords Templeman and Lloyd dissenting on this point.
13 [1975] 2 Lloyd's Rep. 485; S. & T. 343.

was entitled to repudiate the policy on the ground that she had failed to disclose a material fact. Mrs Lambert may well not have realised that the conviction was a material fact, but that was irrelevant—a prudent insurer would have regarded it as material and there was evidence that the company would not in fact have renewed the insurance if they had known of it.

The reason for the rule is stated by Lord Mansfield in *Carter v. Boehm*[14]:

> "Insurance is a contract upon speculation. The special facts, upon which the contingent chance is to be computed, lie most commonly in the knowledge of the *insured* only: the under-writer trusts to his representation, and proceeds upon confidence that he does not keep back any circumstance in his knowledge, to mislead the under-writer into a belief that the circumstance does not exist . . . ".

The rule works harshly in a case like Lambert's. Even if a person is aware of the duty at the outset, he may not realise that it arises on each occasion that the policy is renewed, for that is a new contract. An insured may also be misled because he has answered the specific questions asked of him and supposes, wrongly, that that is the full extent of his duty. Where a question arises as to the materiality of an undisclosed fact, the court will hear expert evidence of insurers and these will be produced by the insurers who will naturally select the most favourable experts to attend. The law has been criticised by the Law Commission, but, to date, remains unamended.[15]

THE MISREPRESENTATION ACT 1967

The 1967 Act affects the law relating to misrepresentation as regards rescission, damages and the effect of exclusion clauses. Exclusion clauses are considered below, page 160.

Rescission

The Act clarifies the law in two respects. (i) A misrepresentation may be incorporated as a term when the contract is concluded. The misrepresentation—*e.g.* "The horse is sound"—then has a dual role: it is both a misrepresentation and a term of the contract. Suppose, however that, as a term, it has the status only of warranty. The buyer cannot avoid the contract for breach of

14 (1766) 3 Burr. 1905 at 1909.
15 Law Com. No. 104 (Cmnd. 8064).

warranty. May he nevertheless rescind the contract for misrepresentation? (ii) After the misrepresentation has been made, the contract is concluded and completely executed—*e.g.* it is a contract to grant a lease and the lease is executed. There was some authority before the Act that the right to rescind was now lost,[16] but Lord Denning strongly resisted that conclusion.[17] May the representee rescind the executed contract?

Section 1 of the 1967 Act answers both these questions in the affirmative:

> 1. Where a person has entered into a contract after a misrepresentation has been made to him, and—
>
> (a) the misrepresentation has become a term of the contract; or
> (b) the contract has been performed;
>
> or both, then, if otherwise he would be entitled to rescind the contract without alleging fraud, he shall be so entitled, subject to the provisions of this Act, notwithstanding the matters mentioned in paragraphs (a) and (b) of this section.

Damages

It will be recalled that, apart from the *Hedley Byrne* principle, damages were not recoverable for a non-fraudulent misrepresentation. The Act creates two new rights to damages.

(i) Section 2(1) provides:

> 2.—(1) Where a person has entered into a contract after a misrepresentation has been made to him by another party thereto and as a result thereof he has suffered loss, then, if the person making the misrepresentation would be liable to damages in respect thereof had the misrepresentation been made fraudulently, that person shall be so liable notwithstanding that the misrepresentation was not made fraudulently, unless he proves that he had reasonable ground to believe and did believe up to the time the contract was made that the facts represented were true.

Suppose the defendant has said to a potential buyer of his house that the drains are in good order, honestly believing this to be true, but it is false. If this misrepresentation causes the plaintiff to

16 *Angel v. Jay* [1911] 1 K.B. 666, DC.
17 In, *e.g. Leaf v. International Galleries* [1950] 2 K.B. 86; S. & T. 350, CA.

enter into the contract to buy the property and he suffers loss (because the property with bad drains is worth less or because he has to spend money having the drains repaired), the Act requires us to ask, Would the plaintiff have been entitled to damages if the defendant had known all along that the drains were not in good order? This sends us to the law of the tort of deceit which is thus incorporated by reference into the Act. The answer appears to be, Yes; so the plaintiff is entitled to his damages, although the misrepresentation was not fraudulent—unless the defendant can prove two things: (a) he had reasonable ground to believe, and (b) he did believe, up to the time the contract was entered into, that the drains were in good order. Note that it is not enough that he had reasonable ground to believe and did believe his representation to be true at the time he made it. As with the principle in *With v. O'Flanagan*, the crucial time is when the contract is entered into. In this section, it seems clear that "misrepresentation" must mean such misrepresentation as would give rise to a right to rescind the contract in equity. It cannot be that the vendor who says, in all good faith, *"In my opinion*, the drains are in good order" should be liable to damages, if they are not. Yet it is clear that if he said this, knowing it to be false, he would be making a misrepresentation of fact (his state of mind) and liable to damages in deceit. If he is not to be liable under the Act, it can only be because the statement is not "a misrepresentation" within the meaning of the Act.

Where a person has entered into a contract after a misrepresentation has been made to him by another party and has suffered loss, he might sue in tort, either in deceit or, where there is a special relationship, in negligence under the rule in *Hedley Byrne v. Heller*; but it would seem that he would now generally be ill advised to do so. If he sues in deceit, he has the heavy burden of proving fraud; and if he sues in negligence he has to satisfy the court that the defendant owed him a duty of care and was in breach of it. Whereas if he sues under section 2(1), he need only prove the facts postulated above and then he is entitled to his damages unless the defendant can prove that he had reasonable ground to believe and did believe the representation to be true.

The misrepresentation which grounds a remedy under section 2(1) is sometimes referred to as "negligent" misrepresentation, but this is slightly misleading because it need not be proved to have been negligent. In *Howard Marine & Dredging Co. Ltd v. A. Ogden & Sons (Excavations) Ltd*[18] Bridge L.J. said:

18 [1978] QB 574, CA; S. & T. 366.

" . . . the liability of the representor does not depend on his being under a duty of care the extent of which may vary according to the circumstances in which the representation is made. In the course of negotiations leading to a contract the 1967 Act imposes an absolute obligation not to state facts which he cannot prove he had reasonable ground to believe."

In that case the letter of two barges told the hirer that their capacity was about 1,600 tonnes. This answer was based on the Lloyd's register "deadweight" figure of 1,800 tonnes, but it was wrong, the true capacity being only 1,195 tonnes. The misrepresentation induced, but was not incorporated in, the contract. The letter had seen the correct figure in the shipping documents but had forgotten it, The Court of Appeal held, Lord Denning dissenting, that the letter had failed to prove that he had reasonable ground for his belief in the truth of his representation and was liable under section 2(1).

(2) Section 2(2) provides:

> (2) Where a person has entered into a contract after a misrepresentation has been made to him otherwise than fraudulently, and he would be entitled, by reason of the misrepresentation, to rescind the contract, then, if it is claimed, in any proceedings arising out of the contract, that the contract ought to be or has been rescinded, the court or arbitrator may declare the contract subsisting and award damages in lieu of rescission, if of opinion that it would be equitable to do so, having regard to the nature of the misrepresentation and the loss that would be caused by it if the contract were upheld, as well as to the loss that rescission would cause to the other party.

This subsection empowers the court to refuse rescission when it would otherwise be available or (a new concept) to reconstitute a rescinded contract and to award damages in lieu. Suppose that an innocent misrepresentation that the drains are in good order has led to a contract for the sale of a house for £100,000. The purchaser either rescinds, or asks the court to rescind the contract. The cost of repairing the drains would be only £1,000. The court might well think it inequitable that the purchaser should be able to get out of the contract altogether when the sum involved is relatively trivial. In that case, it would declare the contract subsisting or refuse rescission, as the case may be, and award damages of, presumably, £1,000. Before exercising its discretion the court must consider:

    (i)   the importance of the representation in relation to the subject matter of the contract;

   (ii)   the loss which would be caused to the misrepresentee by the misrepresentation if rescission were refused; and

   (iii)   the loss which would be caused to the representor by rescission.[19]

If damages are awarded, they should never exceed that which would have been awarded if the representation has been a warranty.

Damages may be awarded under section 2(2) even though the right to rescind has been lost because it has become impossible to restore the parties to the position they were in before the contract was made, at least where the right existed at the time when the claim to rescind was first made.[20]

The question of the measure of damages under the Act is considered below, pages 162 and 217.

RESCISSION AND AVOIDANCE OF CONTRACTS

This is a convenient point at which to consider the nature of rescission for misrepresentation on the one hand and avoidance of a contract for breach on the other. They are different. When a contract is rescinded for misrepresentation, it is wiped out from the start. The parties must be put back into the position in which they were before the contract was made and, if that cannot be done, the contract may not be rescinded. In the case of a contract which continues over a period of time, avoidance for breach terminates it only from the moment of avoidance. It is immaterial that the parties cannot be put back into the position in which they were before the contract was made, and rights and duties which accrued before the moment of avoidance remain good. Where A has entered into a contract to employ B for five years and, after two years, B commits a fundamental breach of contract and A dismisses him, the contract for the final three years is avoided, but everything that was done during the first two years was validly done and stands unimpaired. The parties cannot be restored to the position in which they were before the contract was made—A cannot give back the services which B has rendered to him—but that is immaterial; and B is entitled to

19 *William Sindall plc v. Cambridgeshire County Council* [1994] 3 All E.R. 932; S. & T. 364 and 519.
20 *Witter (Thomas) Ltd v. TBP Industries Ltd* [1996] 2 All E.R. 573 at 590.

retain the salary which he has received during those two years. The two remedies were considered in *Leaf v. International Galleries.*[21] The plaintiff bought a picture from the defendants who represented that it was by Constable. Five years later, the plaintiff discovered that it was not by Constable and claimed rescission of the contract in equity for misrepresentation. The Court of Appeal held that it was too late to rescind the contract not simply (as the County Court judge held) because the contract had been executed, but because the plaintiff had accepted the picture in performance of the contract. This precluded rejection of the picture for breach of condition under section 11(1)(c) of the Sale of Goods Act 1893 (now section 11(4) of the Sale of Goods Act 1979) and it followed that he could not rescind for misrepresentation. Denning L.J. was prepared to assume in the buyer's favour that the statement that the picture was by Constable was a condition. He said:

"Although rescission may in some cases be a proper remedy, it is to be remembered that an innocent misrepresentation is much less potent than a breach of condition; and a claim to rescission for innocent misrepresentation must at any rate be barred when a right to reject for breach of condition is barred. A condition is a term of the contract of a most material character, and if a claim to reject on that account is barred, it seems to me *a fortiori* that a claim to rescission on the ground of innocent misrepresentation is also barred."

Since rescission involves putting the parties back in the position in which they were before the contract was made— usually called *restitutio in integrum*—it follows that, if this is no longer possible, there can be no rescission. So in *Clarke v. Dickson*[22] the plaintiff, who was induced to take shares in a partnership by a misrepresentation, sued unsuccessfully to get his money back after the partnership business had, with his assent, been registered as a company with limited liability. The nature of the thing he bought had changed and he could not return it. The court likened the case to that of a butcher who buys cattle and, after killing them, seeks to get his money back because of a misrepresentation by the seller.

Where the parties are in a fiduciary relationship this rule may be relaxed and rescission allowed even though it is impossible to put the parties in precisely the same position as they were before,

21 [1950] 2 K.B. 86; S. & T. 350.
22 (1858) El. Bl. & Bl. 148; S. & T. 357.

provided the court can achieve what is practically just between the parties: *O'Sullivan v. Management Agency*[23]—a case, not of misrepresentation but undue influence, where it was impossible for the plaintiff to restore the benefit of the work done on his behalf by the defendant, but the court could achieve what was practically just by obliging the defendant to give up the profits and advantages he had obtained, while compensating him for the work he had done under the contract.

Affirmation

The representee loses his right to rescind if, knowing of the facts which give rise to that right and also that he has that right, he affirms the contract. It was decided in *Peyman v. Lanjani*[24] that it is not enough to deprive him of the right that he knows the facts, if he does not also know of his right. The plaintiff, who had entered into a contract to purchase the lease of a restaurant, discovered that he had been induced to do so by misrepresentation. The solicitor who was acting for both parties urged him to proceed with the contract and he agreed to do so. A month later, on the advice of new solicitors, he rescinded and it was held that he was entitled to do so. He was an Iranian who spoke very little English and, when he agreed to proceed he was not aware that he had a right to rescind it. The affirmation was ineffective and the contract was rescinded. The court distinguished an election to affirm from an estoppel. Where there is an operative election to affirm, it is effective as soon as it is made. Once it is communicated to the representor, the right to rescind is gone. It is not necessary to show that the representor acted on the affirmation. An affirmation may, however, be ineffective when made because the affirmer is not aware of his right to rescind; but, if it appears to the representor to be a good affirmation— there is nothing to indicate to him that the affirmer is unaware of his right—and he acts to his detriment in reliance on that affirmation, the affirmer will be estopped from denying the validity of his affirmation.

Where a person has, and knows he has, the right to rescind, he must exercise it within a reasonable time. If he does not do so, he will be taken to have affirmed the contract.

What is rescission?

A person with a right to rescind a contract normally does so

---

23 [1985] Q.B. 428, CA.
24 [1985] Ch. 457, CA; S. 7 T. 352.

simply by informing the other party of his election to rescind the contract. The contract is then wiped out. There is no need to go to court to rescind a contract—though it may be necessary to do so to compel a recalcitrant party to return what he has received under the contract. Rescission is generally a self-help remedy. There may be an exception to this under the principle of *Solle v. Butcher*[25] allowing rescission of a contract for mistake. Here it seems that rescission is allowed only on such terms as the court considers just; and, if that is so, it is plain that a party cannot effect it himself. He must ask the court to do so.

Where a person does have the right to rescind, he must generally actually communicate his decision to do so. One exception appears to be where the contract is one to transfer property and he retakes possession. The contract, it seems, will be rescinded by that act, even before the other party knows of it. Another case where actual communication is not necessary is that where the party at fault has deliberately put it out of the power of the other to communicate, knowing that the other will almost certainly want to do so. Here the contract may be rescinded by an overt act, clearly evincing an intention to rescind. In *Car and Universal Finance Co. Ltd v. Caldwell*[26] the owner of a car which had been obtained from him by deception informed the police and the Automobile Association of the fraudulent transaction. The rogue, of course, was keeping well out of the way. It was held that the plaintiff could not have done more to make his position plain and that the contract was effectively rescinded before the car came into the hands of the BFP[27] who, accordingly, got no title.

25 Below, p. 193.
26 [1965] 1 Q.B. 525, CA; S. & T. 355.
27 Above, p. 58.

CHAPTER FOURTEEN

Exclusion Clauses

1. THE COMMON LAW

'Exclusion" or "exemption" or "exceptions" clauses are terms in a contract which exclude or limit, or purport to exclude or limit, a liability which would otherwise arise. The liability which it is sought to exclude or limit may be a contractual liability, or it may be a liability arising under the common law independently of contract, or a statutory liability. Potential tortious liability may be excluded by a contractual term. So may a liability arising under the common law of bailment and other common law rules. A statutory liability may be excluded unless the terms of the statute preclude exclusion. The Occupiers' Liability Act 1957, s.2(1), imposes on the occupier of premises "a common duty of care" to all his visitors but does not prevent him from excluding this duty "by agreement or otherwise".

Suppliers of goods and services not unnaturally seek to exclude or limit their possible legal liability by the insertion of exclusion clauses in their standard forms of contract. Sometimes these clauses are very far-reaching. The courts have long been hostile to such clauses. Usually, they are not freely negotiated but are, in effect, imposed by the one party on the other. The supplier declares that he will contract on his standard terms and no other and the customer frequently has to accept those terms or go without the service he wants. There is no "equality of bargaining power". Because of their sympathy with the weaker party, the courts have frequently applied the rules concerning the interpretation and formation of contracts strictly in his favour, resolving any doubts against the stronger party. Thus, they have frequently held exclusion clauses to be inoperative:

(1)   by holding the clause not to be part of the contract because notice of it was insufficient or too late;

(2)   by construing the clause strictly against the party relying on it (*contra proferentem*) and holding it to be inapplicable to the events which have occurred; and

(3)   more controversially, by invoking the "doctrine of fundamental breach"—that a person who has committed a breach of a fundamental term or a fundamental breach of an innominate term is precluded from relying on any exclusion clause, at least if the contract has been terminated as a result of the breach.

The Unfair Terms in Consumer Contracts Regulations 1994 now provide:

"**Construction of written contracts**. A seller or supplier shall ensure that any written term of a contract is expressed in plain, intelligible language, and if there is any doubt about the meaning of a written term, the interpretation most favourable to the consumer shall prevail."

The first half of this provision seems to be no more than a pious exhortation; and the second is, in substance, the *contra proferentem* rule which applies at common law to contracts generally, though it may be more strictly enforced in consumer contracts.

The third rule featured largely in the law reports for many years and was the subject of much controversy, but it may perhaps now be considered defunct.

The injustice arising from the use of exclusion clauses has attracted the attention of Parliament from time to time and many statutes contain provisions prohibiting the exclusion or limitation of liabilities arising in particular circumstances. On February 1, 1978, there came into force a much more general and far-reaching statute, the Unfair Contract Terms Act 1977, which applies to contracts made on or after, but not before, that date and to liability for loss or damage suffered on or after, but not before, that date. The title of the Act is misleading in two respects: (i) it is not concerned with all contract terms which might be thought to be "unfair" but with only two types of term: exclusion clauses and indemnity clauses. (ii) It is not confined to contractual terms. It applies to cases where there is no contractual relationship between the parties but an attempt is made to exclude tortious or other liability by means of a notice or other disclaimer.

Far-reaching though the Act is, the common law continues to be of importance because (i) some very important classes of contract are outside the scope of the Act altogether; and (ii) where the Act provides, as in some cases it does, that an exclusion clause is valid if reasonable, the plaintiff may argue (a) that the clause is not part of the contract at all, or (b) that, on its true construction, it does not apply to the situation which has arisen—and in either of those cases it is ineffective, even if it is a reasonable clause. It is probable that the common law principles are not applied with the same degree of strictness after the Act as before—in many cases the Act has diminished or removed the need for the special protection which these rules afforded—but the principles still stand as part of the law. It is therefore convenient to consider them before examining the terms of the 1977 Act.

Was the clause incorporated in the contract?

If the clause is included in a written and signed agreement it is plainly part of the contract and, in the absence of fraud or misrepresentation, it is wholly immaterial that the party has not read the document.[1] The position is the same if the contract has been reduced to writing but not signed, except that it then has to be proved, by some means other than his signature, that the party gave his assent to that paper being the contract. It is here, however, that the difficulties begin. A paper is proffered, or exhibited, by A to B, which A intends to be, either the contract, or a part of it—and it contains an exclusion clause. The question then is whether A did what was reasonably sufficient to give B notice of that term. This principle was laid down in the leading case of *Parker v. South Eastern Railway*[2] where the plaintiff, on depositing a bag in the cloak room at the defendant's station received a ticket with a number, the date, and the words "See back" on the front of it. On the back were printed several clauses, including "The company will not be responsible for any package exceeding the value of £10." The plaintiff did not read the ticket and his bag, valued at £24 10s, was lost. The judge having misdirected the jury, a new trial was ordered so that the jury could answer the question posed above. It was a question of fact. If the notice given was reasonable, the term was part of the

---

1 *L'Estrange v. Graucob* [1934] 2 K.B. 394, DC; S. & T. 135, above, p. 17, *per* Scrutton L.J., who added the reference to misrepresentation to the language of Mellish L.J. in *Parker v. South Eastern Railway* (1877) 2 C.P.D. 416; S. & T. 147.
2 Above, n.1.

contract and liability was limited. Otherwise, it was totally ineffective.

All the relevant circumstances must be taken into account in deciding whether reasonable notice has been given. It has been said that the party giving notice is entitled to assume that those to whom it is addressed speak English and can read. This might now be questioned in areas where there is a large number of recent immigrants—and perhaps in some parts of Wales. Individual handicaps, like illiteracy, not brought to the attention of the other party, though plainly relevant to the question whether the notice was read, may be treated as irrelevant to the issue of reasonable notice. In a tort case, however, Waller L.J. seems to have been regarded the fact that a motorist was feeling ill as relevant to the question whether she had received sufficient notice of a warning that trespassing cars might be clamped.[3]

Mellish L.J., in his classic judgment, distinguished between two types of paper—(i) the type which an ordinary person would not expect to contain contractual terms, and (ii) the type which all reasonably well-informed persons would expect to contain such terms. As an example of the first type, he instanced a turnpike ticket which (in 1877) the reasonable recipient might well put in his pocket unread, assuming that it was merely something he might have to produce to show that he had paid the toll. His example of the second type was a bill of lading which invariably contains the terms of the contract of carriage. A shipper of goods who did not happen to know this and did not read the bill, would, Mellish L.J. thought, have to "bear the consequences of his own exceptional ignorance." He would almost certainly be bound by the terms, but a holder of the unread turnpike ticket probably would not. The law is not stated more positively simply because it is a question of fact and then had to be left to a jury. Even juries, however, did not have unlimited power to decide what was reasonable. Their decisions on questions of fact are always controlled by the judge in two ways. They are not allowed to find a fact proved unless there is evidence on which a reasonable jury could so find; and they must find the fact proved if that is the *only* conclusion to which a reasonable jury could come on the evidence. So in *Thompson v. London, Midland and Scottish Railway*[4] the judge (rightly so the Court of Appeal held) overruled a jury which had found that

---

3 *Vine v. Waltham Forest London B.C.* [2000] 4 All E.R. 169 at 179de. Roch L.J. thought that it must be proved that the motorist saw *and understood the significance of* the notice. Waller L.J. thought that it was sufficient that the notice was seen and known to contain terms although they were not read or understood—which accords with the contract cases.

4 [1930] 1 K.B. 41, CA; S. & T. 151.

reasonable notice had not been given to a passenger (who could not read) whose ticket bore on its face the words "Excursion, for conditions see back", and on the back it was stated that the ticket was issued subject to the conditions in the company's time-tables and excursion bills. Those conditions provided that excursion ticket holders should have no right of action against the company, in respect of any injury, however caused. Such a clause would now be invalid under the Unfair Contract Terms Act, but the case remains an authority on the question of incorporation of terms by the delivery of a ticket. It hardly seems a shining example of the *contra proferentem* rule. The conditions were somewhat far to seek—but a jury which said that reasonable notice was not given was held to be making a perverse decision. Later cases have taken a stricter view of the notice requirement and in *Thornton v. Shoe Lane Parking Ltd*[5] it was held that, the more far-reaching the clause, the greater must be the clarity of the notice to satisfy the requirement of reasonableness. The clause in that case—a car-parking contract, purporting to exclude liability for personal injury (invalid since 1977) would, Lord Denning thought, "need to be printed in red ink with a red hand pointing to it—or something equally startling." The onus on a person relying on a notice to justify clamping a car "must be very high".[6]

However clear the notice may be, it must be given before the contract is entered into. Once the contract has been made, neither side can alter its terms without the consent of the other. In *Chapelton v. Barry UDC*,[7] the Council displayed a notice beside a pile of deckchairs, stating the charge and inviting the public to obtain tickets from an attendant. The plaintiff took a chair and sat in it. Later the attendant came round and gave him a ticket which he put in his pocket unread. The chair gave way and he suffered injury. He claimed damages for negligence and the Council relied on an exclusion clause on the ticket. The clause was held to be ineffective because (i) the ticket (like Mellish L.J.'s turnpike ticket) was not one which a reasonable person would expect to contain contractual terms; and (ii) the contract was made when the plaintiff took the chair and sat in it, thus incurring an obligation to pay the charge when the attendant came to collect it. The ticket came too late. Similarly, in *Olley v. Marlborough Court Ltd*[8] a notice displayed in a hotel bedroom was held to be ineffective when the contract had been made in the

5 [1971] 2 Q.B. 163; S. & T. 152.
6 *Vine's case*, above, at 179d, *per* Waller L.J.
7 [1940] 1 K.B. 532, CA.
8 [1949] 1 K.B. 532, CA.

lobby of the hotel before the guest entered the bedroom. A more arguable point was that, in the course of an extended stay, the contract had been renewed from time to time after the guest had had ample opportunity to read the notice, but the court was unimpressed, taking the view that it was for the hotelier to prove that there had been a change in the terms of the contract made on arrival at the hotel.

If, however there has been a consistent "course of dealing" between A and B of such a nature that any reasonable person would know that A invariably intends to contract only on certain terms, B will be bound by those terms even if he is in fact unaware of them. The leading case is *Hardwick Game Farm v. Suffolk Agricultural Poultry Producers Association*.[9] A farmer ordered feeding stuff from a merchant. It came with a sold note which had an exclusion clause printed on the back. Clearly, that was not part of the contract. As in *Olley's* case, notice was not given until after the contract had been made. But the farmer continued to order feeding stuff from the merchant three or four times a month, for three years. On each occasion a sold note, with same term, came with the goods. Well over 100 sold notes were delivered. There came a day when, as usual, the farmer's order was given and accepted orally, but the stuff delivered with the usual note proved to be poisonous and caused the farmer substantial loss. The merchant relied successfully on the clause. It was immaterial that the farmer had never in fact read it. He had, by now, ample notice that these were the terms on which the seller did business and, if he telephoned an order, it was implicit in his offer that it was to be on those terms.

To have this effect, a course of dealing must be consistent. In *McCutcheon v. David MacBrayne Ltd*[10] the shipper of a car on the carrier's ship was not bound by a clause in the carrier's "risk note" though he had shipped goods on the carrier's vessels on a number of occasions previously. Sometimes he had been asked to sign a risk note and sometimes—probably because of chaotic conditions in the carrier's office—he had not; and on the present occasion he had not been asked to sign. He was not in fact aware of the terms and was not bound by them. Even if the same practice is followed on every occasion, those occasions must be sufficiently numerous and proximate in time to make it clear to the reasonable person who knows what he is about that these, and no other, are the terms on which the other party does business. In *Hollier v. Rambler Motors (AMC) Ltd*[11] it was held that

9 [1969] 2 A.C. 31, HL.
10 [1964] 1 W.L.R. 125, HL; S. & T. 159.
11 [1972] 2 Q.B. 71, CA; S. & T. 162.

three or four transactions over a period of five years was not such a "course of dealing" as to attract the operation of this principle.

A similar principle may operate where both parties are "in the trade" and it is, or should be, well-known to both that a particular term is generally used in the trade. In *British Crane Hire Corporation Ltd v. Ipswich Plant Hire Ltd*[12] both parties were in the business of hiring out heavy earth-moving equipment. The defendants, having an urgent need for a drag-line crane, hired one by telephone from the plaintiffs who sent it, in accordance with the usual practice, with a printed form to be signed by the defendants. Before the form was signed, the crane sank in marshy ground. It was held that the usual conditions (which were in the unsigned form) were incorporated into the contract. As reasonable persons in the trade, the defendants must have known that the plaintiffs would not let out their crane except on some such terms.

Misrepresentation

It has been seen that, apart from statutory provision, the only usual effect of misrepresentation is to create a right to rescind. Misrepresentation requires special mention in this context because it may also limit or exclude reliance on an exclusion clause. In *Curtis v. Chemical Cleaning and Dyeing Co.*[13] the defendants' employee misrepresented the effect of an exclusion clause. On leaving her wedding dress to be cleaned, the plaintiff inquired why she was asked to sign a form and was told it was because the company would not accept liability for certain specified risks, including damage to the beads and sequins with which the dress was trimmed. When the dress came back, the beads and sequins were all right, but the dress had a stain on it. In fact the clause provided that the company was not to be liable for "any damage, however arising". It was held that the employee had unwittingly created a false impression and that the effect was to disentitle the company from relying on the clause, except in regard to the beads and sequins.

The interpretation of the clause

When it has been decided that the clause is part of the contract, the next question is whether it applies to the state of affairs which exists, or the events which have occurred. This is a

---

12 [1975] Q.B. 303, CA; S. & T. 160.
13 [1951] 1 K.B. 805, CA; S. & T. 458.

question of "construction" or interpretation. In dealing with this question, it is important to distinguish between two classes of exclusion clause: (i) clauses which seek to exclude or qualify *obligations* which would otherwise arise under the contract or by virtue of some rule of law; and (ii) clauses which seek to exclude or qualify the *remedies* which would otherwise be available for breach of those obligations. The importance of the distinction is that in the first category there is a direct conflict between the obligation and exclusion clause. If the obligation exists, the exclusion clause, to that extent, is invalid. If the exclusion clause is valid, the obligation does not exist. In the second class of case, this conflict does not arise. The obligation exists all right and, assuming it to be a contractual obligation, if it is broken, the injured party may sue for breach of contract but the clause limits, or purports to limit, the amount of damages recoverable, or the time within which the action must be brought, or the right to rescind or terminate the contract.

A good illustration of the problem which faces the court in the first class of case is *Andrews Bros Ltd v. Singer & Co. Ltd.*[14] It was a case of a written contract for the sale of "new Singer cars". One of the cars delivered was not "new". That looks like a clear case of a breach of an express obligation to deliver a new car. But there was an exclusion clause which stated that "All conditions, warranties and liabilities implied by statute common law or otherwise are excluded." Section 13 of the Sale of Goods Act 1893 (now 1979) provided that "where there is a contract for the sale of goods by description, there is an implied condition that the goods shall correspond with the description." The seller argued that he had excluded all implied conditions, including this one, and so he was not liable. The court's answer was that, notwithstanding the wording of section 13, that the promise that the car would be new was an express, not an implied, term of the contract and the clause did not apply to it. The buyer got his damages. Scrutton L.J. added, however, that if a seller wanted to avoid liability in such a case, "he must do so by much clearer language than this." Too much importance should not be attached to this dictum, but it has been criticised on the ground that it suggests that it is possible to exclude liability for breach of an express term.[15]

"A man cannot in one and same contract expressly include a term (whether condition or warranty) and also exclude it . . . Once the court has decided that the sale was a sale by

14 [1934] 1 K.B. 17, CA; S. & T. 461.
15 *Benjamin on Sale* (Finnemore & James, (8th ed., 1950) p. 622.

description of 'new Singer cars' then nothing else could satisfy the contract and by no artifice could the seller avoid the obligation to provide 'new Singer cars'."

This is surely right. But if the seller had said, "I promise to deliver Singer cars which, to the best of my knowledge, are new", it would be different; and perhaps that is what Scrutton L.J. had in mind. The seller may make it clear that he is giving no promise; but he cannot both promise and not promise.

An aspect of this rule is often called the "main purpose" rule. Once the court has answered the question, "what is the main purpose of the contract?" anything that is inconsistent with the main purpose of contract must give way. If the parties intended the fulfilment of their main purpose—and, *ex hypothesi*, they did—they cannot have intended this clause, at least in its literal sense, to apply, because the clause is incompatible with the main purpose of the contract. In the *Rambler Cycle* case[16] a bill of lading required delivery "unto order or his or their assigns". The main purpose of the contract was that the carrier should carry the goods to their destination and deliver them to the holder of the bill of lading. The bill also provided that the liability of the carrier should "cease absolutely" after the goods had been discharged from the ship. After the goods had been discharged, the carrier delivered them to the consignee who did not produce the bill of lading and never paid for the goods. The Privy Council held the carrier liable. He could not contract to deliver to the holder of the bill of lading (the main purpose) and also contract that he was to be at liberty to deliver to someone who did not hold the bill.

Another way of looking at such cases is to say that the clause must be sensibly interpreted in the light of what reasonable men must have intended. Lord Denning suggested that, if the carrier's argument was right, "by parity of reasoning they would have been absolved if they had given the goods away to some passer-by or had burnt them or had thrown them into the sea." If the officious bystander[17] had suggested to the parties at the time they made their contract that it meant that the carrier was to be at liberty to do such things, it may safely be assumed that, as reasonable men, they would have "testily suppressed him"; of course it did not mean that. And the actual facts were not so different, because the carrier had given the goods to someone he knew was not entitled to have them. It was not

16 *Sze Hai Tong Bank Ltd v. Rambler Cycle Co. Ltd* [1959] A.C. 576, PC; S. & T. 469.
17 Above, p. 129.

necessary to determine what effect, if any, the clause had. It did not apply to *this* event.

An example of the construction of a clause of the second class is *Alderslade v. Hendon Laundry Ltd.*[18] The plaintiff was suing the defendant for damages for the loss of articles sent for laundering. The contract contained the clause, "The maximum amount allowed for lost or damaged articles is 20 times the charge made for laundering." The claim was in negligence and there was nothing in the clause which was inconsistent with the duty of care owed by the laundry. The question was whether the clause was effective to limit liability for negligence. If the clause was intended to do anything at all, it must have been intended to limit liability for negligence because the laundry company could not have been held liable for the loss of the articles otherwise than through its negligence.

It may be different where the defendant, in the absence of any exclusion clause, might be subject to strict liability—*i.e.* liability without any negligence on his part. In such a case, if the clause did not expressly apply to negligence, the court might hold it effective only to exclude the strict liability, leaving the defendant liable in negligence. The clause was clearly intended to do something but, construing it strictly *contra proferentem*, the court decides that sufficient effect is given to it by the exclusion of the strict liability. In *White v. John Warwick & Co. Ltd*[19] the plaintiff hired a cycle from the defendants under a written agreement which provided that "nothing in this agreement shall render the owners liable for any personal injuries." While the plaintiff was riding the cycle, the saddle tilted forward and he was injured. In the absence of the exclusion clause, the defendants might have been held liable: (i) for negligence and (ii) for breach of their undertaking that the cycle was reasonably fit for its purpose. As the clause did not expressly apply to negligence, the court held that it operated only to exclude the second, strict, liability and, negligence being proved, they were liable.[20]

Other distinctions between exclusion and limitation

All exclusion clauses are construed *contra proferentem*, that is, any ambiguity in the clause will be resolved against the party relying on it; but the rule is applied more stringently to a clause which

18 [1945] 1 K.B. 189, CA.
19 [1953] 2 All E.R. 1021, CA.
20 The defendants would now inevitably be liable for negligence causing personal injury under the Unfair Contract Terms Act 1977, s.2(1); but the case remains a useful authority on the general principle.

excludes liability altogether than to one which merely limits liability. The reason is said to be that there is a higher degree of improbability that a party would agree to a complete exclusion than to a limitation: *Ailsa Craig Shipping Co. Ltd v. Malvern Fishing Co. Ltd*[21] where the contract contained both an exclusion clause and a limitation clause. It was held that liability was limited but not excluded.

Another distinction is that an "exclusion" clause may be held to be merely declaratory of the common law—in *Hollier v. Rambler Motors*[22] a clause, stating that a garage proprietor was not responsible for damage by fire to customers cars, was held to be intended to inform the customers of the common law position—*i.e.* that the proprietor was not responsible for damage caused by accidental fires—thus leaving him liable for a fire caused by his negligence. A limitation clause cannot be declaratory because the common law has no rules limiting liability and must therefore have been intended to limit an existing liability.

"Fundamental terms," "fundamental breaches" and exclusion clauses

Over a period of about 15 years before 1966 the courts held in a series of cases that a person who had committed a breach of a "fundamental term" of a contract, or "a fundamental breach" of it was disabled from relying on any exclusion clause in the contract. The proposition was often stated and applied as if it were a rule of law which operated without regard to the intention of the parties as expressed in the contract. The exclusion clause might, on its true construction, apply to the event which had occurred but, if that event constituted a breach of a fundamental term or a fundamental breach, the defaulting party could not rely on it.

A major difficulty inherent in this doctrine was that of determining whether a term, or a breach of a term, was "fundamental." Devlin J. said that a fundamental term must be:

> "something narrower than a condition of the contract for it would be limiting the exceptions too much to say that they applied only to breaches of warranty. It is . . . something which underlies the whole contract so that, if it is not complied with, the performance becomes something totally

21 [1983] 1 W.L.R. 458, HL; S. & T. 471.
22 Above, pp. 165–166.

different from that which the contract contemplates:"[23]
(*Smeaton Hanscomb & Co. Ltd v. Sassoon I. Setty, Son & Co.*)

Yet this attempt to describe a fundamental term is precisely the
same as the classic definition of a condition by Fletcher Moulton
L.J. in *Wallis v. Pratt*.[24] A condition is, by definition, a
fundamental term. Yet Devlin J. was undoubtedly right when
he said that the effect of exclusion clauses could not be confined
to breaches of warranty—or, indeed, breaches of the then
undiscovered innominate term. The doctrine thus made it
impossible to construct a rational theory. This was grossly
inconvenient, not only for academic exponents of the law, but
also for the practitioner. If no rational theory underlies the law, it
becomes impossible to predict the decisions of the courts and to
give reliable advice. Not only did the doctrine of fundamental
breach contain a fundamental flaw but it also contradicted a
basic principle of the law of contract: it is for the parties, not the
court, to make the bargain and, if the parties have clearly agreed
that there should be no, or limited, liability on one of them in
certain circumstances, it is not for the court to overrule that
agreement. Accordingly, in the *Suisse Atlantique* case,[25] the
House of Lords held that there is no such doctrine and "That
the question whether an exceptions clause was applicable where
there was a fundamental breach of contract was one of the true
construction of the contract."[26] Lord Denning and others were,
however, reluctant to see a doctrine which they had carefully
nurtured (and which, no doubt, had achieved fairness in many
cases) die so easily and, in *Harbutt's Plasticine* case,[27] the Court of
Appeal held that the doctrine was excluded only where, as in
Suisse Atlantique itself, the contract was affirmed after the
fundamental breach was committed; and that, if the contract
came to an end as a result of the breach, the effect was to avoid
the exclusion clause *ab initio*, leaving the defendant liable for
breaches which, on its true construction, the clause was intended
to cover. It took a second decision of the House, *Photo Production
Ltd v. Securicor Transport Ltd*[28] to reaffirm the true position as
stated in the headnote to *Suisse Atlantique* quoted above. Whether
the contract is affirmed or not, the question whether the
exclusion applies is always one of construction: was it intended

23 [1953] 2 All E.R. 1471, Q.B.D.
24 [1910] 2 K.B. 1003.
25 *Suisse Atlantique Société d'Armement Maritime S.A. v. N.V. Rotterdamsche Kolen
Centrale* [1967] 1 A.C. 361, HL; S. & T. 472.
26 Headnote to the case, approved in the *Photo Production* case, below.
27 *Harbutt's Plasticine Ltd v. Wayne Tank and Pump Co. Ltd* [1970] 1 Q.B. 447, CA.
28 [1980] A.C. 827; S. & T. 476.

to apply to the breach, fundamental or not, which has occurred? The only proper use now for the expression, "fundamental term," is as the equivalent of "condition"; and the only proper use of "fundamental breach" is to designate such a breach of an innominate term as entitles the injured party to put an end to the contract. But the importance of the term broken, or of the breach, will, of course be of great relevance in answering the question of construction. In the *Rambler Cycle* case,[29] it will be recalled, the court envisaged hypothetical breaches, analogous to the one before the court, and concluded that they were of such a nature that the parties, as reasonable men, could not have intended the clause to apply to them.

If the clause is clearly expressed to exclude negligence then it will also exclude strict liability; but it does not follow that it will always be effective. The defendant may have been guilty of something worse than negligence which the parties, as reasonable persons, could not have intended to be excluded. If, in the *Rambler Cycle* case, the goods had been negligently lost after they were unloaded it may well be that the clause would have been effective to protect the carrier; but that would have been quite different from deliberately throwing them into the sea or burning them, which the court equated with the event which had actually occurred. It is the deliberate character of the breach which takes it out of the protection of the clause. In some of the fundamental breach cases, the breach was said to be fundamental because it was deliberate; but in *Suisse Atlantique* it was pointed out that the mere fact that a breach is deliberate does not mean that it is also "fundamental". A deliberate delay of one day in loading a ship might have little or no effect on the substantial performance of the contract. But the question whether the breach was fundamental is a different question from whether it was intended to be covered by the clause and, in answering the latter question, deliberateness is clearly an important factor.

Where a clause is wide enough to exclude a negligent but not a deliberate breach of contract it becomes vitally important to know what sort of breach occurred and, if this cannot be done, the disposition of the onus of proof is the decisive factor. Paradoxically, if the defendant can show that the breach occurred through his negligence, he escapes liability, because such liability is excluded; but, if he cannot show that, the court may infer that there was a deliberate breach, leaving him liable. It has been held that, when goods in the possession of a bailee are lost or damaged and there is an exclusion clause covering negligence, the onus is on the bailee to prove that the loss

29 Above, p. 168.

occurred either without his fault, or through negligence, and not through something worse. In *Levison v. Patent Steam Carpet Cleaning Co. Ltd*[30] the defendants lost lost the plaintiff's carpet in some unexplained way. Though the agreement exempted them from liability for negligence, they were held liable. They were the ones who should know what happened to the carpet and the onus was on them to prove that the loss was not due to what the court called a "fundamental breach" going beyond mere negligence.

This principle is easily understandable where the fundamental or deliberate breach is committed by the contracting party personally. If I personally undertake to clean your mink stole and then give it away to my girl-friend there is unlikely to be any difficulty in deciding that no exclusion clause, however widely drawn, could reasonably have been supposed to have been intended to cover that. Suppose, however, it has been stolen by one of my employees. Here I, personally, may not even have been negligent, because I may have taken all proper care in employing him. But it seems that the courts will regard this as a worse than negligent breach. My employee is committing the tort of conversion and I am vicariously liable for torts committed by him in the course of his employment. In *Levison's* case, Lord Denning said that the clause would be ineffective if "the goods were stolen by one of his servants; or delivered by a servant to the wrong address; or damaged by reckless or wilful misconduct; all of which the offending servant will conceal and not make known to his employer." The burden on the employer of proving that none of these things happened is therefore formidable.

In the *Photo Production* case Securicor agreed to provide security services, including night patrols, at the plaintiffs' factory. Their employee, Musgrove, while carrying out a night patrol, deliberately started a small fire which got out of control and destroyed the factory, valued at £615,000. Securicor successfully relied on a clause which provided that, under no circumstances, should they be "responsible for any injurious act or default by any employee of the company unless such act or default could have been foreseen and avoided by the exercise of due diligence on the part of the company as his employer . . .". In the Court of Appeal, the doctrine of fundamental breach made what should be positively its last appearance. It was held that there had been a fundamental breach which brought the contract to an end and, following *Harbutt's Plasticine*, the clause could no longer be relied on. The House, however, held that the question

30 [1978] Q.B. 69, CA; S. & T. 468.

was simply one of construction and, on its true construction, the clause applied to the event which had occurred. In commercial transactions, as distinct from consumer contracts (by then regulated by the Unfair Contract Terms Act) there was everything to be said for leaving the parties free to apportion the risks as they thought fit and respecting their decisions. The House was influenced by Securicor's very modest charge—it worked out at 26p a visit—and the relative means of knowledge of the parties. Securicor could know nothing of the value of the factory and efficacy of the fire precautions. It was not reasonable in these circumstances to suppose that the parties could have intended Securicor to assume responsibility for the substantial risk of damage to the premises.

Deliberately starting a small fire is one thing and deliberately burning down the factory is another. It does not necessarily follow that the latter act would have been protected by the clause. Still less does it follow that a deliberate act, done personally by the contracting party, as distinct from one for which he is vicariously liable, would be protected. If Securicor's board of directors had resolved to burn the factory down, clearly Securicor would not have been able to rely on the clause; and it may be that they would not have been able to do so had they—or someone who could be identified with the company—authorised employees to light small fires on the premises to keep warm. The question would be whether the parties, as reasonable commercial men, could have intended the clause to apply in that situation.

Deviation

It is reasonable to suppose that an exemption clause is intended to protect a party only when he is performing the contract and to leave him subject to his usual liability when he is doing something completely outside its terms. If A contracts with B to store B's goods in warehouse X and then proceeds to store them in warehouse Y, where they are destroyed, it may well be that an exclusion clause which would have been effective to protect him against the loss had it occurred in warehouse X will be ineffective.[31] The clause protected him while he was performing the contract, but he was not doing so when the loss occurred. When a shipowner deviates from the contractually agreed voyage he may be disabled from relying on exemption clauses in the contract of carriage. In the *Photo Production* case,

---

31 *cf. Lilley v. Doubleday* (1881) 7 Q.B.D. 510—but there was no exclusion clause in that case.

Lord Wilberforce suggested that it may be preferable to regard the deviation cases as a body of authority *sui generis* with special rules derived from historical and commercial reasons; but, if they can be brought within a general principle of the contract, this would appear to be it.

2. STATUTORY REGULATION OF EXCLUSION CLAUSES

The Misrepresentation Act 1967

Section 3 of the Act, as amended by the Unfair Contract Terms Act 1977, provides:

> 3. If a contract contains a term which would exclude or restrict—
>
> (a) any liability to which a party to a contract may be subject by reason of any misrepresentation made by him before the contract was made; or
> (b) any remedy available to another party to the contract by reason of such a misrepresentation,
>
> that term shall be of no effect except in so far as it satisfies the requirement of reasonableness as stated in section 11(1) of the Unfair Contract Terms Act 1977; and it is for those claiming that the term satisfies that requirement to show that it does.

If then a person brings an action for rescission of the contract for innocent misrepresentation or for damages under section 2(1) of the 1967 Act, the defendant cannot rely on a clause purporting to exclude or restrict his liability for misrepresentation unless he can satisfy the court that the term was a fair and reasonable one to be included, having regard to the circumstances which were or ought reasonably to have been, known to, or in the contemplation of, the parties when the contract was made. Under the 1967 Act as originally passed, the test was whether *reliance* on the term was fair and reasonable in the circumstances of the case. This allowed—and indeed required—the court to take into account relevant events occurring after the contract was made. Clearly this is no longer the case. The court must decide whether the clause was a fair and reasonable one to include in the contract and, if it was, it is valid and must be applied.

Section 3 would also apply if an action were brought for damages for a negligent misrepresentation under the doctrine of

Hedley Byrne.[32] It is not so clear that the section is applicable to an action for breach of contract. We have seen[33] that a misrepresentation may be incorporated into a contract. Suppose there is a clause excluding liability for both misrepresentation and breach of contract. If the representee claims damages under section 2(1), or rescission for misrepresentation, the clause may be struck down under section 3; but what if he claims damages for breach, or to avoid the contract for breach of condition? In some cases, the corresponding provision of the 1977 Act relating to breach of contract will apply and there will be no problem; the same "fair and reasonable" test will apply; but, whereas section 3 applies to all contracts, the 1977 Act does not. If the contract is one of those excluded from the 1977 Act, the scope of section 3 is material. One opinion is that section 3 invalidates the whole clause and that the representee is thus unable to exclude liability for breach of contract to the extent that the relevant term is a misrepresentation for which he cannot do so. But this is not completely clear. If there were two exclusion clauses, one excluding liability for misrepresentation and the other excluding liability for breach of contract, it would be clear that section 3 applied only to the first and not to the second. Why should it be different when the two provisions are put into one clause of a contract rather than into two clauses? The substance is the same. If that view is right, section 3 does not limit the ability of a party to a contract to exclude liability for contractual undertakings as to matters of fact, whether or not they amounted to misrepresentations before the conclusion of the contract. Whether this view is right or wrong, it is of course clear that section 3 does not limit ability to exclude liability for contractual undertakings as to the future, for that does not involve misrepresentation.

The Unfair Contract Terms Act 1977 and the Unfair Terms in Consumer Contracts Regulations 1995[34]

The 1977 Act came into force on February 1, 1978. The original version of the regulations which implement Council Directive 93/13 came into force on July 1, 1995. Those regulations were revoked and re-enacted with modifications and additions by the 1999 regulations which came into force on October 1, 1999. Under the 1995 regulations the Director General of Fair Trading had an obligation to consider any complaint about the fairness of a contract term drawn up for general use and a power to apply

32 Above, p. 147.
33 Above, p. 121.
34 For the full texts see S. & T. 723–738.

for an injunction to prevent the continued use of such a term. That continues but the 1999 regulations provide for the first time that a qualifying body named in Schedule 1 (statutory regulators, trading standards departments and the Consumers' Association) shall have a similar power, provided they give the Director the required notice of their intention. The Regulations also create a new power for the Director and the qualifying bodies to require traders to produce copies of their standard contracts and give informtion about their use. They were enacted without any revision of, and on top of, the statutory protection against unfair terms already existing in English law, including the Misrepresentation Act 1967, section 3 and the 1977 Act. The result is that the 1977 Act and the Regulations (hereafter, "the Act" and "the Regulations") overlap in a rather disorderly way. Some types of contract are covered by both enactments, some only by one and some only by the other. Section 26 of Schedule 1 to the Act and Schedule 1 to the Regulations specify types of contract to which the enactment in question does not apply. The lists do not coincide, so it is necessary to consult both. If the *type of contract* is not excluded by an enactment, then it is necessary to consider whether the *type of term* is covered. It is probably less confusing if the two enactments are discussed separately and the Act taken first.

Clauses affected by the Act

The Act does not provide a definition of an exclusion clause but, by section 13(1), to the extent that [Part I of the Act] prevents the exclusion or restriction of any liability it also prevents—

"(a) making the liability or its enforcement subject to restrictive or onerous conditions;

(b) excluding or restricting any right or remedy in respect of the liability, or subjecting any person to any prejudice in consequence of his pursuing any such right or remedy;

(c) excluding or restricting rules of evidence or procedure;

and (to that extent) sections 2 and 5 to 7 also prevent excluding or restricting liability by reference to terms and notices which exclude or restrict the relevant obligation or duty."

An agreement in writing to submit differences to arbitration, by section 13(2), is not to be treated as excluding or restricting liability and so is unaffected by the Act. The Act does apply to clauses requiring claims or complaints to be made within a specified time or in a specified form (para. (a)), excluding the right to rescind or avoid a contract, precluding a buyer of goods or services from withholding part of the price by reason of defects in the goods or services supplied,[35] (para. (b)) or providing that a customer's signature should be conclusive proof that goods comply with a contract or have a certain value (para. (c)). Whereas a clause which *limits* the amount of damages payable on breach of contract is plainly covered, a clause which *fixes* the amount is probably not,[36] and is valid if it is a liquidated damages clause but void of it is a penalty clause.[37]

An agreement to settle an action for damages is an agreement to exclude or restrict liability but that is an existing liability whereas the Act is concerned with prospective liability—*i.e.* a liability which the parties contemplate might arise under a contract which they are about to enter into. Though section 15 provides that the Act does not affect the validity of such a settlement in Scotland and there is no corresponding provision for England, it has been held that the Act is not intended, and does not apply, to such a settlement.[38]

Contracts affected by the Act

Sections 2 to 7 of the Act apply—

> "(except where the contrary is stated in section 6(4)) only to business liability, that is liability for breach of obligations or duties arising—
>
> (a)   from things done or to be done by a person in the course of a business (whether his own business or another's); or
> (b)   from the occupation of premises used for business purposes of the occupier . . .".[39]

"Business" includes a profession and the activities of any government department or local or public authority.[40] The Act applies then to the obligations of a solicitor, a doctor, the

---

35 *Stewart Gill Ltd v. Horatio Meyer & Co. Ltd* [1992] 2 All E.R. 257.
36 *cf. Suisse Atlantique* [1967] 1 A.C. 361; S. & T. 472, 474.
37 Below, p. 230.
38 *Tudor Grange Holdings Ltd v. Citibank NA* [1991] 4 All E.R. 1, Ch.D. (Browne-Wilkinson V.C.). *cf. Cook v. Wright*, above, p. 73.
39 s.1(3).
40 s.14.

proprietor of a private school operated for profit, a local authority in respect of its schools, swimming baths, etc. but not to a university or a private school which is a charitable foundation. The latter, and any person not carrying on business may continue to exclude liability to the same extent as before the Act; but, of course, it is nearly always in respect of business liability that the matter arises.

There are other limitations. Sections 2–4 do not extend, and sections 5 to 7 are inapplicable, to the contracts listed in Schedule 1, para. 1, which include any contract of insurance, any contract relating to the creation, transfer or termination of an interest in land, or in any patent, trade mark, copyright or other intellectual property, and any contract relating to the formation or dissolution of any company.

The Act does not apply to "international supply contracts" which are contracts for the sale of goods, or under which the ownership or possession of goods passes, made by parties whose places of business (or, if they have none, habitual residences) are in different states *and* either—

(i) the goods are in the course of carriage, when the contract is made, or will be carried, from one State to another; or

(ii) the acts of offer and acceptance are done in different states; or

(iii) the contract provides for the goods to be delivered in a State other than that in which the offer and acceptance took place.[41]

The Act does not apply to contracts which are governed by English law only because the parties have so provided, the substantial connection of the contract being with the law of a country outside the United Kingdom.[42] But it does apply where a term purporting to apply the law of some other country appears to the court or arbitrator to have been imposed wholly or mainly for the purpose of enabling the party imposing it to evade the operation of the Act.

The Act does not preclude the exclusion of liability in certain contracts for the carriage by sea of a passenger and/or his luggage. Nor does it apply to terms (a) authorised or required by any enactment or (b) which impose restrictions no greater than is required to comply with an international agreement to which the United Kingdom is a party.

41 Section 26.
42 Section 27(1).

The effect of the Act

(i) Avoidance of liability for negligence.   Negligence is defined by section 1(1) to include the breach of any duty to take reasonable care or exercise reasonable skill, arising out of a contract, or imposed by the common law or the Occupier's Liability Act 1957. No term of any contract or notice to which section 2(1) applies can exclude or restrict liability for negligence causing death or personal injury and liability for other loss or damage can be excluded or restricted only in so far as the term or notice satisfies the requirement of reasonableness laid down by the Act and considered below.[43] A notice may be relevant evidence that a defendant has satisfied a duty of care by giving warning of a danger; but section 13(1)[44] makes it clear that a term or notice may not negative a duty which would otherwise give rise to a liability which could not be excluded.[45] So the words, "without responsibility, on our part," which saved the defendants in *Hedley Byrne*[46] from liability would no longer be effective unless the defendants persuaded the court—as well they might—that the disclaimer satisfied the requirement of reasonableness.

(ii) Avoidance of liability, otherwise than for negligence, in contract.   This is provided for by section 3 of the Act which operates in favour of two classes of party:

    (i)   One who "deals as consumer" that is, he neither makes the contract in the course of a business nor holds himself out as doing so and the other party does make the contract in the course of a business.[47] If the contract is one of sale or hire purchase, or one under which the title to goods passes, the buyer is a consumer only if the goods are of a type ordinarily supplied for private use or consumption. Sales by auction or competitive tender are not to be regarded as consumer transactions in any circumstances. Where the matter is disputed, the onus of proof is on the party who claims that the other was not a consumer.

    (ii)   One dealing on the other's written standard terms of business. The party proffering such terms is, *ex*

43 p. 183.
44 Above, p. 177.
45 *Smith v. Eric S. Bush (a firm)* [1990] 1 A.C. 831, HL; S. & T. 490.
46 Above, p. 147.
47 section 12(1).

hypothesi, making the contract in the course of a business but the other party may or may not be. Terms will not fail to qualify as "standard" because particular matters are negotiated, *e.g.* price, time of performance, etc. If the whole of the written terms have been written for this particular contract, clearly they are not "standard." Standard terms may be prepared by a trade or professional organisation, for example, the RIBA, or by the individual contractor. They are not necessarily signed.

The effect of section 3 is that the business party, or the party proffering the standard terms, cannot—

(a) when in breach of contract, exclude or restrict liability, except in so far as the contract term satisfies the requirement of reasonableness; or

(b) claim to be entitled to render a contractual performance substantially different from that which was reasonably expected of him, or to tender no performance at all, except in so far as the contract term authorising him to do so satisfies the requirement of reasonableness.

But paragraph (a) applies only when the defendant is in breach. We have seen[48] that a term may exclude an alleged promise, in which case there is no breach. Section 13, which prevents the exclusion or restriction of duties, does not apply to section 3.

If a term purports to exclude or restrict liability for breach of the promise, it is caught by paragraph (a) and is ineffective unless it satisfies the requirement of reasonableness.

The importance of the limitation on the effect of paragraph (a) is, however, much diminished, if not entirely eliminated by paragraph (b). The different performance, or non-performance, contemplated by (b) is not a breach of contract. If it were, it would be covered by (a). Paragraph (b) therefore assumes that there are two ways of performing the contract. Each is a "contractual performance" but only one is "reasonably expected". Performing the contract in the other way will be a statutory breach of contract, unless the term authorising that performance satisfies the requirement of reasonableness. An example may make this clearer. Suppose that standard terms provide:

48 Above, p. 167.

"(i) Accommodation will be provided in the Majestic Hotel
. . .
(ix) If accommodation in the Majestic Hotel is not available it
will be provided in another hotel of comparable quality."

If clause (ix) is held to be an attempt to exclude liability for
breach of a promise to provide accommodation in the Majestic, it
is caught by paragraph (a) and is ineffective unless it satisfies the
requirement of reasonableness; but if it is held to provide for an
alternative mode of performance of the contract, and the plaintiff
reasonably expected to be accommodated in the Majestic, it is
caught by paragraph (b) and there is a statutory breach of
contract unless the defendant shows that the term satisfies the
requirement of reasonableness.

**(iii) Contracts under which possession or ownership of goods
passes.**   By section 6, the seller or supplier of goods cannot, by
any contract term, exclude or restrict his undertaking as to title
implied by section 12 of the Sale of Goods Act 1979 or section 8 of
the Supply of Goods (Implied Terms) Act 1973—though he may
still contract to give only such title as he has.[49] As against a
consumer, the seller or supplier cannot exclude or restrict
liability for the implied undertakings as to conformity of goods
with description, or sample, or as to their quality or fitness for a
particular purpose and, as against others, he may do so only in
so far as the clause satisfies the requirement of reasonableness.
Section 7 makes similar provision for other contracts under
which ownership or possession of goods passes.

(iv) Indemnity clauses.   By section 4, a consumer may not be
required by any contract term to indemnify any other person
against a liability incurred by that other for negligence or breach
of contract, unless the term satisfies the requirement of
reasonableness. For example, D, the owner of a car ferry,
obtains from P, the owner of a car, a promise to indemnify D, or
D's servants, against claims arising from negligent manoeuvring
of the car. If injury is caused to a third party (whether to his
person or to his property) P can be required by D to indemnify D
only if D shows the clause satisfies the requirement of
reasonableness.

(v) Guarantees of consumer goods.   A manufacturer or
distributor of goods may seek to exclude or limit his liability in
tort in return for a "guarantee" of the goods. Section 5 protects

49 Above, p. 131.

the consumer's rights. It does not apply as between the parties to a contract under or in pursuance of which ownership or possession of goods passes. If goods are manufactured by A, distributed by B, and retailed by C to the consumer, D, the section may apply as between A and D, or B and D, but not as between C and D. D will have ample remedies against C under the Sale of Goods Act. A or B may offer D a guarantee of the goods in consideration of D's surrendering his potential rights of action in tort under *Donoghue v. Stevenson*[50] or under any collateral contract that may arise between them. If death or personal injury is caused, the term or notice is invalid under section 2 of the Act. Reliance need be placed on section 5 only in respect of damage to property or such other economic loss as may be recoverable at common law. The section does not create any new liability, it merely prevents the exclusion or restriction of a liability resulting from the negligence of a person concerned in the manufacture or distribution of goods which prove defective while in consumer use.

The requirement of reasonableness

In relation to a contractual term, the requirement is that the term shall have been a fair and reasonable one to be included having regard to the circumstances which were, or ought reasonably to have been, known to, or in the contemplation of the parties when the contract was made.[51] In determining for the purposes of sections 6 and 7 (sale, hire-purchase and miscellaneous contracts under which goods pass) whether a term satisfies the requirement of reasonableness a court or arbitrator must have regard to the matters specified in Schedule 2.[52] These include the relative bargaining power of the parties; whether there was an inducement to agree to the term or an opportunity to enter into a similar contract without such a term; whether the customer knew, or ought reasonably to have known, of the term; whether the goods were manufactured, etc., to the special order of the customer; and where the term applies if some condition is not complied with, whether it was reasonable to expect that compliance with the condition would be practicable.

In determining whether the requirement of reasonableness is satisfied for the purpose of other sections, there are no statutory guidelines; but a court will naturally take account of the matters

50 [1932] A.C. 562, HL.
51 Section 11.
52 S. & T. 734.

mentioned in Schedule 2 where they are relevant. Whatever section is in issue, the list is not exclusive.

The Regulations

The Regulations apply only to "consumer contracts". A term is "unfair" if, "contrary to the requirement of good faith [it] causes a significant imbalance in the parties' rights and obligations under the contract to the detriment of the consumer." "Good faith" is not defined but Schedule 2 states some considerations to which regard shall be had in making the assessment. An unfair term is not binding on a consumer. "Consumer" means a natural person acting for purposes which are outside his business making a contract with a seller or supplier acting for business purposes. "Business' is defined in the same way as in the Act. A corporation, not being a "natural person", cannot benefit from the consumer provisions of the Regulations but may be protected by the Act. A corporation which is a charity probably does not carry on a business and so could be a "consumer" for the purposes of the Act but not the Regulations. The Regulations apply to all terms in consumer contracts except:

   (i)   terms which have been individually negotiated;
  (ii)   terms defining the subject-matter of the contract; and
 (iii)   terms fixing the price or remuneration where its adequacy is in issue.

It appears that the Regulations, unlike the Act, may apply to an arbitration clause or a liquidated damages clause; but not a contract for the settlement of a dispute, because that could hardly be called a consumer contract. A long "indicative and non-exhaustive list of terms which may be regarded as unfair" is provided in Schedule 2.[53]

---

53 S. & T. 737.

CHAPTER FIFTEEN

Contracts Void for Failure of a Basic Contractual Assumption

> "Whenever it is to be inferred from the terms of a contract or its surrounding circumstances that the consensus has been reached upon the basis of a particular contractual assumption, and that assumption is not true, the contract is avoided: *i.e.*, it is void *ab initio* if the assumption is of present fact and it ceases to bind if the assumption is of future fact."

This proposition was formulated by Sir John Simon for the assistance of the House of Lords in *Bell v. Lever Bros Ltd*[1] and was thought by Lord Atkin to be a statement to which few would demur, though its value depended upon the meaning of "contractual assumption" and "basis".

It is established that, although the parties are in perfect agreement, the contract may be invalid from the start, or being initially valid, may become invalid through the failure of a basic contractual assumption. Where such an assumption fails, it seems an entirely reasonable conclusion that the parties, as reasonable men, do not intend the contract to operate. When the failure occurs before the contract is made, the case is traditionally treated in the books under the rubric, "mistake"; but, where it occurs after the contract is made, it is a case of frustration and usually treated under the general heading of "Discharge of contract". Historically, the frustration of a contract was based on an implied term and the same explanation has been offered to

1 [1932] A.C. 161, HL; S. & T. 503.

account for the initial invalidity of a contract through "mistake". The implied term theory is generally regarded sceptically by modern writers, but it is, in the writer's opinion, the best explanation and it has the virtue of being equally applicable to initial and subsequent invalidity. Implied terms in the form of promises are an established part of the law and there is no reason why conditions other than promises should not be equally acceptable. Both are, in a sense, fictions, since the courts impute to the parties intentions which they may never in fact have held; but the one type of term is no more fictional than the other. The implied term theory in fact makes for consistency of approach and is followed in this book. It is useful to consider the matter in the light of the problem which arises in the case of the most common alleged failure of a basic assumption—that where the subject-matter of the contract has ceased to exist, either before the contract was made, or before it was fully performed. Assume the thing ceased to exist before the contract was made. An implied term theory admits of three possible solutions.

(i)   A impliedly promised B that the thing existed or would continue to exist.

(ii) A impliedly promised B that he had taken reasonable care to find out whether it existed.

(iii) A and B proceeded on a common assumption, for which neither was more responsible than the other, that thing existed.

In determining whether (i) or (ii) applies, the court must necessarily decide whether it is appropriate to imply a promissory term in accordance with the principles already discussed. If the court decides that it is not appropriate and proceeds to solution (iii), is it not the natural and rational conclusion that solution (iii) depends on an implied condition precedent? If the existence of the thing is the basic assumption on which they have proceeded, then the contract is void. A similar analysis may be made of the case where the subject-matter of the contract ceases to exist after the contract is made, though (ii) is inapplicable and it is much less probable that a person would promise that a thing would continue to exist, than that it does exist.

INITIAL FAILURE OF A CONDITION

What is the right sort of term to imply depends on the circumstances, particularly the relative means of knowledge of the parties and whether one was relying on the other. Where A has all the means of knowledge and B has none, and A asserts that the thing exists when he knows, or ought to know, that B will act on this assertion in entering into and performing the contract, it will probably be held that A has promised B that the thing exists so that, if it appears that it does not, A will be in breach of contract. If, on the other hand, A and B have, and know they have, equal knowledge about the existence of the thing and contract on the basis of their common assumption that it exists, the contract is likely to be held to be void if it does not. In the former case, A has accepted responsibility for the existence of the thing, in the latter case it is no more the responsibility of the one than the other.

The best example of the former case is *McRae v. Commonwealth Disposals Commission.*[2] The defendants invited tenders for the purchase of an oil tanker described as lying on Jourmand Reef off Papua, together with its contents, which were stated to be oil. The plaintiffs made a tender of £285 which was accepted. They then incurred considerable expense in modifying a vessel for salvage work, etc. There was in fact no such tanker nor, indeed, was there a place known as Jourmand Reef. The plaintiffs sued for damages. The defendants argued that the contract was void because the subject-matter did not exist. The High Court of Australia held them liable. They had promised that the tanker existed and were in breach of contract. There was no "common assumption" here that the tanker existed. The Commission stated that it did exist and *McRae* was relying entirely on that assertion.

Compare a case in which A and B travel from Nottingham to London to view A's theatre which B is thinking of hiring. It appears suitable and, in the course of the rail journey back to Nottingham, they sign a contract under which A agrees to let the theatre, and B to hire it, for three months. Five minutes before they sign the agreement, the theatre is completely destroyed by an explosion for which neither A nor B is in any way responsible. Here there is a common assumption that the theatre exists. B is not relying on A for his belief in its existence—he has just seen it with his own eyes. It is true that A is unable to perform his contract. He has contracted to provide a theatre and now he cannot do so. He can escape only if there is some unexpressed but implied condition in the contract, but it would be a harsh law of contract which held him liable in these circumstances. The common law takes the view that reasonable men would not consider A's promise binding.

In *McRae's* case the Australian courts were much troubled by

2 (1951) 84 C.L.R. 377, High Court of Australia, S. & T. 499.

the decision of the House of Lords in *Couturier v. Hastie*[3] which had long been believed to lay down a proposition of law that, where the subject matter of a sale, without the knowledge or fault of the seller, had ceased to exist, the contract was void. The High Court demonstrated convincingly that *Couturier v. Hastie* decided nothing of the sort. It concerned the sale of a cargo of corn which had been shipped from Salonika and was believed by the parties to be at sea at the time of the sale. In fact, the cargo had fermented so the captain had put into port and sold it. On the day of the contract there was no cargo. The question was whether the buyer was liable to pay the price. The seller argued that the buyer was liable because, in truth, it was a contract for the sale of "the adventure"—the commercial enterprise which the seller had set in train—and that the seller's obligation was to deliver, not a cargo of corn, but the shipping documents representing the adventure—the bill of lading which would enable the buyer to get possession of the cargo if it arrived and the policy of insurance which would enable him to claim the insurance moneys if it did not. The buyer, on the other hand, said that it was a contract for the sale of cargo of corn which had not been delivered and so he did not have to pay for it. That was the question which was considered in the Court of Exchequer, which decided that it was a contract for the sale of the adventure, and the Court of Exchequer Chamber and the House of Lords, both of which held that it was a contract for the sale of the cargo. The seller had not performed his contract and was therefore obviously not entitled to the price.

The question whether the contract was void did not arise. It would have arisen if the buyer had sued the seller for failure to deliver the promised cargo, but that did not happen and it is impossible to be certain what the outcome would have been had it happened. It seems quite likely that the right answer is that the contract was void, for it was made on the common assumption that a cargo was at sea in the course of a voyage from Salonika to England. The seller (in 1853) could know no more than the buyer what might have happened to the cargo in the course of the voyage. But the case did not decide that the contract was void and is certainly not authority for that general proposition which, before *McRae*, was attributed to it. Even though the High Court then regarded itself as bound by a House of Lords decision, that decision left them quite free to decide as they did.

A more serious matter is section 6 of the Sale of Goods Act 1979. This provides, re-enacting section 6 of the Sale of Goods Act 1893:

---

3   (1856) 5 H.L.C. 673, HL; S. & T. 495.

"Where there is a contract for the sale of specific goods and the goods without the knowledge of the seller have perished at the time the contract is made, the contract is void."

This provision seems to have got into the law because the draftsman of the 1893 Act misunderstood *Couturier v. Hastie*. He thought it established that proposition, which it did not; but section 6 now represents the law. The High Court in *McRae* avoided it neatly by noting that the Australian equivalent of section 6, like section 6 itself, applied only to goods which have perished, whereas the tanker had never existed; but that is not a rational basis for such a distinction. If section 6 is taken to lay down a rule of law which applies in all circumstances, including those where a seller with all the means of knowledge asserts the existence of the thing to a buyer whom he knows to have no such means, then the common law, as described above, has been altered. But it may be that section 6, like many of the provisions of the Sale of Goods Act, will be so interpreted that it gives way to a contrary intention of the parties. Suppose that a seller assures a doubting buyer that a thing is in existence in order to persuade him to buy and perhaps gives an undertaking to that effect in the written contract. Surely the court would give effect to the express undertaking rather than to section 6; and if the section can be excluded by an express term, then it can also be excluded by an implied one, for there is no difference in principle.

WHEN IS A COMMON ASSUMPTION "BASIC"?

Parties to a contract may make many assumptions which are unfounded, without impairing the validity of the contract. They may, for example, make a common assumption as to the value of the goods they are buying and selling—the goods are in fact worth much more, or much less than they assumed—but they are both bound by the contract they have made.[4] The courts have taken a very strict and limited view of the "basic" common assumption.[5] In *Bell v. Lever Bros* Lord Atkin gave only two clear examples. The first was the case of non-existent subject-matter. Lord Atkin, following the then prevailing view of *Couturier v. Hastie*, thought that this necessarily invalidated the contract. We now know that this is not so. The existence of the subject-matter

---

4 But see *Solle v. Butcher* and cases following it, below, p. 193.
5 In *Rose v. Pim* (above, p. 21) the common assumption that the feveroles were horsebeans, though regarded by Lord Denning as "fundamental," did not avoid the contract.

may or may not be a basic common assumption, depending on the circumstances. The second was the case of a contract of sale by A to B when it turns out that the property in question belongs not to A but to B. It certainly seems reasonable to suppose that a basic assumption of a contract of sale by A to B is that the property to be sold belongs to A and not to B. In *Cooper v. Phibbs*[6] where such a situation arose in relation to the lease of a fishery, the House of Lords treated the contract as voidable; but several distinguished judges—Scrutton L.J., Lord Atkin and Lord Wright—have since said, *obiter*, that such an agreement is more properly regarded as void. The basic assumption has failed. It should be noted however that this must be subject to the same qualification as *McRae* makes to *Couturier v. Hastie*. If the right construction of the agreement is that A is promising B that he is the owner, the contract is not void but is broken by A.

Where the common error of the parties is not as to the existence or ownership of the thing but as to some quality of it, it seems that the courts will not regard the contract as void. It is true that in *Bell v. Lever Bros* Lord Atkin did say that a mistake would have that effect where it is "as to the existence of some quality which makes the thing without that quality essentially different from the thing as it was believed to be"; but this dictum is difficult, perhaps impossible, to reconcile with the decision.

Bell was employed by Lever Bros at a salary of £8,000 a year. When his appointment had some years to run, he became redundant. Lever Bros offered, and Bell accepted £30,000 as compensation for terminating his services. Lever Bros then discovered that Bell had committed breaches of his contract of service for which they could and, as the jury found, would, have dismissed him without paying him a penny, had they known what he had done. Lever Bros sued to get their money back, claiming rescission of the contract on the ground of fraud. The jury found there had been no fraud. Bell did not fraudulently conceal the breaches of his contract of service. They were not present to his mind and he did not appreciate their effect.

However, Wright J. and the Court of Appeal held that Lever Bros succeeded on the ground that the compensation agreement was void, having been made under a common mistake. The House of Lords, Lords Warrington and Hailsham dissenting, allowed the appeal. The subject-matter of the contract was Bell's contract of service. It definitely existed, but both parties were making a mistake about a fundamental quality of it; they thought it was not terminable at will by Lever Bros, whereas it was terminable at will by them. The terminability of the contract of

6 (1867) L.R. 2, HL 149.

service was the quality which mattered above all else. Negotiations would never have started if Lever Bros had known the true quality of Bell's contract of service; they would simply have dismissed him. That Bell was not dismissable at will was certainly the basic assumption made by Lever Bros and it seems not unreasonable to say that it was also Bell's basic assumption—that he went into the negotiations on the assumption that he had something to sell—his right to continue in Lever's employment—and he had nothing to sell, he had no right to continue in their employment. He got £30,000 for nothing. The thing with the quality it was believed to have was worth £30,000; without that quality it was worth nothing. Lords Warrington and Hailsham were surely right in saying that the erroneous assumption made by both parties was as fundamental to the bargain as any that could be imagined but, contrary to their view, the contract was not void. If Bell's contract of service had been *void*—*i.e.* non-existent—and not merely voidable, presumably the decision of the majority would have been different; yet there would have been no difference in substance—it was £30,000 to nothing. The House did not look at the case from the point of view of *Cooper v. Phibbs*; was not Bell, in substance, selling to Lever Bros the right to put an end to his contract—something that, unknown to them, they already owned?

As it is impossible to envisage a mistake as to quality which is more fundamental than that in *Bell v. Lever Bros*, it appears that, while that decision stands, no common assumption as to the quality of the subject-matter of the contract will be regarded as sufficiently basic to render the contract void. It does not follow that initial voidness is confined to the two cases recognised by Lord Atkin. In *Griffith v. Brymer*[7] the plaintiff entered into an oral agreement at 11 a.m. on June 24, 1902, for the hire of a room to view the coronation procession of Edward VII. A decision to operate on the King had been made at 10 a.m., rendering the procession impossible. Wright J. held that the contract was void and the plaintiff was entitled to recover his money. The common assumption was that there was going to be a coronation procession. It was mistaken and it was basic. Other cases recognised that the cancellation of the procession frustrated similar contracts which had already been made; and it seems right that an event which, if it occurs after the making of the contract, will frustrate it, should, if it occurs before, render the contract void from the start.

In *Associated Japanese Bank (International) Ltd v. Credit du Nord SA*[8] Steyn J. condemned as "too simplistic" an analysis of *Bell v.*

7 (1903) 19 T.L.R. 434.

Lever Bros similar to that made above. It is true that the analysis is inconsistent with a passage in Lord Atkin's speech in which he said:

> "Mistake as to the quality of the thing contracted for . . . will not affect assent unless it is the mistake of both parties, and is as to the existence of some quality which makes the thing without the quality essentially different from the thing as it was believed to be."

Steyn J. suggests that there was a doubt whether Lever's decision to enter into the compensation agreement would have been affected if they had known that the service agreement was voidable—*i.e.* that this quality did not make the service agreement essentially different from what it was believed to be. But this contradicts the finding of the jury that Lever would have dismissed Bell without compensation if they had known the truth. In no case since *Bell v. Lever Bros* has it been held that a mistake as to quality rendered a contract void and it seems, notwithstanding the above dictum, that there can be no such case. Steyn J. also suggested that the compensation was intended as: (i) a tangible recognition of Bell's outstanding services to the company and (ii) an inducement to him to co-operate in the re-organisation of the company. But the former would be a past consideration; and a letter to Bell stated plainly that the payment was made in consideration of his retirement and made no mention of future collaboration.

In the *Japanese Bank* case Steyn J. held that a guarantee of a lessor's performance of his agreement to lease four machines was void because there was an implied condition precedent that the machines existed and they did not. That accords with the theory described above; but, in case he was wrong in so deciding, Steyn J. went on to consider whether the guarantee was void "for mistake". It is submitted that there is no room for such an inquiry. Once it is found that there was no unsatisfied express or implied condition precedent to the existence of a contract, it is established that the parties intended the contract to exist; and the most that any mistake can do is to make it voidable.

MISTAKE RENDERING A CONTRACT VOIDABLE

In *Bell v. Lever Bros* Lord Atkin said, "If mistake operates at all it operates so as to negative or in some cases to nullify consent".

8 [1988] 3 All E.R. 902, Q.B.D.; S. & T. 510.

That is, mistake prevents any agreement from arising (as, for example in *Raffles v. Wichelhaus*),[9] so there is no contract; or it nullifies the agreement which has been arrived at, so there is no contract; or it has no effect at all. Lord Atkin did not allow for the possibility of mistake rendering a contract voidable; but we must now take account of the decision of the Court of Appeal in *Solle v. Butcher*,[10] that a common mistake as to the quality of the subject-matter may render the contract not void but voidable.

The defendant leased a flat to the plaintiff for seven years at a rent of £250 per annum. Both parties believed that the flat was not bound by the Rent Restriction Acts and that they were at liberty to negotiate such rent as they thought fit. In fact, the flat was bound by the Acts, with the effect that the standard rent of £140 applied, notwithstanding their agreement to the contrary. The plaintiff, having paid rent at £250 p.a. for some time sued for a declaration that the standard rent was £140 and to recover the amount overpaid. The Court of Appeal, Jenkins L.J. dissenting, held that the contract was voidable for mistake on the terms laid down by the court. The figure of £250 was a fair one and, if the defendant had given notice of his intention to raise the rent in accordance with the Acts before granting the lease, he could properly have done so; but, once the lease was granted, it was too late. So the terms imposed by the court were that the lease would be rescinded on the defendant's undertaking to permit the plaintiff to remain as a licensee pending the grant of a new lease and to serve the proper notice to raise the standard rent and to grant a new lease at the full permitted rent, not exceeding £250 p.a.

This was a case where, in Lord Denning's words, the parties "were agreed in the same terms on the same subject-matter." There was no question of the lease being void, or of consent being negatived or nullified. But they were mistaken as to a quality of the subject matter, important but not by any means so fundamental as that in issue in *Bell v. Lever Bros* Looked at in economic terms, the difference here was between £250 and £140 p.a. compared with £30,000 and nothing. The landlord in *Solle v. Butcher* was getting a substantial rent for his flat, even though it fell well short of what he had bargained for and of what the flat was really worth. So, if the contract was voidable in *Solle v. Butcher* it should, *a fortiori*, have been voidable in *Bell v. Lever Bros*—yet none of the Law Lords even considered the possibility. Lord Denning's explanation of this was that the House was, once

9 Above, p. 15.
10 [1950] 1 KB 671; S. & T. 513.

again,[11] overlooking equity. He relied in particular on *Cooper v. Phibbs* where the House of Lords did indeed say that the contract was voidable for mistake, and a line of similar cases. But *Cooper v. Phibbs* has in modern times been regarded as a case of a void contract,[12] and, in any event, its facts bear little resemblance to those of *Solle v. Butcher*. The fact seems to be that Denning L.J., assisted by Bucknill L.J., invented a new principle, namely:

> "A contract is . . . liable in equity to be set aside if the parties were under a common misapprehension either as to the facts or as to their relative and respective rights, provided that the misapprehension was fundamental and the party seeking to set it aside was not himself at fault."

Denning L.J. remarked that "there was a good deal to be said for the view that the lease was induced by an innocent material misrepresentation by the plaintiff." The parties had been in partnership as estate agents, the plaintiff, a surveyor, knew at least as much about the flat as the defendant and he had told the defendant that he could charge a rent of £250. But the court did not find it necessary to reach a conclusion on that point, deciding the case on the ground of mistake. Had the decision been put on grounds of misrepresentation, it would have been uncontroversial; but it must be taken to be a decision on a case where the parties were making a common assumption for which neither party was more responsible than the other. Denning L.J. expressed the opinion that a material misrepresentation need not be "fundamental" to ground rescission; but, for mistake to justify rescission, the misapprehension must be fundamental. It is not clear what "fundamental" means. The mistake need not be so fundamental as to render the contract void because then the question of rescission would not arise; yet it apparently means something more than "material" for Denning L.J. contrasted these two qualities. Perhaps "fundamental" here means only sufficiently important to satisfy the court that it is fair to rescind the contract.

The principle stated above can be supported only by recognising that *Bell v. Lever Bros* was based on an incomplete statement of the law. This was acknowledged by Goff J. in *Grist v. Bailey*.[13] The defendant, believing that a house he owned was occupied by a tenant entitled to the protection of the Rent Restriction Acts, contracted to sell it for £850, "subject to the

11 See his Lordship's treatment of *Foakes v. Beer*, above, p. 84.
12 Above, p. 190.
13 [1967] Ch. 532, S. & T. 520, Ch.D., doubted in *William Sindall plc*, below, p. 196.

existing tenancy thereof." It turned out that the tenant was not entitled to the protection of the Acts and the value of the property with vacant possession was about £2,250. On discovering the truth, the defendant declined to complete and the plaintiff sued for specific performance. The defendant counterclaimed for rescission for mistake. Goff J. said that *Bell v. Lever Bros*, "if exhaustive", was fatal to the defendant. The mistake in *Bell v. Lever Bros* was more fundamental than any mistake made in the present case. But *Solle v. Butcher* was also binding on Goff J. In the present case, there was a common mistake which was, in view of the difference in price, "fundamental" and there was no evidence of any such fault as would debar the defendant from relief in equity.

Solle v. Butcher was followed by the Court of Appeal, Winn L.J. dissenting, in *Magee v. Pennine Insurance Co. Ltd.*[14] Following an accident to his car, Magee claimed £600 from his insurers. They offered him £385 which he accepted. This was held by Lord Denning, with some doubt, to be a contract of compromise— Magee was abandoning his claim to £600 in consideration of the company promising to pay him £385. The company then discovered that Magee had made an innocent misrepresentation when entering into the contract of insurance. Had they only known, they could have rescinded the contract on that ground. They need not have paid or offered to pay anything. The contract of compromise had been made by both sides on the mistaken common assumption that the contract of insurance was not voidable at the will of the insurers. There is an obvious similarity to the situation in *Bell v. Lever Bros* but Lord Denning repeated his opinion that "A common mistake, even on a most fundamental matter, does not make the contract void at law: but it makes it voidable in equity." But voidable, apparently, not at the will of the party prejudiced by the mistake, but at the discretion of court, for Lord Denning said that he had hesitated over the question whether the court ought to set the agreement aside. He did so on the ground that it was not equitable that the plaintiff should have a good claim to money promised under a "fundamental" mistake, and it was not fair to hold the company to it.

The status of *Solle v. Butcher* is doubtful not only because of the difficulty of reconciling it with *Bell v. Lever Bros* but also because it is hard to reconcile with fundamental principles of common law, such as the principle of *caveat emptor*. If A sells to B an old picture which both believe to be of small value, is the contract to be voidable if it turns out to be an old master? If A contracts to

14 [1969] 2 QB 507; S. & T. 520.

sell to B land which both believe to be of no great value, is the contract voidable if it is discovered to be sited over a great oil well? If these contracts are voidable so, *a fortiori*, must be those where B is aware of A's mistake of fact—B has realised that the picture is an old master, or that the land is oil bearing, before the contract is concluded. The contract in *Smith v. Hughes*[15] must have been voidable if the seller knew the buyer was making a mistake as to the age of the oats. But *Smith v. Hughes* is generally regarded (though not by Lord Denning!) as a pillar of the law of contract.

These problems have at last been noticed in *William Sindall plc v. Cambridgeshire County Council.*[16] The trial judge held that the buyer of land for development for £5m was entitled to rescind the contract of sale for common mistake as to the existence of a sewer. The development was impossible unless the sewer was diverted. The cost would be £18,000. The value of the land had fallen to less than half the price paid, which, of course, was why the buyer wanted to rescind and get his money back. The Court of Appeal allowed an appeal. They held that if the risk of a mistake was allocated by the contract, that allocation must prevail and that, said Hoffman L.J., meant not just allocation by the terms of the contract but also the "rules of general law applicable to the contract and which, for example, provide that, in the absence of express warranty, the law is *caveat emptor*". The general law allocated the risk to the buyer. If we apply the rules of general law, it is not clear what room, if any, that leaves for the application of *Solle v. Butcher*.

Equally problematical is the effect of *Solle v. Butcher* on contracts of compromise such as that in *Cook v. Wright.*[17] The parties there were certainly under a fundamental misapprehension as to their relative and respective rights—it was indeed very close to the facts of *Bell v. Lever Bros* because the commissioners were getting a substantial sum of money when they were, in fact and in law, entitled to nothing. The law encourages the settlement of disputes and it is important that settlements should be binding and final.

---

15 Above, p. 16.
16 [1994] 3 All E.R. 932, S. & T. 519.
17 Above, p. 73. If both parties had wrongly believed that the defendant was liable to pay the charges, the agreement for reduced payment by instalments would apparently have been void—presumably for failure of a common basic assumption that the debt existed. See S. & T. 219 Note.

CHAPTER SIXTEEN

Contracts Avoided for Failure of a Basic Contractual Assumption—Frustration

FRUSTRATION OF CONTRACTS

The starting point is that a party is not excused from performing his contract merely on the ground that performance turns out to be unexpectedly burdensome or difficult. The closure of the Suez Canal in 1956 gave rise to a series of cases in which sellers in Port Sudan, who had agreed to ship goods to various European ports for a fixed price, found that, instead of being able to send the goods through the Canal, as they had expected, they had to send them round the Cape—which in one case was more than four times as far. The cost to the sellers was obviously much greater than they had expected but their argument that the contract of sale was frustrated failed. The contract was still capable of performance, for the goods were not so perishable that they would not survive the journey round the Cape. The bargain had turned out to be a very bad one; but it was still capable of being performed and the sellers must perform it or pay damages.[1] In *Davis Contractors Ltd v. Fareham Urban District Council*[2] a contract to build houses for £92,000 within a period of eight months took 22 months to complete and cost £17,000 more than estimated because of an unexpected shortage of skilled labour and building

---

1 *Tsakiroglou & Co. Ltd v. Noblee Thorl GmbH* [1962] A.C. 93, HL, *Note*, S. & T. 543.
2 [1956] A.C. 696; S. & T. 540.

materials. That was bad luck for the contractor but the contract was not frustrated. In the famous old case of *Paradine v. Jane*[3] a tenant was held bound to pay three years' arrears of rent although throughout that time he had been expelled from the premises by Prince Rupert "an alien born, enemy to the King" and his army. The court distinguished between duties imposed by law and duties undertaken by contract. Whereas performance of the former might be excused by circumstances, the latter would not be unless the contract so provided—the contracting party could have qualified his undertaking when he gave it and, if he had not, it was taken to be absolute. The tenant would have taken the benefit of "casual profits"—if Rupert had, uncharacteristically, offered gold for the privilege of camping on the land, the tenant would have kept that—and he must bear the burden of casual losses. The rule stated was hard and uncompromising: " . . . though the land be surrounded, or gained by the sea, or made barren by wildfire, yet the lessor shall have his whole rent".

IMPLIED CONDITIONS

The existence of a person or thing

In the leading case of *Taylor v. Caldwell*[4] Blackburn J. stated the general rule that the contractor must perform a contract which had become unexpectedly burdensome "or even impossible"; but he went on:

> "But this rule is only applicable when the contract is positive and absolute, and not subject to any condition either express or implied: and there are authorities which, as we think, establish the principle that where, from the nature of the contract, it appears that the parties must from the beginning have known that it could not be fulfilled unless when the time for the fulfilment of the contract arrived some particular specified thing continued to exist, so that, when entering into the contract, they must have contemplated such continuing existence as the foundation of what was to be done; there, in the absence of any express or implied warranty that the thing shall exist, the contract is not to be construed as a positive contract, but as subject to an implied condition that the parties shall be excused in case, before breach, performance becomes impossible from the perishing of the thing without default of the contractor."

3 (1647) Aleyn 26; K.B.; S. & T. 523.
4 (1863) 3 B. & S. 826 Q.B.; S. & T. 523.

The defendants had agreed to "let" a music hall and gardens for a period of four days for the purpose of concerts and fetes for £100 a day. Before the day arrived the hall was destroyed by fire without the fault of either party. The plaintiffs sued for damages for breach of contract in failing to provide the hall. Applying the principle stated above, the court held that the contract was frustrated. It had come to an abrupt end and each party was discharged from liability to perform.

Exceptionally, Blackburn J. relied heavily on Roman law for the proposition that the contract was subject to a condition that its subject matter should continue to exist, but he did not, in that case, invent the English doctrine of frustration. There was ancient authority to show that contracts requiring personal performance, including contracts to marry, were terminated by the death of the promisor before the time for the fulfilment of the promise, although there was no express exception in the contract. This was understood—it was something that went without saying, as every reasonable man would agree. Mrs Cutter[5] could not recover any part of her late husband's wages but at least she was not liable as his personal representative for any breach of contract in failing to serve as mate for the whole voyage. He was, of course, discharged from his obligation by death. Similarly it was established that if a painter who had contracted to paint a picture went blind, the contract came to an end. The contract might similarly be conditional on the continuing life of a third party. A father who had covenanted that his son would serve as an apprentice for seven years was not liable for breach of contract if the son died within that period. It was settled that a seller of goods was discharged from his duty to deliver the goods and bound to refund the price paid if, before the ownership (and, with it, the risk) had passed to the buyer, the goods were destroyed without his fault. Similarly, a borrower or bailee of goods was discharged from his duty to return the goods if they were destroyed without his fault. So Blackburn J. was able to find authority for a general principle that:

> "in contracts in which the performance depends on the continued existence of a given person or thing, a condition is implied that the impossibility of performance arising from the perishing of the person or thing shall excuse the performance."

It will be noted, however, that Blackburn J. did not treat this as an absolute rule of law. It applied only "in the absence of any

5 Above, p. 142.

express or implied warranty that the thing shall exist."[6] Thus he recognised that just as in the case of initial impossibility of performance (*McRae's* case, above, p. 187) the implied condition precedent would give way to a implied promise, if that was the right construction of the contract. It is less likely that a person will promise that a thing will continue to exist than that he will promise that it does exist and, to that extent, a promise will less readily be imputed; but it is not impossible.

The impossibility of "an adventure"

In *Taylor v. Caldwell* Blackburn J. concentrated on impossibility arising from the non-existence of a person or thing because that was the nature of the case before him, but frustration is not confined to that case. Commercial men may contract with a particular "adventure"—a particular commercial enterprise—in view, and that adventure may, without their fault, become impossible of performance although all the physical features required for performance—the ship, the goods, the ports of loading and discharge—all remain in existence. This will usually arise from some factor which causes inordinate delay. If there were a contract for "a spring voyage" by a particular vessel and an accident postponed the availability of the vessel until the autumn, the spring voyage contemplated by the parties has become impossible and, in the absence of an absolute promise that, come what may, the vessel would be available, this is likely to be regarded as a frustrated contract. That was the situation which Bramwell B. thought had, in effect, arisen in *Jackson v. Union Marine Insurance Co. Ltd.*[7] A ship was chartered to proceed with all possible dispatch (dangers and accidents of navigation excepted) from Liverpool to Newport and there to load a cargo of iron rails for San Francisco. The ship sailed on January 2, 1872 but ran aground on January 3. She was got off on February 18 but required repairs which took until the end of August. On February 15, the charterers threw up the charter and chartered another ship. It was held that they were entitled to do so. A voyage after the repairs had taken place, though carrying the same rails in the same ship between the same ports, would have been a different adventure. "If the charter were read as a charter for a definite adventure there was *necessarily* an implied condition that the vessel should arrive at Newport in time for it." The identity of the "adventure" is, of course, less precise than "a spring voyage", and whether the delay is such as to

6 Above, p. 198.
7 (1874) L.R. 10 C.P. 125; Exchequer Chamber, S. & T. 528.

destroy its identity is a question of degree and one for the judgment of the court, which must try to put itself into the position of commercial men at the relevant time. Would the reasonable charterer, on February 15, believe the adventure was now impossible?

The principle is not confined to commercial contracts. We would not describe the hiring of an opera singer as "an adventure"; but the principle upon which the contract in *Poussard v. Spiers* was held to be frustrated by illness and that in *Bettini v. Gye* to be not so frustrated[8] is the same. A contract by which the plaintiff (professionally known as "Charlie Chester"), a music hall artiste, appointed the defendant his agent for a term of 10 years was held to be frustrated when, in 1940, the plaintiff was called up for service in the army for the duration of the war. The invasion of the contract was likely to be so great that it had come to an end.[9] A contract for a four-year apprenticeship as a plumber was frustrated when, after about 21 months, the apprentice was sentenced to Borstal training which would last probably 39 weeks and possibly more.[10]

The occurrence of an event

The fundamental common assumption of the parties may be that a particular event is going to occur so that, if the event is cancelled, the contract is frustrated. In *Krell v. Henry*,[11] that event was to be the coronation procession of King Edward VII. The defendant saw an announcement in the windows of the plaintiff's flat in Pall Mall to the effect that windows to view the procession were to be let. The housekeeper pointed out to the defendant what a good view of the procession could be had from the premises and he agreed in writing to take the suite for June 26 and 27, the days of the processions, and to pay £75. £25 was paid immediately and £50 was to be paid on June 24. The writing did not mention the procession. Early in the morning of June 24 the procession was cancelled. The plaintiff sued for £50 and the defendant counterclaimed £25. If the court was confined to the written contract, the plaintiff would obviously succeed. He had agreed to provide the defendant with the use of the rooms on two days, no more and no less, and he was ready and willing to do so. There could be no question of frustration. But when the surrounding circumstances are looked at, it is apparent that the

8 Above, p. 137.
9 *Morgan v. Manser* [1948] 1 K.B. 184, Streatfeild J.
10 *Shepherd F. C. & Co. Ltd v. Jerrom* [1986] 3 All E.R. 589, CA.
11 [1903] 2 K.B. 740, CA; S. & T. 529.

plaintiff was not simply selling the use of two rooms; he was selling a view of the coronation procession and he was unable, through no fault of his own, to provide that. The parol evidence rule did not apply so as to prevent the court from learning the true purpose of both parties to the contract. The common and fundamental assumption was not merely that the rooms at 56A Pall Mall would exist on June 26 and 27 but also that a procession would be passing.

The court distinguished an example put in argument of a cabman engaged to take someone to Epsom on Derby Day when the Derby is cancelled. The cabman is simply selling a ride to Epsom. The ride is a valuable service which he offers every day whereas we may be sure that the plaintiff in *Krell v. Henry* was not in the habit of letting out the view from his windows—there was no market for it. The happening of the Derby might be the foundation of the contract from the point of view of the hirer, but it is not clear that it would be so from the point of view of the cabman. He is not generally concerned with his customer's reasons for wishing to go to a particular destination—and, for all he knows, the customer may be going to Epsom to visit his aunt whose birthday happens to be on Derby Day. If a bus company were to advertise "an excursion to Epsom on Derby Day", the cancellation of the Derby might well frustrate the contract for the company now appears to be offering to sell a visit to the Derby. The fact that a particular customer hated horse-racing and bought a ticket in order to visit his aunt would make no difference for the matter would be judged objectively and his secret intention would be irrelevant.

The cabman example was thought to be persuasive in another case which was under consideration at the same time by the same court and which reached a different result—*Herne Bay Steam Boat Company v. Hutton.*[12] The contract was for a steamboat to take a party for the purpose of viewing the naval review at Spithead and for a day's cruise round the fleet. The review was cancelled because of the King's illness but the fleet was still there. The consideration had not wholly failed. No one in his right mind would want to spend two days looking out of the windows of 56A Pall Mall at the ordinary traffic, but, in those days when Britannia ruled the waves, the fleet was well worth seeing. In the court's opinion, the happening of the naval review was not the foundation of the contract.

12 [1903] 2 K.B. 683; S. & T. 534.

Sale of goods

A contract for the sale of specific goods is generally frustrated if, without the fault of either party, the goods are destroyed before the ownership passes to the buyer. Section 7 of the Sale of Goods Act 1979 provides:

> "Where there is an agreement to sell specific goods and subsequently the goods, without any fault on the part of the seller or buyer, perish before the risk passes to the buyer, the agreement is avoided."

If the ownership has passed to the buyer—*i.e.* the agreement to sell has become a sale—before the goods perish, the contract has not been frustrated because its main purpose—the transfer of ownership—has been accomplished; and unless the parties have agreed otherwise, the risk passes with the ownership so the buyer must bear the loss. Just as section 6 may be capable of exclusion[13] by a promise that the thing exists, so section 7 might be capable of exclusion by a promise that it will continue to exist; but for obvious reasons, such a promise is less likely.

Where the contract is to sell, not specific goods, but goods of a particular description, the contract will not be frustrated because the particular goods which the seller had in mind are destroyed. He must get other goods answering the description. The contract is not impossible of performance as it is where specific goods are destroyed. A fundamental assumption of the seller may have failed, but this is not true of the buyer. In *Blackburn Bobbin Co. Ltd v. T. W. Allen & Sons Ltd*[14] the seller was liable for a breach of contract to sell Finnish birch timber when the outbreak of war prevented him from importing timber from Finland as he had contemplated. The custom of English timber merchants was to import Finnish timber as required, not to hold stocks; but as the buyer neither knew nor had reason to know of the custom, it was wholly immaterial. If the buyer had been a timber merchant the result might have been different.

A contract for the sale of goods by description may be frustrated in some other way, as by legislation prohibiting dealing in the goods in question. Legislation rendering the performance of a contract illegal necessarily frustrates it.

13 Above, p. 184.
14 [1918] 2 K.B. 467; S. & T. 535.

Leases

It was once thought that a lease can never be frustrated because a lease is something more than a contract, it conveys an estate in land, which continues regardless of fundamental changes in the circumstances. The hard line taken by the court in the old case of *Paradine v. Jane*[15] will be recalled. But a lease may be terminated prematurely by reason of an express term, so why not by an implied term, if that is the proper construction of the contract? The circumstances in which such a term is necessarily implied in a lease are likely to be rare and in neither of the two leading cases in which the House of Lords has considered the matter was the lease held by any of their lordships to be frustrated. In the *Cricklewood*[16] case the lease was granted in 1936 for a term of 99 years, the land to be used as sites for shops which the lessee covenanted to erect within a time limit. When war broke out in 1939 no building had been done and it then became impossible because of government restrictions. The lessee's claim that the lease was frustrated failed. This is clearly right under the principles already discussed. Though prospects seemed bleak in the early days of the war, no one then contemplated that there would not be plenty of time before the year 2035 when the shops could be built and enjoyed. The invasion, actual or contemplated, of the contract period was not such as to prevent substantial performance. Two of their lordships thought, *obiter*, that a lease could never be frustrated, but two others took a different view. Suppose that legislation had permanently prohibited building, declaring the area an open space for ever? If the common purpose of the lease were the erection of buildings, it would have failed.

This seems the better view and in *National Carriers Ltd v. Panalpina (Northern) Ltd*[17] four out of five of the House agreed that a lease might be frustrated, though it would rarely happen and certainly had not happened in that case. It concerned the lease of a warehouse for 10 years. After a little more than five years the local authority closed the street giving the only access to the warehouse because of the dangerous condition of a listed building opposite. It seemed likely that the closure would last just over 18 months, leaving the lease with three more years to run. It would cause a severe interruption of the lessee's business and put him to considerable expense and inconvenience, but this

---

15 Above, p. 198.
16 *Cricklewood Property and Investment Trust Ltd v. Leighton's Investment Trust Ltd* [1945] A.C. 221.
17 [1981] A.C. 675, S. & T. 536.

is not enough to frustrate a contract.[18] The interruption was for
one-sixth of the total term and (perhaps more to the point) one-
third of the remainder of the term and had not:

> "so significantly changed the nature of the outstanding
> contractual rights and obligations under the lease from what
> the parties could reasonably have contemplated at the time
> of its execution that it would unjust to hold them to the
> literal sense of its stipulations."[19]

Clearly the result might have been different if it had appeared
that the road would be closed for the whole, or substantially the
whole, of the remainder of the term.

It appears then that where a lease has a particular purpose—
building, warehousing, dwelling, etc.—an event which prevents
the fulfilment of that purpose may frustrate it. If property is let as
a warehouse, it certainly seems reasonable to conclude that the
basic common assumption of the parties is that the property is,
and will remain, capable of use as such. Lord Russell, dissenting
on the issue of principle, thought that the purchaser of a
leasehold interest, like the purchaser of a freehold, takes the risk
that the property may become quite unsuitable for the purpose
he has in mind.

SELF-INDUCED FRUSTRATION

The essence of frustration is that performance has been rendered
impossible without the fault of either party and so it is said
"reliance cannot be placed on a self-induced frustration". On the
contrary, a party who causes a "frustrating" event will usually
be in breach of contract. If the father who had contracted that his
son would serve as an apprentice for seven years had, during
that time, killed or incapacitated the son, he could not have
relied on frustration; nor presumably could the widow of the
second mate, Cutter, if he had jumped overboard and she had
been sued as his personal representative. If Caldwell had
deliberately burnt down the music hall, he would certainly have
been liable to Taylor for failure to provide it. In *The Eugenia*[20] a
charterparty forbade the charterers from bringing the vessel into
a dangerous zone. In breach of contract, they sailed it to Port Said
at a time when it was a dangerous zone. The ship was trapped in
the Suez Canal and it became impossible to carry out the

18 Above, p. 197.
19 *per* Lord Simon of Glaisdale, at 707.
20 [1964] 2 Q.B. 226, CA; S. & T. 544.

charterparty; but the charterers could not rely on this self-induced frustration to say that the contract was at an end. In *Maritime National Fish Ltd v. Ocean Trawlers Ltd*[21] the appellants chartered the respondents' trawler, the St Cuthbert, for 12 months, for use in the fishing industry only. Both parties knew that the vessel could only be used with an otter trawl and that it was an offence to use a vessel with an otter trawl without a licence from the appropriate Canadian minister. The appellants, who were operating five trawlers, applied for five licences but were granted only three and asked to name the three trawlers. They named three other than St Cuthbert. The Privy Council held that they could not rely on the lack of a licence as frustration of the contract, because it was self-induced: the appellants could have named St Cuthbert for a licence. Presumably it would have been different if the minister had named the trawlers and had excluded St Cuthbert.

The *Ocean Trawlers* case was followed by the Court of Appeal in *The "Super Servant Two"*.[22] The defendants contracted to carry the plaintiffs' rig from Japan to Rotterdam on either the *Super Servant One* or the *Super Servant Two*. They intended to use *Two*, but that vessel sank. The defendants had entered into other contracts and decided to use *One* to perform those. It was held that the contract with the plaintiffs was not frustrated. The defendants could not perform all their contracts and may have acted reasonably in the circumstances; but the fact that it was the result of their choice that that contract could not be performed was fatal to the plea of frustration.

Where it is uncertain whether the alleged frustrating event was or was not due to the "fault" of a party, the disposition of the onus of proof is decisive. If it is for the party claiming that the frustration was self-induced to prove that it was so, he will fail; but if it is for the other party to prove that it was not self-induced, he will fail: neither party is able to establish what happened. This situation arose in *Joseph Constantine Steamship Line Ltd v. Imperial Smelting Corporation Ltd*[23] where the event was an explosion in a ship which prevented the shipowners from delivering it in accordance with the terms of a charterparty. The charterers claimed damages. The explosion may or may not have been due to the fault of the shipowner. It was impossible to say. The House of Lords held that the onus of proof lay on the charterer to show that the shipowner was at fault; so the charterer's action failed. Some of their lordships put the decision

21 [1935] A.C. 524, PC.
22 [1990] 1 Lloyd's Rep. 1; S. & T. 547.
23 [1942] A.C. 154, HL; S. & T. 551.

on the ground of a general principle that the party who brings a matter into issue must prove it; and it was the charterers who were saying that the shipowner was at fault. But, equally, it might be said that the shipowner, simply by raising the defence of frustration was asserting that he was not at fault, because the whole essence of a frustrating event is that it is one which occurs without the fault of either party. There are policy considerations. It was a wartime case and Viscount Simon envisaged the case of a ship being torpedoed and sinking immediately. Is the shipowner to be liable because he cannot prove affirmatively that the crew were behaving with all proper care, keeping a good look-out, obscuring lights, etc.? It would seem unreasonable that he should bear that onus.

THE EFFECT OF FRUSTRATION

The occurrence of the frustrating event brings the contract to a summary end. It is not, however, invalidated from the start. Everything that was done from the making of the contract up to its frustration was, and remains, validly done in pursuance of it. At one time, the courts drew from this premise the conclusion that money paid in pursuance of the contract before the frustrating event was necessarily irrecoverable and that promises to pay before that event remained enforceable. In *Chandler v. Webster*[24] the plaintiff made a contract for the hire of a room to view the coronation procession for £141 15s, payable immediately. He paid £100. Subsequently the procession was cancelled. It was held that not only was he not entitled to recover the £100 but he was bound to pay the additional £41 15s. This was a valid obligation incurred while the contract was still alive and the consideration had not totally failed because he had received a perfectly good and—at the time—binding, promise to provide the view of the procession in return for his promise to pay. That decision was overruled by the House of Lords in the *Fibrosa* case.[25] It failed to distinguish between two meanings of "consideration". When we are discussing the formation of contract, it means the promise but when we are concerned with the quasi-contractual or restitutionary action based on failure of consideration, it means the performance of the promise. The promise to provide a view of the procession, though a perfectly good promise and consideration for the promise to pay, was wholly unperformed. The plaintiff ought to have recovered his

24 [1904] 1 K.B. 493.
25 *Fibrosa Spolka Akcyjna v. Fairbairn Lawson Combe Barbour Ltd* [1943] A.C. 32; S. & T. 552.

£100 and been discharged from his obligation to pay the £41 15s.

In *Fibrosa* a contract by an English company to sell machinery to a Polish company was frustrated by the outbreak of war. The price was £4,800, one-third of which was payable immediately, but, in fact, only £1,000 was paid. The House of Lords, reversing the Court of Appeal which had followed *Chandler v. Webster,* held that the Polish company was entitled to recover the £1,000. Although the English company had done a considerable amount of work on the machinery before the frustrating event, none had been delivered and the House treated this as a total failure of consideration. This remedied an injustice but, as the House recognised, it left the law in an imperfect state, particularly because (i) money was recoverable only where the failure of consideration was total—the performance of a small part of the consideration would defeat the claim—and (ii) it might be unfair to a party who had prudently stipulated for a payment in advance to meet expenses and who had to repay it. It may be that the English company was left with a lot of useless half-built machinery on its hands.

Parliament acted swiftly by passing the Law Reform (Frustrated Contracts) Act 1943.[26] This Act has nothing to say about when a contract is frustrated—that remains a matter of common law—but is concerned with adjusting the rights of parties as fairly as possible after frustration has occurred. Section 1(2) provides that all money paid or payable before frustration shall be recoverable or cease to be payable. It is unnecessary that the consideration should have totally failed. But there is a proviso that, if the party to whom money was paid or payable under the contract has incurred expenses for the purpose of the performance of the contract, the court may, if it thinks it just to do so, allow him to retain or recover a sum not exceeding that payable under the contract and not exceeding the amount of expenses incurred. So, if *Fibrosa* occurred today and the English company had incurred expenses amounting to £1,200, the court might, in its discretion, allow it to retain the £1,000 paid and to recover a further £200. But if the expenses incurred amounted to £1,800 the maximum sum which the court could require the Polish company to pay would be £600, because only £1,600 was payable before the frustrating event.

Section 1(3) of the Act provides that where one party (A), in performing the contract, has conferred a valuable benefit on the other (B) (not being a payment of money to which section 1(2) applies) the court may allow A to recover from B such sum, if any, as the court considers just, not exceeding the value of the benefit to B. In estimating the just sum, the court must take into account expenses incurred by B, including any money which he has paid, or is required to pay, to A under section 1(2), and the effect of the circumstances giving rise to the frustration of the contract. The value of a benefit conferred may be recovered even though there is no provision for an advance payment. If, in a case like *Fibrosa* the English company had delivered machinery which was worth £3,000 to the Polish company, the court could, if it thought it just to do so, allow the English company to retain the £1,000 paid and to recover not more than a further £2,000; and if there had been no provision for payment, and no payment made, before the frustrating event, it could have allowed recovery of up to £3,000. Where the Act applies to a contract like that in *Cutter v. Powell*,[27] the effect would be that the widow might recover from the master the value to him of the mate's services up to the time of his death—if he had served for about three-quarters of the voyage, something like £6, the proportion of the usual wage, not of the exceptionally large sum which the master had agreed to pay. But in a case like *Appleby v. Myers*[28] it appears that the unfortunate plaintiff would recover nothing. The night before the fire, he had indeed conferred a benefit—the premises with the machinery were worth more than the premises without it— but the benefit was destroyed by the frustrating event.[29] The court is required to take into account "the effect, in relation to the said benefit, of the circumstances giving rise to the frustration of the contract."

The Act applies only in the absence of any provision to the contrary: section 2(3). If the parties agree on some different solution to the problems arising on the occurrence of a frustrating event, their agreement, and not the Act, prevails. This raises a serious doubt whether the Act would apply at all to the contract in *Cutter v. Powell*, as it was construed by the King's Bench. Lord Kenyon C.J. said that "[Cutter] stipulated to receive the larger sum if the whole duty were performed, and nothing unless the whole of that duty were performed: it was a kind of insurance". If that is the right construction of the contract, the parties had provided for the event which occurred and their provision must prevail. A similar view might be taken of *Appleby v. Myers*; but in *B.P. v. Hunt*[30] Robert Goff J. thought that the fact

27 Above, p. 142.
28 Above, p. 142.
29 *cf. B.P. Exploration Co. (Libya) Ltd v. Hunt (No. 2)* [1981] W.L.R. 232, affirmed, [1983] A.C. 352. The case is summarised at S. & T. 558.
30 Above, n.29.

that a contract is "entire" should not automatically preclude an award under section 1(3).

There are some important contracts to which the Act does not apply at all—charterparties, except time charterparties or charterparties by way of demise, contracts of insurance and contracts for the sale of specific goods which are frustrated by the perishing of the goods, where section 7 of the Sale of Goods Act 1979 applies, or any other contract for the sale of specific goods which is frustrated by the perishing of the goods.

CHAPTER SEVENTEEN

Anticipatory Breach of Contract

One party cannot, by his wrongful act, bring a contract to an end without the consent of the other. If A commits a breach of a condition, or a fundamental breach of an innominate term of his contract with B, it is for B to decide whether to terminate the contract or not.

The same applies to what is known as "anticipatory breach" as to other breaches. Before the time comes for A to perform his part of the contract, he declares that he is not going to do so. This repudiation of the contractual obligation is itself a breach of contract—a breach of an implied promise to maintain the contractual obligation intact from the making of the contract until it is performed. B may choose to ignore A's anticipatory breach. If, when the time for performance comes, A has changed his mind and carries out the contract, well and good—all obligations under the contract are satisfied. But if, on the day, A fails to perform then B may sue him for the breach he then commits.

B, however, does not have to wait. As soon as A repudiates the contract, B may sue him for damages. The peculiarity of anticipatory breach is that, if B does so, he is said to "accept" the breach and this brings the contract to an end. This seems to mean that B accepts *the fact* that A is not going to perform the contract and that he is accordingly free from his own obligations and able to sue for the injury he will incur through A's non-performance. It is often said that "an unaccepted repudiation is a thing writ in water and of no value to anybody"[1]; but

---

1 *Howard v. Pickford Tool Co.* [1951] 1 K.B. 417 at 420.

repudiation by A gives B a right, which he previously lacked, to terminate the contract and sue for damages. An unaccepted anticipatory breach is a breach,[2] no less than any other breach of condition which the injured party chooses to ignore. With an ordinary breach of condition or fundamental breach of an innominate term, the injured party may sue for damages, *and* keep the contract alive or terminate it, as he thinks fit. This is not so with anticipatory breach. B's claim for damages terminates the contract. When he gets his damages he is compensated in advance for A's anticipated failure to perform. It follows that A's duty to perform must now be abrogated.

In the leading case of *Hochster v. De la Tour*[3] the defendant had agreed to employ the plaintiff as a courier on June 1, 1852 but, on May 11, 1852, he told the plaintiff he had changed his mind and did not require his services. The plaintiff began an action on May 22. The defendant's objection that there could be no breach before June 1 was rejected. Lord Campbell C.J. said that the contract constituted a relation between the parties and each impliedly promised the other that he would not do anything inconsistent with that relationship. In *Frost v. Knight*[4] A promised B that he would marry her when his father died. During his father's lifetime, A broke off the engagement. It was held that there was no difference between the case where the time for performance was a certain day and that where it depended on a contingency, such as the death of the father. B was entitled to her damages. It was pointed out that this procedure may be for the benefit of both parties. The promisee (B) may then take steps to mitigate the damage which would occur if it were necessary to wait until the time for performance.

If B elects not to sue but to keep the contract alive, it subsists for the benefit of both parties. If a frustrating event occurs before the time for performance arrives, the contract terminates and B's right to "accept the breach" and claim damages is gone. In *Avery v. Bowden*[5] the defendant chartered the plaintiff's ship, *Lebanon*, to load a cargo at Odessa within 45 days. The ship proceeded to Odessa and remained there a great part of the 45 days, during which the defendant repeatedly told the captain he had no cargo for him and advised him to go away. Before the 45 days elapsed, the Crimean War broke out and frustrated the contract. No breach, other than the anticipatory breach, had occurred, or could occur before the end of the 45 days. The defendant's

2 *Tilcon Ltd v. Land and Real Estate Investments Ltd* [1987] 1 All E.R. 615, CA.
3 (1853) 2 E. & B. 678.
4 (1872) L.R. 7 Exch. 111, S. & T. 565.
5 (1855) 5 E. & B. 714.

declaration that he would not be able to provide a cargo, may have been an anticipatory breach but, even if it was, the plaintiff now had no right to damages.

In most of the cases there could be no doubt that A knew very well that he was announcing his intention to commit a breach of contract. Suppose, however, that he mistakenly believes he has a right to repudiate the contract. In fact, he has no such right, and he is therefore announcing his intention to commit a breach of contract—if he puts his intention into effect, he will commit such a breach. Is this an anticipatory breach which entitles B to treat the contract as repudiated and claim damages? Lord Denning thought so: "I have yet to learn that a party who breaks a contract can excuse himself by saying that he did it on the advice of his lawyers; or that he was under an honest misapprehension. Nor can he excuse himself on those grounds from the consequences of a repudiation."[6] But in *Woodar Investment Development Ltd v. Wimpey Construction U.K. Ltd*[7] the House of Lords, Lords Salmon and Russell dissenting, took a different view. A clause in a contract for the sale of land provided that the buyer, Wimpey, should be entitled to rescind it in certain specified circumstances. Wimpey, because they misconstrued the contract, thought those circumstances had arisen and purported to rescind. Woodar alleged that this amounted to a repudiation and claimed damages. The view of the majority was that Wimpey thought they were acting on the terms of the contract and it followed that they were not repudiating it. It does not necessarily follow that the result would have been the same if Wimpey had purported to determine the contract in the mistaken belief that some action of Woodar's amounted to a breach of condition or fundamental breach; but it is difficult to see why there should be any difference in principle. Arguably, the better view is that of the minority.

Does "acceptance of the breach" require communication? Where B has expressly renounced the contract, it must surely be terminated by A's then so acting as to make performance impossible. Suppose that, in a case like *Frost v. Knight*, A wrote to B that he would never marry her and she did not reply but promptly married another. If A's father had died the next day and A had then called on B to marry him, he could surely not have succeeded in an action for breach of promise. A could hardly complain that B had taken him at his word. It is different where A has not declared the contract to be at an end but has committed a "repudiatory breach"—a breach entitling B to

6 *Federal Commerce Navigation Co. Ltd v. Molena Alpha Inc.* [1978] Q.B. 927, at 979.
7 [1980] 1 W.L.R. 277; S. & T. 570.

terminate the contract. Here A, far from intending to repudiate the contract, may be very anxious that it should continue. As with rescission for fraud or misrepresentation, if B wants to terminate the contract, he must tell A.

The question has arisen whether B can "accept the breach" simply by not performing his own obligations. The answer seems to be that it may where B's non-performance would make it clear to a reasonable person that he accepted that the contract was at an end. In *Vitol SA v. Norelf Ltd*[8] Lord Steyn put the case of an employer telling a contractor that he is repudiating the contract and he need not return the next day. If the contractor does not return the next day, or at all, his failure to perform conveys a decision that the contract is at an end.

In *Hochster v. De la Tour, Avery v. Bowden* and *Frost v. Knight* the courts were insistent that the respective plaintiffs had an option; they could "accept" the breach by suing for damages, or they could keep the contract alive and wait and see whether the defendant performed on the due date. There was no question of the plaintiff going ahead and performing on his own—Hochster could not act as courier until he was given something to carry nor could Avery sail away with a cargo which had not been supplied, while Frost could not marry without Knight's co-operation and, anyway, the day had not yet come. Suppose, however, that the victim of an anticipatory breach is able to perform his part without the co-operation of the other—may he simply ignore the anticipatory breach, fulfil his own contractual obligation and claim the consideration promised? In *White & Carter (Councils) Ltd v. McGregor*,[9] a Scottish case, the House of Lords answered this question in the affirmative, subject, perhaps, to "a general equitable principle, or element of public policy":

> "It may well be that if it can be shown that a person has no legitimate interest, financial or otherwise, in performing the contract rather than claiming damages, he ought not to be allowed to saddle the other party with an additional burden with no benefit to himself."[10]

The defender's sales manager, acting within his ostensible authority, contracted with the pursuers that the pursuers would display advertisements for the defender's business on litter bins for three years. The defender immediately cancelled the

8 [1996] 3 All E.R. 193 at 200, HL.
9 [1962] A.C. 413; S. & T. 573.
10 *per* Lord Reid, at 431.

contract—an anticipatory breach. The pursuers refused to accept the breach and proceeded to display the advertisements which they were able to do without any further co-operation from the defender. A term of the contract provided that the first annual payment was due seven days after the first display and, if it remained unpaid for four weeks, the whole amount due for the three years became payable. The pursuers sued under this term for the full amount. The courts were faced with a conflict of principles: (i) that the victim of an anticipatory breach has an option; (ii) a party injured by breach of contract has a duty[11] to mitigate the damage. If there is, in these circumstances, a duty to mitigate, there is no real option. The defender could mitigate the pursuer's loss by abandoning his "right" to perform the contract and claiming his loss of profits. The majority held that the pursuers who were suing, not for damages, but for the price of services rendered, had no duty to mitigate but had a right to perform the contract. Lords Morton and Keith, dissenting, held that the pursuers' only claim was in damages and they had a duty to mitigate.

The decision has been heavily criticised. The contract was not, in its nature, specifically enforceable; yet the pursuer, because he could do his part without the co-operation of the defender, was able to achieve the same effect—a sort of self-help specific performance. Megarry J. stated that "the decision is one which I should be slow to apply to any category of case not fairly within the contemplation of their lordships"[12]; while Lord Denning said that he would follow it only in a case which was precisely on all fours with it.[13] In *White & Carter* the House discussed the example of a person who contracts to go to Hong Kong at his own expense and make a report in return for £10,000 and who, before he sets out and before he has incurred any expense is informed by the other party that the report is no longer required. Is he entitled to go to Hong Kong and prepare a report which is no longer required and claim in debt for his fee? It seems that, even allowing for Lord Reid's qualification,[14] he would, for he has a legitimate interest in performing, in keeping himself in work and perhaps enhancing his reputation by producing a good report. A shipbuilder who contracts to build a ship and who is immediately informed that the ship is no longer required would certainly have an interest in performing the contract, as

---

11 Below, p. 228.
12 *Hounslow London Borough Council v. Twickenham Garden Developments Ltd* [1971] Ch. 233; S. & T. 578.
13 *Attica Sea Carriers Corporation v. Ferrostaal Poseidon Bulk Deederei GmbH* [1976] 1 Lloyd's Rep. 250; S. & T. 581.
14 Above, p. 214.

distinct from merely claiming the profit he would have made, particularly if he has no other orders, for he is enabled to keep his shipyard working as a going concern. Yet it makes no economic sense that he should build a ship which is no longer required and be able to claim the price. *White & Carter* remains the law; but it is likely that courts will strive to avoid applying it.

CHAPTER EIGHTEEN

Remedies for Breach of Contract

DAMAGES

The purpose of the law of contract is, as far as possible, to fulfil the reasonable expectations of the contracting parties. The object of damages is, so far as money can do it, to put the party injured by a breach in the same position as he would have been in had the contract been performed. How well off would he have been if the contract had been performed? How well off is he now? The difference is the measure of damages. The principle is well illustrated by the law of sale of goods. Suppose that the buyer refuses to accept and pay for the goods. If there is a market for the goods, the seller can sell them to another; so the measure of damages is the difference between the market or current price of the goods at the time when they ought to have been accepted and the contract price.[1] This assumes that the market price is the lower. If it is the same as, or higher than, the contract price, then the seller has suffered no loss, and will be entitled only to nominal damages. Similarly where the seller refuses to deliver the good. If there is a market for similar goods, the buyer can buy them and recover from the seller the difference between the contract price and (assuming it to be greater) the market or current price of the goods at the time when they ought to have been delivered.[2]

---

1 Sale of Goods Act 1979, s.50(2) and (3).
2 *ibid*., s.51(2) and (3).

Where, however, a seller of Vanguard cars could sell all the Vanguards he could lay his hands on, he was entitled only to nominal damages from a buyer who refused to take delivery. As there was a waiting list of buyers, he simply sold that car to someone else. If he could get, say, 20 Vanguards a year, he could make 20 times the profit on a Vanguard, no more and no less, and it made no difference to whom he sold them.[3] Where, however, there were more cars than buyers, the seller was entitled to the loss of profit from a defaulting buyer. He sold, say, 20 Hillmans in that year; but, if the defendant had not defaulted, he would have sold 21. He was entitled to be put into the position he would have been in if the contract had been performed.[4]

There are, however, limits to the application of this principle. The law has long recognised that it would be too harsh to make a contracting party liable for all loss which results in fact, however unpredictable and vast that loss might be. The contract-breaker is liable only for such part of the loss actually occurring as, at the time of the making of the contract, was reasonably foreseeable as a likely result of the breach. The classic statement of the rule is that of Alderson B. in *Hadley v. Baxendale*[5]:

"Where two parties have made a contract which one of them has broken, the damages which the other party ought to receive in respect of such breach of contract should be such as may fairly and reasonably be considered as either arising naturally, *i.e.* according to the usual course of things, from such breach of contract itself, or such as may reasonably be supposed to have been in the contemplation of both parties, at the time they made the contract, as the probable result of the breach of it."

This proposition has been customarily analysed into two rules, one for loss "arising naturally" and the second for loss "which may reasonably be supposed to have been in the contemplation of both parties." Analysis in later cases shows that there is really a single principle—that of foreseeability as a likely result. But what a person foresees depends on what he knows. Everyone is taken to know "the ordinary course of things", whether he does so in fact or not. That is provided for by the "first rule". But a person may have special knowledge, over and above that which every reasonable man is presumed to have. One with that special

---

3 *W. L. Thompson v. Robinson (Gunmakers) Ltd* [1995] Ch. 177.
4 *Charter v. Sullivan* [1957] 2 QB 117; *cf.* S. & T. 604.
5 (1854) 9 Exch. 341.

knowledge may reasonably be expected to foresee as likely a loss which, without that knowledge, would not have been reasonably so foreseeable. This is provided for by the "second rule". The person with the special knowledge may be liable for the further loss. The "rules" are well illustrated by *Hadley v. Baxendale* itself. The owners of a mill driven by steam engine delivered a broken crank shaft to carriers for carriage from Gloucester to engineers in Greenwich. A delay of five days in delivery was held to be a breach of contract by the carriers. The mill owners claimed £300 loss of profit for the five days by which the resumption of work was delayed. It appeared that the broken shaft was sent as a pattern for a new one, and, until that was received, the mill could not operate. The only facts communicated to the carrier were that the article was the broken shaft of a mill and that the plaintiffs were millers. In the opinion of the court, in the great majority of cases it would not have followed that the mill would be stopped. Presumably they considered that the great majority of millers were sufficiently prudent to own a spare shaft. So this was not a loss occurring "in the ordinary course of things". Had the carrier been told, "The mill is stopped and cannot operate until we receive a new shaft, for which this broken one is a pattern", presumably the result would have been different.[6] The carrier would then have had special knowledge, outside the ordinary course of things, from which it would have been readily foreseeable that loss of profits was likely, if there was a delay in delivery.

How likely must the loss be? This question was debated in the two modern leading cases on the subject. In *Victoria Laundry (Windsor) Ltd v. Newman Industries Ltd*[7] Asquith L.J. said that it is enough that the loss is one foreseen as "liable to result" but in *The Heron II*[8] Lord Reid criticised the word "liable" both as too vague and as including possible but improbable loss. In *Hadley v. Baxendale* itself it was certainly *possible* that the delay in delivery would result in closure of the mill. Lord Reid was also critical of Asquith L.J.'s use of the phrases, "a real danger", "a serious possibility", or "on the cards" to describe the necessary degree of likelihood. His own preference was for "likely' or, better, "not unlikely"; but it should be observed that the remainder of their Lordships were not so critical of Asquith L.J.'s formulation of the test, though all deprecated the use of the phrase, "on the cards," as capable of denoting a most improbable and unlikely event.

6 The headnote to the case is misleading in so far as it suggests that this information was given.
7 [1949] 2 K.B. 528, CA; S. & T. 592.
8 [1969] 1 A.C. 350; S. & T. 597.

In the *Victoria Laundry* case damages for loss of profits arising from the delay of five months in delivering a boiler were held to be recoverable; but in that case, the defendants were not carriers but the sellers of the boiler, they were an engineering company who might be expected to know more about the use of boilers than the plain man, and they knew they were selling the boiler to a laundry company who obviously, as the court thought, wanted the boiler to boil water, to wash clothes, to make profits. The plaintiffs might, conceivably, have wanted the boiler to replace another which was functioning satisfactorily in the meantime. In fact, they wanted it to expand their business. The sellers were not informed of this; but there was at the time "a famine in laundry facilities" and, in the court's opinion, reasonable persons in the defendants' shoes would have foreseen that a five months delay was "likely" to result in financial loss—and certainly there was a "real danger", "a serious possibility" and it was "liable" to happen.

This was a case of the application of the "first rule;" but it illustrates the fact that there is no hard and fast line between the two so-called rules. The fact that the defendant was a seller rather than a carrier is significant, for a seller is likely to be much more aware of, and concerned with, the purposes to which an article is to be put than is a carrier; and an engineering company might be expected to be more aware than some other seller. So we are looking at all the relevant circumstances in order to determine what is reasonably foreseeable as "likely" or "not unlikely".

It is clear than an event may be "not unlikely" although there is a substantially less than an even chance that it will occur. In the *Heron II* the contract was to carry a cargo of sugar to Basrah or, at the option of the plaintiff, the owner of the sugar, to Jeddah. The option was not exercised and the ship arrived at Basrah, but nine days late, the carrier having made deviations in breach of contract. It was always the intention of the plaintiff to sell the sugar immediately on arrival in Basrah. He did so, but the price had fallen substantially during the nine days and he claimed the difference in damages. The defendant did not know of the plaintiff's intention to sell but he knew there was a market for sugar in Basrah and, if he had thought about the matter, he must have realised that it was "not unlikely" that the sugar would be sold on arrival. He must also have known that market prices fluctuate; but he had no reason to suppose that the price would go down rather than up. If the price had gone up, the plaintiff would actually have made a profit as a result of the breach. The sugar might not have been intended for sale on arrival; and, if it was, the price might have gone up or down.

Nevertheless, it was held that the loss which the plaintiff had actually incurred was "not unlikely" and he was entitled to the damages claimed. The courts avoid laying down precise mathematical rules. But Lord Reid thought a one in four chance "not unlikely". It was not unlikely that the top card of a well-shuffled pack would prove to be a diamond. A one in fifty-two chance, however, was unlikely—it was not likely that the top card would be the nine of diamonds (though, in his Lordship's opinion, "on the cards", "a serious possibility" or "a real danger"). Somewhere in between a line is drawn. We cannot expect the courts to tell us precisely where. It is a matter for the judgment and the sense of fairness of the particular court in determining where the loss should lie.

What must be foreseen?

It seems that it is enough that the defendant should have foreseen a head or type of damage, not its quantum. In *Wroth v. Tyler*[9] where a defendant failed to complete his contract to sell a house for £6,050 he was held liable to pay damages of £5,500 when the value rose to £11,500 by the day of judgment. A rise in the price of houses was in the contemplation of the parties when the contract was made and it was immaterial that they never contemplated a rise which would nearly double the price. In *Parson (Livestock) Ltd v. Uttley Ingham & Co. Ltd*[10] it was held that the seller of a defective hopper must have foreseen, had he been aware of the defect, that it was not unlikely that the pig nuts to be stored in the hopper would deteriorate and cause the pigs to be ill; and it was immaterial that the very serious illness which in fact resulted to the pigs was not at all likely—the defendant was liable for its consequences. These decisions seem irreconcilable with the holding in the *Victoria Laundry* case[11] that, while the defendants were liable for the loss of dyeing contracts reasonably to be expected, they were not liable for the loss of certain particularly lucrative dyeing contracts: the latter was not damage "arising naturally . . . according to the usual course of things" and, as the defendant had no knowledge of these contracts, he was not liable under the "second rule" in *Hadley v. Baxendale*. Yet the damages seem to be of the same type and, if so, they would be recoverable under the principle of the later cases.

9 [1974] Ch. 30, Megarry J.
10 [1978] Q.B. 791, CA; S. & T. 604.
11 Above, p. 219.

Is mere knowledge sufficient?

In *British Columbia Sawmill Co. Ltd v. Nettleship*[12] there is a suggestion by Willes J. that it is not. The defendant carrier lost a box which he knew to contain part of the machinery of a sawmill to be erected in Vancouver Island. He did not know that the part was essential to the working of the machinery and he was held not liable for loss of profits when the operation of the mill was in fact prevented by the lack of the missing part. Willes J. said that knowledge of the use to which the article would be put was not enough—

> "there must have been knowledge under such circum-
> stances as would raise the presumption that he intended to
> make himself liable for the special consequences and that
> the person contracting with him believed, and had reason-
> able grounds for believing that he intended to undertake
> such liability and unless there was a special payment it
> would be very difficult to get a jury to come to such a
> conclusion."

This suggests that there has to be, in effect, a term in the contract, imposing this exceptional liability. Subsequent cases do not seem to insist on so strict a requirement. At the same time, it may be questioned whether a casual remark to the defendant's clerk— "The mill is stopped till we get the shaft back, you know"— should suffice to impose liability on the defendants in a case like *Hadley v. Baxendale.*

Recovery of wasted expenditure

There are cases in which it would be very difficult for the victim of a breach of contract to prove that he would have been better off if the contract had been performed, but he can prove that he has, quite properly, incurred expenditure in, or for the purpose of, the performance of the contract and that, as a result of that breach, the expenditure will be wasted. In such a case he is permitted to claim his "reliance" damages in lieu of "expecta-tion" damages. He has incurred expenditure in reliance on the other party's promise to perform and he claims compensation for that, abandoning his right to be compensated for the disappoint-ment of his legitimate expectations that the contract would be performed. He cannot have both, because, if his expectations had been fulfilled, he would have incurred the expenditure. If he

12 (1868) L.R. 3 C.P. 499.

were put in the position in which he would have been had the contract been performed, he would have incurred that expenditure; so he cannot have both. But it seems that he may choose. In *McRae v. The Commonwealth Disposals Commission*[13] the facts of which are given above, p. 187, the plaintiff would have found it very difficult if not impossible to prove any "expectation" loss because, even if there had been a tanker at the latitude and longitude specified, this entirely mythical vessel might have been worthless, or not capable of profitable salvage, or of salvage at all. The courts will award damages for loss of a chance to earn a reward and must not be deterred from doing so because of the difficulty of assessing the value of the chance[14]; but in this case the court thought that the plaintiffs could not show that the absence of a tanker caused them any loss. They could show that they had incurred expenditure in reliance on a broken promise and that the breach of promise made it *certain* that the expenditure would be wasted. This shifted the burden to the Commission to prove that, if there had been a tanker there, the expenditure would equally have been wasted; and it was, of course, just as impossible for the Commission to prove this as it was for McRae to prove the contrary.

The plaintiff's claim to recover his expenditure will fail to the extent that the defendant can prove that, even if he had performed his contract, the plaintiff would not have succeeded in recouping his outlay. If the plaintiff's outlay was £1,000 and the defendant proves he would have made nothing out of the transaction, the plaintiff can recover nothing; but if the plaintiff would have made £400 then he is entitled to £400 of wasted expenditure. The result in those circumstances is the same, of course, as if he had been awarded "expectation" damages; the difference is in the onus of proof.[15] If the plaintiff would not have recovered his expenditure even if the defendant had performed, the plaintiff has made a bad bargain and the law should not, and does not, shift the loss resulting from the plaintiff's bad bargain to the defendant. In *C. & P. Haulage (A Firm) v. Middleton*[16] the defendant was ejected, in breach of a contractual licence renewable on a six-monthly basis, ten weeks before the end of a six-month period. He claimed the cost of improvements he had made to the premises. But the contract provided that any fixtures

---

13 (1951) 84 C.L.R. 377; S. & T. 499 and 613.
14 *Chaplin v. Hicks* [1911] 2 K.B. 786, CA; S. & T. 595 (plaintiff deprived, in breach of contract, of opportunity to participate with a limited class of persons in a beauty competition).
15 *cf. Albert & Son v. Armstrong Rubber Co.* (1949) 178 F.2d 182, cited in *CCC Films Ltd v. Impact Quadrant Films Ltd* [1984] 3 All E.R. 298; S. & T. 618.
16 [1983] 1 W.L.R. 1461; S. & T. 616, CA.

he put in were not to be removed at the end of the licence. If the contract had not been broken but had been lawfully determined at the end of the period, there could have been no question of his recovering his expenditure. He may have made a bad bargain in agreeing that the fixtures should belong to the defendant and it was not the function of the court to put him in a better position that he would have been in if the contract had been performed.

Where expenditure is recoverable, it must, of course, be expenditure which it was reasonable to incur. In *Mason v. Burningham*[17] the buyer of a second-hand typewriter who had to return it to the true owner because the seller had no title to it, was held by the Court of Appeal to be entitled to recover not only the price of the typewriter but also the cost of having it overhauled. The county court judge had dismissed the claim, saying that if the buyer had had the machine gold-plated, she could not recover the cost of that. Of course she could not; but having the typewriter overhauled was "the ordinary and natural thing" to do in the circumstances.

More controversially, it has been held that damages may be recovered for costs incurred *before* the contract was made if they are:

(i)   legal costs of approving and executing the contract; or
(ii) costs of performing an act required to be done by the contract, notwithstanding that the act was done in anticipation of it; or
(iii) such costs "as would reasonably be in the contemplation of the parties as likely to be wasted if the contract was broken": *Anglia Television v. Reed.*[18]

In that case the plaintiffs incurred expense in preparation for filming a television play. Subsequently they entered into a contract with the defendant to play the lead. He repudiated the contract and the plaintiffs were unable to find a substitute. It was held that they were entitled to recover the whole of the wasted expenditure: the defendant must have known that the expenditure, whether incurred before or after the contract was made, would be wasted if he broke his contract. This is more controversial because it is arguable that a person who incurs expenditure before a contract has been entered into does so at his own risk. The expenditure is not incurred in reliance on the contract-breaker's promise. On the other hand, it may be said that the asset represented by the expenditure is put at risk in reliance on the promise and that this is enough.

17 [1949] 2 K.B. 545, CA.
18 [1972] 1 Q.B. 60.

Recovery for non-economic loss

The cases considered so far have all related to economic loss of some kind. It is no longer the law, if it ever was, that damages are confined to such loss. Damages are generally not recoverable for disappointment or injured feelings resulting from the breach. But, if the purpose of a contract is to provide pleasure and, because of a breach, it fails to do so, damages are recoverable. In *Jarvis v. Swan's Tours*[19] travel agents were held liable to pay the plaintiff damages of £125 when a holiday costing £63.45 fell disastrously short of what was promised. The plaintiff would not be adequately compensated merely by giving him back his money. The only fortnight holiday he received, and to which he looked forward all the year, had been ruined. *Dicta* of the court went further. A man has a ticket for Glyndbourne. It is the only night he can get. He hires a car to take him. The car does not turn up. It was said he can recover from the car-hire firm damages for his disappointment and loss of entertainment. Presumably it would be necessary to show that the firm knew he was going to the performance at Glyndbourne; but, even so, their business is to provide a ride from A to B, not to provide entertainment. So, if the dicta are right, they go well beyond the actual decision. It is sufficient if a major or important part of the contract is to give pleasure, relaxation or peace of mind. In *Farley v. Skinner*[20] a surveyor wrongly and negligently advised the buyer of a house in the country that it was unlikely to be affected by aircraft noise. He was liable to pay £10,000 damages for the buyer's discomfort and inconvenience.

Again, if the purpose of the contract is to provide protection from harassment and, because it is broken, the plaintiff is harassed, damages for the resulting distress are recoverable: *Heywood v. Wellers (A firm)*[21] where solicitors negligently failed to obtain and enforce an injunction to restrain a man from molesting the plaintiff. The court was prepared to assume that the injunction would be effective unless the defendants proved that it would not.

Dicta in *Cook v. Swinfen*[22] go beyond this. Lord Denning M.R. said that a solicitor who conducted litigation negligently would be liable for the client's consequent breakdown in health if it could be proved that this was a reasonably foreseeable consequence of the breach of contract. In that case it was not

19 [1973] 1 Q.B. 233; S. & T. 628.
20 [2001] 3 W.L.R. 899.
21 [1976] Q.B. 446, CA.
22 [1967] 1 W.L.R. 457.

reasonably foreseeable. The plaintiff was peculiarly liable to nervous shock but it was not proved that this was known to the defendants. If it had been so proved, damages for the breakdown might have been recoverable. Where the contract is to supply a "pleasurable amenity" which the supplier fails to deliver, the plaintiff is entitled to damages for loss of the anticipated pleasure, however difficult it may be to assess these. He is not entitled to recover the cost of providing the amenity where to do so would be wholly disproportionate to the non-monetary loss he has suffered. In *Ruxley Electronics and Construction Ltd v. Forsyth*[23] F contracted with R to build a swimming pool in F's garden with a maximum depth of 7ft 6 in. When it was complete, F discovered that it was only 6ft 9 in. deep. It was perfectly safe for diving and of no less financial value that if it had been in accordance with the contract. The cost of rebuilding the pool would have been £21,500, and F claimed that sum. The judge was not satisfied that, if F recovered it, he would spend it on rebuilding and awarded £2,500 for loss of amenity. The House of Lords agreed. The cost of rebuilding would have been wholly disproportionate to F's loss of the pleasure he would have taken in his larger pool. The sum awarded may have been on the high side but the House did not interfere with it.

It is different where the service provided has a commercial value lower than that contracted for. "If A hired and paid in advance for a four-door saloon at £200 a day and received delivery of a two-door saloon available for £100 a day, he suffered loss."[24] This is so even if A did not intend to carry any passengers and the car provided was just as good for all practical purposes as the car contracted for. A would be entitled to recover £100 per day—or more if the difference in market value was greater.

Accounting for profits obtained by breach of contract

There are cases in which D's breach of contract causes no loss to the other party, P, but the breach enables D to make a profit. Exceptionally, the court may order D to account to P for the profit so obtained. In *Att.-Gen. v. Blake*[25] B had been a member of the secret service. In breach of the Official Secrets Act 1989 he divulged information to the Soviet Union and, in 1961, was sentenced to 42 years imprisonment. In 1966 he escaped and took

23 [1995] 3 All E.R. 268, HL, S. & T.629.
24 *per* Bingham M.R. in *White Arrow Express Ltd v. Lamey's Distribution Ltd* [1995] T.L.R. 430.
25 [2000] 4 All E.R. 385.

refuge in Russia where he remains. In 1989 he entered into a contract with an English publisher to publish his book, which included an account of his activities in the secret service. This was a breach of his contract with the Crown, never to publish such material. The publishers were to pay him royalties amounting to £150,000. B's employment by the Crown had long since ceased and the material was no longer confidential; so the publication was not a breach of a fiduciary duty which might have resulted in a trust. It was merely a breach of contract. The House of Lords nevertheless held that the Attorney General was entitled to an account of profits and to be paid a sum equal to that owed by the publisher to B. This newly recognised discretionary remedy will be granted only in exceptional circumstances, where the usual remedies for breach of contract are inadequate and the claimant has a legitimate interest in preventing the defendant's profit-making activity and depriving him of his profit. Lord Hobhouse forcefully dissented, holding that compensation is the intellectually sound and just remedy for breach of contract and warning that there are dangers in introducing new restitutionary rights into commercial law.

All their Lordships were disposed to approve of the *Wrotham Park case*.[26] A vendor sold land subject to a restrictive covenant limiting building on the land to a particular layout. A purchaser built 14 houses in breach of the covenant This caused no loss to the vendor but Brightman J. held that he was entitled to recover the profits resulting from the development in breach of contract. Lord Hobhouse interpreted this decision as an application of the compensation principle: "What the plaintiff has lost is the sum which he could have exacted from the defendant as the price of his consent to the development."[27]

Injury for which damages may not be recovered

In *Addis v. Gramophone Co Ltd*[28] the House of Lords held that damages in contract are for pecuniary loss caused by the breach and that nothing can be recovered for mental distress, anxiety or injury to feelings. The plaintiff was not entitled to compensation for the harsh and humiliating manner of his dismissal from employment by the defendants. The House also said that the plaintiff could not, in an action for breach of contract, recover

---

26 *Wrotham Park Estate Co. Ltd. v. Parkside Homes Ltd.* [1974] 2 All E.R. 321. The *Wrotham case* is preferred to *Surrey C.C. v. Bredero Homes Ltd.* [1993] 3 All E.R. 705, CA, S. & T. 591.

27 [2000] 4 All E.R. at 410 e-f.

28 [1909] A. C. 488; S. & T. 622.

damages for injury to his reputation. In *Johnson v. Unisys Ltd.*[29] the House, Lord Steyn dissenting, recently declined to reconsider *Addis*, but the possibility that injury to reputation resulting in damage to the claimant's employment prospects may still be open.

As we have seen damages may be recovered for non-pecuniary injury where the breach results in the loss of the pleasure,[30] or the peace of mind and freedom from distress,[31] which it was the object, or an important object, of the contract to provide. Damages for physical inconvenience resulting from breach—*e.g.*, having to walk five miles home on a wet night— have long been recoverable.[32]

Mitigation of damage

The plaintiff is entitled only to such damages as would have been suffered by a person acting reasonably after the breach. If it is possible for the injured party to take steps which will result in no loss whatever occurring *and* if it is reasonable for him to take those steps, then he is entitled only to nominal damages. if taking those reasonable steps will reduce the loss which would otherwise occur, then he is entitled to damages only for that reduced loss. This principle is usually described in terms of the plaintiff's "duty to mitigate" the damage. But the term "duty" is loosely used. The plaintiff commits no wrong by choosing not to mitigate. He may act as he thinks best in his own interest; but whether he mitigates the damage or not, he will recover only those damages which would have been incurred had he done so.[33] This is sometimes explained on the ground that the defendant is liable for such damages only as he has caused by his breach of contract, and that the additional damage arising from a failure to mitigate has been caused by the plaintiff's own unreasonable behaviour.

Whether loss is avoidable by reasonable action by the plaintiff is a question of fact to be decided in the light of all the circumstances of the particular case. If an employee is dismissed immediately and in breach of a contract to give him three months' notice, he loses three months' pay; but if he is offered immediate re-employment in similar work at the same or a

---

29 [2001] 2 All E.R. 801, above, p. 132.
30 *Jarvis v. Swan's Tours*, above, p. 225.
31 *Bliss v. South East Thames Regional Health Authority* [1987] I.C.R. 700 at 718.
32 *Hobbs v. L. & S.W.Rly. Co.* (1875) L.R. 19 Q.B. 111, Q.B. (contract to carry family from Wimbledon to Hampton Court; train terminating at Esher resulting in family having to walk home).
33 *The Solholt* [1983] 1 Lloyds' Rep. 605; S. & T. 637.

higher rate of pay, it is likely (for all the circumstances must be taken into account) that he will be entitled only to nominal damages, whether he accepts the offer or not. Thus in *Brace v. Calder*[34] where the dismissal was of a technical nature, resulting from the dissolution of a partnership, and the continuing partners offered to re-employ the plaintiff, he was entitled, on declining that offer, to only nominal damages against the original firm. It might have been different, of course, if the continuing partners had been in breach of good faith or had acted in any such way as to make it unreasonable to expect the plaintiff to enter into their employment. In *Payzu Ltd v. Saunders*[35] a seller, in breach of his contract to deliver goods over a period of nine months, payment to be made within one month of delivery of each instalment, declined to deliver any more after the first instalment; but he offered to continue deliveries at the contract price if the buyers, the plaintiff, would agree to pay cash with each order. The plaintiffs rejected the offer. Their claim for the difference between the contract price and the market price, which had risen, failed. The reasonable buyer would have accepted the seller's offer. In the *Solholt*[36] the sellers of a ship failed to deliver on the due date and the buyer properly cancelled and claimed the difference between the contract price and the market price which was $500,000 higher. But the sellers' ship was available shortly after the due date and they were still prepared to sell it to the buyers at the contract price. The buyers offered a lower price which was refused. It was held that the buyers were entitled only to nominal damages. Although accepting the ship at the contract price would have, in effect, nullified the decision which they were entitled to make to cancel the contract, it was still the reasonable thing to do and they were entitled only to the damage they would have incurred if they had done it.

Mitigation and anticipatory breach

It will be recalled that in *White & Carter (Councils) Ltd v. McGregor*[37] the House of Lords decided that the victim of an anticipatory breach has a true option and is not precluded from deciding to perform the contract, where he can do so without the co-operation of the party in breach, merely by reason of the fact that, to do so, will aggravate the loss which will be suffered by

34 [1895] 2 Q.B. 253.
35 [1919] 2 K.B. 581, CA; S. & T. 635.
36 [1983] 1 Lloyd's Rep. 605, S. & T. 637.
37 Above, p. 214.

the party in breach. It is different where the injured party "accepts" the breach as putting an end to the contract. He is then under the so-called "duty" to mitigate—he will recover only such damages as he would have incurred if he had taken reasonable steps. Where a person who has agreed to buy goods at a future date declares that he will not accept the goods when that date arrives, the seller who accepts the breach as putting an end to the contract will be treated, for the purpose of assessing damages, as if he had sold the goods at the first opportunity, if that is the course which a reasonable business man who desired to mitigate the loss would take. If the price is falling dramatically, the seller cannot sit back and charge the buyer with the difference between the contract price and the much reduced market price at the time fixed for delivery.[38] But the standard required of the injured party is not a strict one. His "duty" is only to act not unreasonably. The wrongdoer has no right to expect from the man whom he has wronged the utmost amount of diligence, the utmost amount of skill and the most accurate conclusion in a matter of judgment.[39]

Liquidated damages and penalties

The parties to a contract may anticipate the possibility of a breach of contract and include a term that a certain sum shall be paid by the defaulting party in the event of a specified breach or breaches. If the sum is a genuine estimate of the actual damages likely to be suffered in the event of breach, the term, known as a "liquidated damages clause", is enforceable. If, however, the sum fixed is not a genuine estimate but is greater than any loss likely to be caused and is intended to operate as a threat to keep a potential defaulter to his bargain, it is described as a "penalty clause" and is not enforceable. The injured party can recover no more than the loss actually sustained by him as a result of the breach, estimated in accordance with the usual principles, discussed above.

Whether a particular clause provides for liquidated damages or for a penalty is a question of construction and the fact that the parties have called it the one or the other is far from conclusive. If the sum fixed is "extravagant and unconscionable in amount in comparison with the greatest loss that could conceivably be proved to have followed from the breach" it is a penalty.[40]

38 *Roth & Co. v. Tayson, Townsend & Co.* [1895] 1 Com.Cas. 240.
39 *Dunkirk Colliery Co. v. Lever* (1880) 41 L.T. 633, *per* James L.J.
40 *Dunlop Pneumatic Tyre Co. Ltd v. New Garage and Motor Co. Ltd* [1915] A.C. 79, HL; S. & T. 641.

Likewise if the breach consists in a failure to pay a sum of money and the sum fixed is a greater sum. It is said that "when a single lump sum is made payable by way of compensation, on the occurrence of one or more or all of several events, some of which may occasion serious and others but trifling damage," there is a presumption that it is a penalty.[41] But, on the other hand, it is said that the case where damage from any particular breach would be difficult to forecast is an appropriate one for use with a liquidated damages clause. In the *Suisse Atlantique* case[42] the provision requiring the charterers to pay demurrage of $1,000 a day was held to be a liquidated damages clause, although a delay of one day, or a few days, might cause the shipowners no loss of freight and only a small amount by way of increased overheads in port. Sometimes the clause will work to the advantage of one party, sometimes to that of the other. In such a case, each side derives an advantage from having the figure fixed and knowing in advance what the consequences of a breach will be. If litigation occurs, it eliminates what might have been the heavy cost of proving, or disproving, the amount of damage claimed. These are significant advantages and the courts should not be astute to categorise such clauses as penalties and so nullify their effect. Where the clause is likely to benefit one party only, then it is likely to be a penalty clause. In *Lamdon Trust Co. v. Hurrel*[43] a hire-purchase agreement provided that if, as a result of a breach by the hirer, the letter terminated the agreement, the hirer should pay as compensation for depreciation 75 per cent of the total sum due under the agreement. The Court of Appeal held that this was a penalty and unenforceable. If the hirer had failed to pay the first instalment, the letter, according to the agreement, could have recovered a car which had hardly depreciated at all *and* 75 per cent of its value.

If a plaintiff sues for a penalty, he can recover no more than the sum stipulated, even though he has suffered damages in excess of that sum. It is been held in one case that it is open to him to ignore the penalty clause and sue for damages, in which case he can recover the whole of his loss; but there are conflicting authorities and the House of Lords has left the matter open.

The same principles apply to a clause which provides that, in the event of a breach, the defaulting party shall transfer to the injured party property other than money. If the value of the property to be transferred is proved to be less than the actual

41 Lord Watson in *Lord Elphinstone v. Monkland Iron and Coal Co.* (1886) 11 App. Cas. 332, HL (Sc.), cited by Lord Dunedin in the *Dunlop* case, above, n.40.
42 Above, p. 171.
43 [1955] 1 W.L.R. 391.

232 Remedies for Breach of Contract

loss, then the clause does not operate as penalty and must be enforced. It is different if the value is, or may be, greater, than the actual loss. In *Jobson v. Johnson*[44] an agreement for the sale of shares in Southend Football Club for £350,000 by £40,000 down and six half-yearly instalments provided that, if the buyer defaulted on the second or a subsequent instalment, he must return the shares to the seller for £40,000. The seller was not required to refund instalments paid. When, after the buyer had paid £140,000 he defaulted and the seller claimed specific performance of the agreement to re-transfer the shares, it was held that this was a penalty clause. The form of relief to be granted to the buyer was complicated by the fact that there was no evidence as to the value of the shares. The court offered alternatives to the buyer, one involving the sale, and the other the valuation, of the shares, with the object of compensating the seller for the loss actually caused by the buyer's breach and no more.

Money payable otherwise than on breach

Penalties and liquidated damages have one thing in common: they are both money, or other specified property, which, by the terms of a contract, is payable on breach of that contract. A term which provides that a sum of money shall be payable on some event other than a breach of contract cannot be either a penalty or a liquidated damages clause. The £100 "reward" in the *Carbolic Smoke Ball* case was payable on the plaintiff catching 'flu; but that event was not a breach of contract, because the defendants had not undertaken that the users of the ball would not catch 'flu. If they had so promised, then the money would have been payable on a breach of contract and the question whether it was a penalty or liquidated damages would have arisen.

In *Alder v. Moore*[45] a professional footballer was insured by his union against permanent total disablement from playing professional football. He suffered an injury which the insurers were satisfied amounted to permanent total disablement. As required by the policy, he signed a declaration that he would take no part, as a playing member, in any form of professional football and that "in the event of the infringement of this condition, he will be subject to a penalty of the amount paid to him in settlement of his claim." He started playing football again and the insurers sued to recover £500. The Court of Appeal, reversing Paull J.,

44 [1989] 1 All E.R. 621, CA; S. & T. 646.
45 [1961] 2 Q.B. 57, CA.

held that this was a contract for the payment of a sum in a certain event which was not a breach of contract—there was "no *contractual* ban upon the defendant from playing professional football again" said Slade J. Devlin L.J. dissented, holding that as the clause was described as "a penalty", the onus was on the insurers to prove that it was not; and they had in fact exacted a promise from the defendant that he would not play again.

These principles produce a strange anomaly: the defendant who has committed a breach of contract is better off than the defendant who has not. The former can say to the plaintiff, "You are trying to enforce a penalty", the latter cannot say that. In *Bridge v. Campbell Discount Co. Ltd*[46] the hirer of a car had a right under the hire-purchase agreement to return it at any time but, if he did so he was required by the agreement to pay "by way of agreed compensation for depreciation" such sum as would make his payments up to two-thirds of the purchase price. He returned the car after paying only one monthly instalment. The Court of Appeal held that this was not a breach of contract and therefore the company's claim for the "agreed compensation" was not a claim for a penalty: the defendant had to pay. But the majority of the House of Lords managed to find that the defendant was not exercising his contractual right to return the car, but was breaking his contract; so the claim was for a penalty and he was not liable. Lord Denning fairly said that this meant that "equity commits itself to this absurd paradox: it will grant relief to a man who breaks his contract but will penalise the man who keeps it."

The reason, of course, is the exceptional nature of the rule by which the court grants relief against penalties—the court has no general jurisdiction to decline to enforce contractual terms because they are onerous or unfair. Penalty clauses are unique, and to treat one class of term in a radically different way from any other cannot fail to produce anomalies.

Damages under the Misrepresentation Act 1967, s.2(1)

The right to damages under the 1967 Act is described above.[47] Section 2(1) appears to create a new statutory tort with the consequence that the tort and not the contract rules concerning damages apply. The object of damages in tort is to put the claimant into the position he would have been in if the tort had not been committed. If that is applied to the case where S sells to B a machine for £1,000, having misrepresented that it will fulfil a

46 [1962] A.C. 600, HL; S. & T. 644.
47 See p. 153.

certain function whereas it proves to be useless, B will be entitled to recover £1,000 to be put back where he started from. But if the misrepresentation was a term and a machine capable of fulfilling that function would be worth £5,000, B would be entitled to £5,000 to put him in the position he would have been in if the contract had been performed. If, on the other hand, demand for the machine's product had diminished so that, even if it had worked, it would have been worth only £500, the contractual measure of damages would be only £500; and if the demand had evaporated altogether, so that the machine was worthless, the contractual damages would be nominal. Whether the tortious or the contractual measure of damages is the more advantageous to the claimant depends on the circumstances.

The tortious measure of damages for fraudulent misrepresentation is different from that applicable to negligent misrepresentation under *Hedley Byrne* (above, p. 147). In the case of fraud, the defendant is liable for any loss, foreseeable or not, which flowed from the fraud; but in the case of mere negligence only foreseeable loss is recoverable. In *Royscot Trust Ltd v. Rogerson*[48] it was held that the plain words of section 2(1) require the application of the fraud rule. Academic opinion that so harsh a rule should apply only where actual fraud was proved was not followed.

SPECIFIC PERFORMANCE

A decree of specific performance is an order by the court directing a party to a contract to carry it out. If he fails to do so, he will be in contempt of court. Equity acts *in personam*. Specific performance is an equitable remedy and courts of equity intervened only when the common law was considered to be inadequate. So specific performance is available only when damages are not an adequate remedy. It is rarely available in a contract for sale of goods. The injured seller can obviously be fully compensated by money and so too may the buyer if he can buy similar goods elsewhere. The contract might be specifically enforceable if it was for the sale of some unique thing. Contracts for the sale of land are generally specifically enforceable because each piece of land is unique.

Equitable remedies are discretionary. A party injured by a breach of contract is entitled to damages as a matter of right, but the court will grant specific performance only if it considers it just and equitable to do so. The discretion is, however, exercised in accordance with principles, so the decision is not an arbitrary

48 [1991] 3 All E.R. 294, CA.

one; but it allows the court to take into account a wide range of considerations. "Mutuality" is said to be a condition of specific performance. If one party to a contract is entitled to it, then so too, in equity, should be the other party. The vendor of land could be adequately compensated by damages; but since the purchaser would be entitled to specific performance, the vendor is entitled to it as well. But the principle has another, apparently inconsistent, aspect. If one party could not have specific performance, then, in equity, neither should the other party. A minor will not be granted specific performance even of a contract in its nature specifically enforceable, because specific performance could not be ordered against him. Contracts for personal services are not specifically enforceable.

There is a settled practice, now confirmed by the House of Lords in *Co-op Insurance Society Ltd v. Argyll Stores Ltd*,[49] that an order requiring the carrying on of a business will not be made. The House reversed a majority decision of the Court of Appeal, who had ordered the defendant to comply with a covenant to keep open a supermarket, then making a substantial loss, from 1995 until 2014. The Court of Appeal thought damages would not be an adequate remedy, partly because the departure of the defendants would have a serious effect on the plaintiff's other tenants of neighbouring shops. The traditional reason for the practice is that the enforcement of the order would require the constant supervision of the court, which is impracticable. The powerful weapon of contempt of court is an unsuitable instrument for overseeing the carrying on of a business and there would be the possibility of repeated applications which would be costly to the parties and the judicial system. The loss which the defendant may suffer by running a business at a loss for a long time may be far greater than the loss which the plaintiff will suffer from the breach, for which he may recover damages. There is a difference, however, between orders to carry on an activity, which will usually not be made, and orders to achieve a result, which well may be.

49 [1997] 3 All E.R. 297, HL.

CHAPTER NINETEEN

Contracts by Minors

At common law persons under the age of 21 were categorised as "infants" and had only a limited capacity to contract. Section 1 of the Family Law Reform Act 1969 reduced the age to 18 and authorised the use of the term, "minor", as an alternative to "infant". "Minor" is now the preferred term. The capacity of a minor to contract is still regulated by the common law, now modified only by the Minors' Contracts Act 1987 which repealed a troublesome statute of 1874, the Infants Relief Act. The 1987 Act applies to contracts made on or after June 9, 1987. For contracts made before that date, it may be necessary to refer to the provisions of the 1874 Act, which are not dealt with in this book.[1]

CONTRACTS GENERALLY NOT BINDING ON MINORS

The general principle is that contracts made by a minor with an adult are binding on the adult but not on the minor. The contract becomes binding on him only if, after attaining his majority, he ratifies it. Ratification is an act confirming the minor's earlier promise. It requires no fresh consideration from the adult[2] and makes the contract fully binding on the former minor party.

Although the contract is not binding on the minor it is not void and money paid or property transferred under it can be recovered by the minor only if he can show that there has been a total failure of consideration. A minor who bought and enjoyed the use of

---

1 See *Cheshire, Fifoot and Furmston* (13th ed.), Chapter 13.
2 The position was different under the Infants Relief Act.

furniture for some months was not allowed to recover the price[3] and a minor who exchanged his motor cycle for a car could not get the cycle back when the car broke down.[4] These decisions were made, notwithstanding the provision of the Infants Relief Act that contracts for such non-necessary goods were "absolutely void" and should, *a fortiori*, be the same after the repeal of that Act.

CONTRACTS "VOIDABLE" BY THE MINOR

Where a minor acquires an interest in "a subject of a permanent nature . . . with certain obligations attached to it"—such as a leasehold or shares in a company—he is bound by the obligations so long as he retains the "subject". It was so held in *North Western Railway v. M'Michael*[5] where the defendant was held liable to pay calls on shares although he was a minor at the time he bought the shares and when the calls were made and he had never ratified the purchase. Equally, however, he had never repudiated it. He was at liberty to avoid the contract during minority or within a reasonable time thereafter but he had not done so. It was no answer to the claim that the transaction was a disadvantageous one—"why, in such a case, does not the infant disagree to and avoid the purchase, and so get rid of the obligation?". "Avoid", as we have seen[6] is an ambiguous word and the court in *M'Michael's* case used it in the sense of "rescind"—the minor might avoid the contract *ab initio*, getting rid not only of his liability to pay future calls but also of his liability to pay calls already due, but unpaid. Others have taken the view that obligations are avoided only for the future and that the minor, or former minor, remains liable to meet obligations already accrued at the time of avoidance. The observations in *M'Michael* were *obiter*, there is no modern authority and the matter remains open.

If the right to repudiate is not exercised within a reasonable time after majority, it lapses. What is a reasonable time depends on all the circumstances of the case; but the House of Lords in *Edwards v. Carter*[7] was in no doubt that a party to a marriage settlement made a month before his majority was much too late when he repudiated the contract four-and-a-half years after attaining it.

Whether avoidance is retrospective or not, it seems clear that the minor cannot recover money which he has already paid,

3 *Valentini v. Canali* (1889) 24 Q.B.D. 166.
4 *Pearce v. Brain* [1929] 2 K.B. 310.
5 (1850) 5 Ex. 114.
6 Above, p. 156.
7 [1893] A.C. 360.

unless he can show that there has been a total failure of consideration. If that is the position for the first category of minors' contracts considered above, it should, *a fortiori*, be so for this category. In *Steinberg v. Scala Ltd*[8] a minor's action to have her name removed from the register of shareholders succeeded, but she was not allowed to recover money paid by way of calls. She had got the very thing she bargained for, and it was immaterial whether she had derived any real advantage from the contract. In an action to recover money for a total failure of consideration there was no difference between a minor and an adult plaintiff.

CONTRACTS FOR NECESSARIES

The principal exception to the common law rule of the immunity of the minor is that he is liable to pay for "necessaries" supplied to him. Since 1893 liability for necessary goods supplied to a minor has been regulated by the Sale of Goods Acts and the 1979 Act, re-enacting the 1893 Act, provides by section 2:

" . . . where necessaries are sold and delivered to an infant (or minor) . . . he must pay a reasonable price therefor.
    'Necessaries' in this section mean goods suitable to the condition of life of such infant (or minor) . . ., and to his actual requirements at the time of the sale and delivery."

"Necessaries" are those things without which a person cannot reasonably exist and obviously include food, clothing, lodging and essential services. In *Chapple v. Cooper*[9] a widow who was a minor was held liable to an undertaker for his work in connection with the funeral of her late husband. The law allowed minors to marry and a minor who did so might unhappily find it necessary to bury her spouse. She must pay for it. Education or training in a trade has also always been regarded as necessary.

The nature of the necessary thing was held to depend to some extent on the "station in life" of the minor. "His clothes may be fine or coarse according to his rank; his education may vary according to the station he is to fill; and the medicines will depend on the illness with which he is afflicted, and the extent of his probable means when of age." The application of the principle must vary with changing social conditions. A servant in livery may have been a necessary for a rich minor in 1844 but

8 [1923] 2 Ch. 452, CA.
9 [1844] 13 M. & W. 252. The illustrations below are taken from Alderson B.'s judgment.

it is impossible that it would be so today. Alderson B. said that "articles of mere luxury are always excluded, though luxurious articles of necessity are sometimes allowed." A well-to-do minor would have to pay for his Savile Row suits but a poor boy would not. The High Street shop would be quite good enough for him. The Saville Row tailor would supply him at his peril; but the High Street shop would not run the same degree of risk.

As the Sale of Goods Act makes clear, goods supplied must be suitable, not only to the condition in life of the minor, but also "to his actual requirements at the time sale and delivery." If the minor has enough of the articles in question, more cannot be necessary to him. So in *Nash v. Inman*[10] an undergraduate at Trinity College, Cambridge was not liable to pay for clothing, including 11 fancy waistcoats, when his father gave evidence that his son was already amply supplied with clothes. The onus of proof was on the plaintiff to prove that the defendant minor was not adequately supplied.

Nature of the minor's liability for necessaries

It will have been noted that the Sale of Goods Act declares the infant to be liable only where the goods are "sold and delivered" and that he is liable to pay, not any agreed price, but a reasonable price. In *Nash v. Inman* Fletcher Moulton L.J. said that this was a codification of the common law and that the basis of the action is "hardly contract. Its real foundation is an obligation which the law imposes on the infant to make a fair repayment in respect of needs satisfied. In other words the obligation arises *re* [by virtue of something done] and not *consensu* [by virtue of agreement]." The practical significance of this (apart from any difference between an agreed and a reasonable price) is that the minor would not be liable on an executory contract in damages. The seller, even of necessary goods, would have no claim if the minor, in breach of the agreement, refused to accept delivery. Fletcher Moulton L.J.'s opinion has the support of other eminent judges,[11] as well as the Sale of Goods Act. On the other hand, Buckley L.J. in *Nash v. Inman* thought that the action was "in contract on the footing that the contract was such as the infant, notwithstanding infancy, could make. The defendant, though he was an infant, had a limited capacity to contract". Then there is *Roberts v. Gray*.[12] The plaintiff recovered damages from the

10 [1908] 2 K.B. 1, CA.
11 Cotton L.J. in *Re Rhodes* (1890) 44 Ch.D. 94, 105 and Scrutton L.J. in *Pontypridd Union v. Drew* [1927] 1 K.B. 214, 220.
12 [1913] 1 K.B. 520, CA.

defendant, a minor, for breach of a contract to join him in a world tour, playing billiards. Though the plaintiff had expended time and trouble and incurred liabilities in making the arrangements, it seems a plain case of a minor being held liable for breach of an executory contract for necessaries. It was not a contract of employment but one for the teaching and instruction of the minor, the plaintiff being a noted billiards player. Hamilton L.J., rejecting the argument that the defendant would have become liable only on actually receiving the plaintiff's instruction, held that the contract was binding on the minor from its formation. It does not seem possible to justify a distinction between necessary goods and necessary services on either a historical or a logical basis. *Roberts v. Gray* might have been justified as concerning a contract belonging to the next category, beneficial contracts of service, except that the court specifically held that it was not a contract of employment but a contract for necessary instruction.

A contract is not binding on a minor merely because it is proved that it is for the minor's benefit. But a contract, which would otherwise be for necessaries is not one if it contains harsh or onerous terms. A contract by a minor for the hire of a taxi to go five or six miles to collect his bag might be a contract for a necessary; but if it contains a term purporting to impose liability on him for any damage to the car, whether due to his negligence or not, it is not such a contract.[13]

BENEFICIAL CONTRACTS OF SERVICE

It is for the minor's benefit that he should be able to obtain employment, which he could hardly do if he could not make a binding contract. The law therefore allows him to do so, provided that the contract, taken as a whole, is manifestly for his benefit. Whatever the position regarding necessaries, here the liability is plainly contractual. The service is one to be rendered by the minor. In *Clements v. London & North Western Railway*[14] the plaintiff, a minor, was employed as a porter and had agreed to join an insurance scheme to which his employers contributed and to forgo any claims he might have against them under the Employers' Liability Act. On sustaining an injury, he claimed under that Act. His action failed. The term by which he agreed to forgo his rights was obviously not to his advantage; but the contract must be looked at as a whole, and, when it was so regarded, the court found it to be for his advantage and therefore binding. A minor pursuing a career as a professional boxer was

---

13 *Fawcett v. Smethurst* (1914) 84 L.J.K.B. 473.
14 [1894] 2 Q.B. 482.

held to be bound by his contract to observe the rules relating to that sport, not being of a harsh or onerous character. The contract enabled him to earn his living and so was for his benefit.[15] The same principle was applied to a contract with a young author to publish his book and to take an assignment of the copyright. The contract, judged at the date when it was made, was for the author's benefit. It was immaterial that it turned out later to be less beneficial than had been thought.[16]

RESTITUTION BY THE MINOR

The law is capable of producing injustice where a minor has obtained property under a contract which is not enforceable against him. He may get the property for nothing and the adult party, who may be in no way at fault, is the loser. This may be so even where the minor has lied about his age. It was held that the minor was not estopped from denying that he was an adult, so as to avoid the effect of the Infants Relief Act 1874[17] and it is likely that the court today would similarly decline to allow the policy of the common law against the imposition of liability on minors to be defeated by estoppel. It has been decided that an action in deceit will not lie against the minor because that too would enable the contract to be indirectly enforced against him. However, the Minors' Contracts Act 1987 now affords a limited measure of redress to the adult party. By section 3, where a contract, made after the commencement of the Act, is unenforceable against a defendant because he was a minor when it was made:

"the court may, if it is just and equitable to do so, require the defendant to transfer to the plaintiff any property acquired by the defendant under the contract, or any property representing it."

Suppose A, a minor, has bought from B some non-necessary thing, *e.g.* a racehorse, for £10,000. He refuses to pay or to return the horse. The court now has a discretion to order him to do so. If A has exchanged the racehorse for a car, or he has sold it and paid the proceeds into his bank account, the court may require him to hand over the car or an appropriate part of the bank balance; but, if the proceeds of the sale have been dissipated and

---

15 *Doyle v. White City Stadium Ltd* (1929) [1935] 1 K.B. 110, note, CA.
16 *Chaplin v. Leslie Frewin (Publishers) Ltd* [1966] Ch. 71, CA, Lord Denning M.R. dissenting on the question whether the contract was beneficial.
17 *Levene v. Brougham* (1909) 25 T.L.R. 265.

can no longer be identified in A's possession, B has no redress under the section.

If B lends money to A, a minor, he will be unable to sue for the recovery of the money lent unless he is able to prove that he made the loan for the express purpose of enabling A to buy necessaries and that A in fact did so.[18] Equity gives relief on the ground that the money has in fact been expended on necessaries. If the money lent is identifiable in A's hands—*e.g.* it is part of A's credit balance at his bank—the lender might be able to invoke section 3, for example where the minor had fraudulently misrepresented that he was of full age.

Restitution in equity

By section 3(2) of the 1987 Act, "nothing in this section shall be taken to prejudice any other remedy available to the plaintiff." Accordingly, B might still rely on the equitable doctrine which required a fraudulent minor to disgorge property which he had obtained by deception and which was still identifiable in his possession.[19] Clearly there is an overlap between the statutory and equitable remedies and the former is wider in that it does not depend on proof of fraud. It is not clear that there would be any advantage in invoking the equitable remedy since that too is discretionary. And with equity, as with the statute, "restitution stopped where repayment began."[20]

GUARANTEES OF MINORS' CONTRACTS

C promises B that, if he will enter into a contract with A, a minor, he, C, will guarantee performance by A. B enters into the contract with A who fails to perform or repudiates the contract and B then calls on C to honour his guarantee. Before the 1987 Act came into operation C might have argued that, since A's promise was, in law, a nullity, there was nothing to guarantee and his own promise was equally void. Section 2 of the 1987 Act rules out any such argument. A guarantee of a minor's contract is not unenforceable merely because the contract with the minor is not enforceable against him on the ground that he is a minor. The section does not apply if A's promise is not enforceable against him for some reason other than the fact that he is a minor, *e.g.* that he was induced to enter into the contract by misrepresentation or duress. In such a case, C would not be liable either.

---

18 *Earle v. Peale* (1711) 1 Salk. 386; *Lewis v. Alleyne* (1888) 4 T.L.R. 560.
19 *Leslie (R.) Ltd v. Sheill* [1914] 3 K.B. 607, CA.
20 [1914] 3 K.B. 607 at 618, *per* Lord Sumner.

CHAPTER TWENTY

Contracts Requiring Writing

The general principle is that contracts may be made entirely orally, however valuable or important the subject-matter. Occasionally legislation requires that a particular category of contract must be in writing. In addition, contracts of certain classes are not enforceable by action unless evidenced in writing. The contract may be made orally but neither party can sue on it unless and until he can produce the appropriate written evidence of it—which may come into existence after the contract has been made. These two classes of contracts are the subject of the present chapter.

CONTRACTS UNENFORCEABLE FOR LACK OF WRITING

The origin of the unenforceable contract is to be found in sections 4 and 17 of the Statute of Frauds 1677. The purpose of the statute was to prevent fraud by requiring written evidence of certain types of promise which were considered then to be particularly vulnerable to dishonest claims. Throughout its history the statute was heavily criticised both for its drafting and its substance and it was often thought to assist rather than to prevent fraud. It was not, however, until 1954 that the Law Reform (Enforcement of Contracts) Act repealed important parts of it. From 1677 to 1954 the statute applied to—

    (i)   A promise by an executor or administrator to pay damages out of his own property.

    (ii) A promise made in consideration of marriage. This referred not to the mutual promises of the engaged couple (which was an enforceable contract until the Law Reform (Miscellaneous Provisions) Act 1970, s.1(1)) but to marriage settlements and ancillary agreements, such as that alleged in *Shadwell v. Shadwell.*[1]

(iii) A promise not to be performed within one year of its making; and

(iv) A contract for the sale of any goods of the value of £10 or upwards. This provision was re-enacted in the Sale of Goods Act 1893, s.4.

For contracts made after the 1954 Act came into force, these provisions are of no significance; but the student needs to be aware of them for the proper understanding of cases such as *Shadwell v. Shadwell, Jorden v. Money*[2] and *Felthouse v. Bindley*[3] which, while affected by the repealed parts of the Statute of Frauds, remain authorities on general principles still applicable

The 1954 Act left unrepealed the requirement of writing in respect of two classes of contract. One was any contract for the sale or other disposition of an interest in land. Since 1989 these contracts are governed by a new rule, considered below, p. 247. The only survivor of the Statute of Frauds is now—

A "special promise to answer for the debt, default or miscarriage of another person."

The antique language of section 4 of the 1677 Act is still in force but it has been heavily overlaid with case law. As interpreted, it applies only where three persons are involved. A is, or may become, under a liability (whether in contract or in tort) to B and C promises B for consideration that, if A does not discharge his liability, he, C, will so do. C's promise to B is not enforceable unless evidenced in writing. A promise made by C to A (the person primarily answerable for the "debt, default or miscarriage") is not within the statute and is enforceable (if given for consideration) without written evidence.[4]

Nor does the statute apply where C promises B to meet A's liability in any event, not only conditionally upon A's failing to do so. The unconditional promise is called "an indemnity", the conditional promise "a guarantee"; and the statute applies only to guarantees. But the fact that the parties use the one term rather

---

1 Above, p. 66.
2 Above, p. 84.
3 Above, p. 30.
4 *Eastwood v. Kenyon* (1840) 11 Ad. & E. 438.

than the other is not conclusive; the question is as to the true meaning of the promise.[5] If the effect of C's promise is to end A's obligation, or prevent it ever arising, there is no guarantee but merely a substitution or ascertainment of the obligor.

These restrictions on the meaning of the statute are not easy to justify, but they do not end there. Even where C's promise is undoubtedly a guarantee it is held to be outside the statute if it is part of a wider transaction. Notably, the statute does not apply to *del credere* agency. A *del credere* agent is one who guarantees the performance of their contracts by persons whom he introduces to his principal. The main object of the contract is the introduction and the guarantee is incidental to it.[6] Nor, it has been held, does the statute apply where C gives the guarantee in order to secure the release by A of an encumbrance affecting C's proprietary rights. In *Fitzgerald v. Dressler*[7] A sold goods to B who resold to C. A was still in possession and, not having been paid by B, had a lien on the goods. C, being anxious to obtain possession, guaranteed payment by B if A would deliver directly to him. A did so and C relied, unsuccessfully, on the statute.[8] Such decisions are explicable only on the ground of the courts' understandable dislike of a statute which, if applicable, enables a party to dishonour with impunity an obligation which he has clearly undertaken. This provision of the statute was retained in 1954 for the protection of the public against unscrupulous persons who might claim that guarantees had been given when they had not; but it is doubtful whether this is a good reason for the retention of the strange and illogical law which has grown up around the words of the statute.

The requirement of writing

Section 4 of the 1677 Act provides that no action may be brought on the guarantee—

> "unless the agreement . . ., or some memorandum or note thereof, shall be in writing and signed by the party to be charged therewith or by some other person thereunto by him lawfully authorised."

5 *Mountstephen v. Lakeman* (1874) L.R. 7 HL 17; *Guild v. Conrad* [1894] 2 Q.B. 885.
6 *Couturier v. Hastie* (1852) 8 Exch. 40; S. & T. 495.
7 (1859) 7 C.B.N.S. 374.
8 C, having bought the goods, was the owner of them. Where C had no proprietary, but only a personal interest to protect, *Fitzgerald v. Dressler* was distinguished and the statute applied: *Harburg India Rubber Comb Co. v. Martin* [1902] 1 K.B. 778, CA.

The note or memorandum may take any form—it might, for example, be a letter—but it must identify the parties and include all the express terms of the contract. It need not contain any terms which are implied by law. It is permissible to join several documents, each in itself insufficient, to form a complete memorandum, provided that there is an express or even an implied reference in the signed document to the others. The courts have allowed a letter to be joined with an envelope proved orally to have enclosed it, and an agreement to buy land to be joined with a receipt for the deposit signed by the vendor. Similar laxity has been shown in respect of the signature. A manual subscription is not essential. Any representation of the defendant's name is sufficient if the court is satisfied that it is intended to authenticate the whole document.

Effect of non-compliance

For many years the courts held that the effect of non-compliance with the statute was to render the contract void. As late as 1862 in *Felthouse v. Bindley*[9] it was held that the lack of a memorandum at the date of the auction prevented the property in the horse passing from the nephew to his uncle although there was a memorandum at the time the action was brought. But, already, in 1852 in *Leroux v. Brown*[10] it had been held that the effect of the statute was not substantive but procedural. A contract made in France and governed by French law was not enforceable in an English court without a memorandum because English procedural rules applied. This was confirmed by the House of Lords in *Maddison v. Alderson* in 1883.[11]

The oral contract is valid and may be enforced against any party so soon as he has signed a sufficient memorandum but not against a party who has not. Acts done in performance of the unenforceable contract are validly done so that a party who has paid money under the contract cannot recover the money as he could if the contract were void. The payee, while he could not sue on the contract, may rely on it to justify his retention of the money, so long, at least, as he remains ready and willing to perform his own obligations.

As the requirement is procedural, the defendant may waive it and rules of court in fact require that, if he wishes to rely on the statute, he must plead it.

---

9 Above, p. 30.
10 (1852) 12 C.B. 801.
11 (1883) 8 App.Cas. 467, at 488, *per* Lord Blackburn.

CONTRACTS REQUIRED TO BE IN WRITING

The most important contract in this class is a contract for the sale or other disposition of an interest in land. Until 1989 these contracts could be made orally but contracts made between 1677 and September 29, 1989 were, and remain, unenforceable unless evidenced in writing. The requirement was imposed by section 4 of the Statute of Frauds which was re-enacted in more modern language by section 40 of the Law of Property Act 1925. Section 40 was repealed and replaced by section 2 of the Law of Property (Miscellaneous Provisions) Act 1989 which provides:

> 2.—(1) A contract for the sale or other disposition of an interest in land can only be made in writing and only by incorporating all the terms which the parties have expressly agreed in one document or, where contracts are exchanged, in each.
>
> (2) The terms may be incorporated in a document either by being set out in it or by reference to some other document.
>
> (3) The document incorporating the terms or, where contracts are exchanged, one of the documents incorporating them (but not necessarily the same one) must be signed by or on behalf of each party to the contract.

If the parties wish to change a term in a contract they have made for the sale of land—*e.g.* to change the completion date—the contract as varied must satisfy the formalities of section 2. If it does not, the original contract remains valid.[12]

The section has caused difficulty in connection with the exercise of an option to buy land. In *Spiro v. Glencrown Properties Ltd*[13] the plaintiff (S) granted the first defendant (G) an option to buy land for £745,000. The agreement was in two parts, each signed by both parties and exchanged. The option was exercisable by notice in writing to S on the same day. G duly delivered a letter exercising the option. This letter was signed on behalf of G but not, of course, by S. G failed to complete the alleged contract for the sale of the land and S sued for damages. G's defence was that, applying section 2, there was no contract for the sale of the land since the letter concluding the contract was not signed by S. This was a formidable objection and one with grave consequences. If it were upheld, options to buy land would be invalid unless some new and cumbersome procedure

---

12 *McCausland v. Duncan Lawrie Ltd* [1996] 4 All E.R. 995.
13 [1991] 2 W.L.R. 931, Ch.D; S. & T. 107.

were introduced. Hoffmann J. thought that this could not have been intended by Parliament. He held that section 2 was intended to apply to the agreement which created the option and not to the notice by which it was exercised. The grant of the option was the *only* "contract for the sale or other disposition of an interest in land" within the meaning of the section.

This decision no doubt produced a sensible result, but there are serious theoretical difficulties. It may be fair to say that the option was a *contract to sell*—S was conditionally bound, for his offer to do so was irrevocable; but could it fairly be said that there was a contract to buy? G was not bound to buy—whether he exercised the option was entirely at his discretion. It will be noticed that it was G's contract to buy which was enforced. If the grant of the option was the only contract for the sale of land, by what process did G become bound to buy? A "lock-out" agreement,[14] whereby a prospective vendor agrees that for a specified period he will not deal with anyone other than a particular purchaser, is not covered by section 2: the vendor does not agree to sell to anyone, nor does the purchaser agree to buy.[15]

The long history of the Statute of Frauds shows that procedural requirements often stand in the way of justice and that courts strive to find a way around. Sometimes this can be done without undue strain, as in the use of the collateral contract which has already proved its utility in relation to section 2.[16]

In other circumstances, such as those in *Spiro*, it seems to involve distortions which are hard to justify.

---

14 Above, p. 47.
15 *Pitt v. PHH Asset Management Ltd* [1993] 4 All E.R. 961, above, p. 51.
16 See *Record v. Bell*, above, p. 127.

CHAPTER TWENTY-ONE

Duress and Undue Influence

It is not surprising that A is not bound by a contract with B if he entered into it only because B was holding a pistol to his head and threatening to blow out his brains if he did not. What is surprising is that it is always said that duress makes the contract not void but merely voidable. The logical consequence would seem to be that, if it is a contract for the sale of A's car and B leaves A trussed up while he finds a bona fide purchaser to whom he sells the car, the BFP would get a good title; A has done nothing to rescind the contract. Yet is seems nonsensical to require A to notify B that he does not wish to be bound by the contract in circumstances such as these; B knows that very well, right from the start—otherwise why produce the pistol? Perhaps nothing more is meant than that, though A is not bound by the contract, B would be bound if A decided he wished to hold him to it. Obviously it should not be a good defence for B to say, "But A only agreed to the contract because I threatened to shoot him." But the fact that B cannot be heard to say that the contract is void does not mean that it should not be regarded as void for all other purposes. Even Blenkarn[1] would surely have been liable on the contract to buy the linen if Lindsay had chosen to sue him for it, yet the contract was, otherwise, certainly a nullity.

Contracts at pistol point may sound fanciful but this is what happened in the Australian case of *Barton v. Armstrong*[2]; and, even more remarkably, the Australian courts and a minority in the Privy Council held that the contract was binding because

1 Above, p. 59.
2 [1975] 2 W.L.R. 1650; S. & T. 658.

Barton had entered into the contract, not because he was overborne by the threat, but for reasons of commercial necessity. All the judges agreed on the principle: that, just as a misrepresentation does not make a contract voidable if it has no effect on the mind of the representee, so too a threat which does not affect the judgment of the person threatened is inoperative. The onus is, however, on the threatener to prove that his threats made no contribution to the decision of the other to contract. If the threat was one reason among others for entering into the contract, the person threatened is entitled to relief, even though it may be that he would have entered into the contract in the absence of any threat. The majority of the Privy Council held that Armstrong had not satisfied the onus which lay on him to prove that the threat did not influence Barton; but the minority thought there was no justification for interfering with the finding of fact by the courts below.

Duress is not limited in the law of contract to physical threats of this kind. In *Williams v. Bayley*[3] the threat was to prosecute Bayley's son for felony ("a case of transportation for life") if he did not meet promissory notes on which the son had forged his signature. In recent years, some courts have gone further and recognised a category of "economic duress" which makes a contract voidable. A threat to break a contract may fall into this category. In *North Ocean Shipping Co. v. Hyundai Construction Co.*[4] shipbuilders without justification demanded an additional 10 per cent on the contract price of a ship they were building for the plaintiffs, who reluctantly acceded to the demand because a delay in delivery of the tanker might have had very serious consequences for them. Mocatta J., with some hesitation, found that there was consideration for the promise to pay the additional 10 per cent because the builders, in return, had complied with the plaintiffs' request to increase by 10 per cent the letter of credit which they had opened to provide security for repayment of instalments in the event of their default in the performance of the contract. But he held that the builders' threat to break their contract unless they were paid the additional money constituted economic duress which rendered the contract voidable. Since, however, the owners had waited for eight months after delivery of the tanker before making any claim, they must be taken to have affirmed the contract and lost their right to rescind. In the *North Ocean* case, the builders were not merely taking advantage of a strong bargaining position but were threatening to commit a legal wrong—to break their

3 (1866) L.R. 1, HL; 200 HL; S. & T. 658.
4 [1979] Q.B. 705; S. & T. 241.

contract—unless their demand was met.

Economic duress was the principal *ratio decidendi* in *Atlas Express Ltd v. Kafco*.[5] Kafco (K), a small company secured and was ready to fulfil a large contract to supply goods to Woolworths. K made a contract with Atlas (A), a national road carrier, to distribute the goods to Woolworths' shops at an agreed price per carton. Because A had underestimated the size of the cartons, the price they had quoted and which had been agreed was uneconomically low. After the first delivery, A realised this. They then sent an empty vehicle to K's premises. The driver carried a document amending the contract so as to provide better terms for A. His instructions were to take the vehicle away unloaded unless the amended agreement was signed. It was essential to K's commercial survival that they should meet delivery dates. If they had not done so, Woolworths would have cancelled the contract and sued for loss of profit. K. signed. Tucker J. held that K were not bound by the amendment to the agreement, (i) because it was procured by economic duress and (ii) there was no consideration for it. Comparison may be made with *Williams v. Roffey*.[6] In each case the party who had made a bad bargain was seeking better terms. It was an enormous benefit to K to have A carry out their contract rather than break it, so it is hard to see that there is any difference regarding consideration. But K (the little company) was in a hopeless bargaining position whereas that of Roffey (the larger concern), though difficult, was by no means so desperate; and A proceeded by ultimatum whereas Williams negotiated and, so far as appears, made no threats. If the cases are distinguishable, it must be on grounds of economic duress.

The limits of economic duress are uncertain. It is said that there must be some factor "which could in law be regarded as a coercion of his will so as to vitiate consent"[7]; but such propositions are of very limited assistance. In the *North Ocean* case the owners did consent, albeit reluctantly; and they knew exactly what they were consenting to. In such circumstances— and they will be the usual circumstances—a phrase like "vitiate consent" tells us nothing. Lord Denning in several cases repeatedly stressed the importance of "inequality of bargaining power" but it is quite clear that mere inequality of bargaining power, even where the stronger party takes advantage of his

---

5 [1989] Q.B. 833, Q.B.D.; S. & T. 672.
6 Above, p. 78.
7 *Occidental Worldwide Investment Corporation v. Skibs A/S Avanti* [1976] 1 Lloyd's Rep. 293 at 336, *per* Kerr J., approved in *Pao On v. Lau Yiu Long* [1980] A.C. 614; S. & T. 233.

position, is not, in itself, sufficient to make the contract voidable. A person wanting to borrow money in order to meet pressing liabilities will have virtually no bargaining power and will have to accept the terms on which the bank or building society is willing to deal with him, or do without. The courts will interfere only in exceptional cases where the conduct of the stronger party has been "oppressive or unconscionable."[8] In *CTN Cash and Carry Ltd v. Gallagher Ltd*[9] Steyn L.J. said that the common law does not recognise a doctrine of inequality of bargaining power in commercial dealings. G, who had a monopoly in respect of the distribution of popular brands of cigarettes, demanded payment of £17,000, the price of a stolen consignment which G believed, wrongly but in good faith, to be at C's risk. C refused to pay until G threatened to withdraw credit facilities, which they had a right to do, unless C paid. This would have been very damaging to C and they paid as the lesser of two evils. C's action to recover the money on grounds of economic duress failed. The court recognised that the result was "unattractive"—G was allowed to retain £17,000 which was not due to them—but found that the law compelled this result. It is possible, however, that a different claim, *i.e.* in restitution, might have succeeded.

A threat to break a contract will not invariably amount to economic duress. In *Payzu v. Saunders*[10] the refusal of the seller to deliver further instalments of the goods was a threat to break his contract to deliver on credit terms; yet the court held that the buyer was under a "duty" to mitigate the damage by agreeing to a contract for cash sales—*i.e.* to yield to the threat. But in that case, the buyer had committed a breach of contract by failing to pay within one month of the delivery of the first instalment and the seller may well have believed, though wrongly, that this entitled him to insist on cash in future, so his conduct could not be described as oppressive or unconscionable.

UNDUE INFLUENCE

Alongside the common law relating to duress there exists an equitable doctrine of "undue influence" which has been exercised primarily in relation to gifts but which is equally applicable to contracts. Undue influence has been the subject of four recent decisions of the House of Lords. The first three of these must now be read in the light of the fourth, *Royal Bank of*

---

8 *Alec Lobb (Garages) Ltd v. Oil G.B. Ltd* [1985] 1 W.L.R. 173, CA; S. & T. 670.
9 [1994] 4 All E.R. 714; S. & T. 675.
10 [1919] 2 K.B. 581, S. & T. 635, above, p. 229.

Scotland v. Etridge[11] in which the House, considering eight appeals, thoroughly reviewed and clarified the law.

In these cases P claims that a transaction should be set aside because he reposed trust and confidence in D which D abused; that, in this transaction, D took unfair advantage of the influence P's trust gave him. It is for P to prove that this occurred. The cases fall into two categories.

(i) Where P and D are in one of certain legally recognised relationships there is a conclusive presumption that P has put trust and confidence in D. These relationships include parent and child, guardian and ward, trustee and beneficiary, solicitor and client and medical advisor and patient. There is no presumption that the confidence has been abused; that depends on the facts of the particular case. It would be absurd if every gift by a child to his parent or every fee paid by a client to his solicitor were presumed to have been obtained by the exercise of undue influence. If a transaction is one that is readily explicable by the relationship, there are no grounds for an inference that something untoward has occurred. But if the transaction is not so explicable—for example it is manifestly disadvantageous to P—there is a presumption that D has exercised undue influence and an onus on him—an "evidential burden"—to tender evidence showing that he has not done so. The greater the disadvantage to P, the more cogent must be the evidence to rebut the presumption. If D does not offer such evidence, he loses—the transaction wil be set aside. If he does offer such evidence there is a question of fact for the court and the ultimate burden is on P. Only if, at the end of the case, the court is satisfied on the balance of probabilities that D did abuse his trust will the transaction be set aside.

(ii) Where the relationship between the parties is not one which is presumed by the law to involve trust and confidence, P must prove both (i) that, in fact, a relationship of trust and confidence existed and (ii) that it was abused by D. Relationships in this category which frequently come before the courts include husband and wife and banker and customer. There is nothing unusual or strange in a wife, from motives of affection or otherwise, conferring substantial benefits on her husband. Nevertheless a wife may have

11 [2001] 4 All E.R. 449, HL.

confidence in her husband, especially in financial matters, which is open to abuse. The relationship between banker and customer is a commercial one; but a bank manager may in fact inspire trust in a customer and acquire great influence over him. Before the *Etridge* case, it was thought essential, in certain types of case, for P to prove that the transaction was "manifestly disadvantageous" to him. It now appears that manifest disadvantage is only evidence—important evidence—that undue influence has been exercised. Where there is no manifest disadvantage, that fact might be proved by other evidence.

Where, in the course of the trial, P has established, whether by presumption, as in (i) above or inference as in (ii), that undue influence was exercised, D can rebut the presumption or inference by evidence that P entered into the transaction with a full understanding of its nature and by a free and voluntary exercise of will. The best, and possibly the only, way of proving this is to show that P had the benefit of independent and competent advice. Independent advice, even when it shows that the wife fully understood the situation, does not necessarily establish that she was not acting under undue influence. All the evidence must be taken into account. If, in the end, the court is not satisfied on the balance of probabilities that undue influence was exercised in fact, P fails.

In the typical case considered in the recent decisions a husband (D) and wife (P) obtained money from a bank on the security of the jointly-owned matrimonial home. D initiated the transaction, usually for purposes of his business, and now P sought to set it aside on the ground of undue influence by either D or the bank. As already noted, neither husband and wife nor banker and customer is a relationship in which trust and confidence is presumed. In the *Nat West case*[12] P had no confidence in her husband's business abilities and acted on the advice of the bank manager. The House was not satisfied that her relationship with the bank ever went beyond the normal business relationship of banker and customer, or that the transaction was disadvantageous to her. The House therefore reversed the decision of the Court of Appeal setting the transaction aside. In the *CIBC case*[13] P was entitled to set aside the transaction as against D, because was D was guilty of misrepresentation and actual undue influence; but this was not

---

12 *National Westminster Bank v. Morgan* [1985] A.C. 686; S. & T. 663.
13 *CIBC Mortgages plc. v. Pitt* [1993] 4 All E.R. 433; S. & T. 666.

effective against the bank. D was not the bank's agent, nor did the bank have actual or constructive notice of D's misconduct, the advance being made to P and D jointly. But in *Barclays Bank plc v. O'Brien*[14] the money was borrowed, not for the benefit of P and D, but for D's company; and D and P had guaranteed repayment. The bank had constructive notice of D's exercise of undue influence because a wife's guarantee of her husband's commercial debts is not for her financial benefit and there is a greater risk of undue influence. The guarantee was not enforceable.

Where a husband and wife give a bank a legal charge over the matrimonial home and the wife claims that she was induced to sign by the misrepresentation or undue influence of her husband, the burden is on her to prove that the bank had constructive notice; but it is easily discharged by showing that the bank knew that she was a wife living with her husband and that the transaction was not to her financial advantage. The burden is then on the bank to to show that it took reasonable steps to satisfy itself that her consent was properly obtained.[15] The steps required are set out in great detail in *Etridge*. They generally involve a solicitor explaining the transaction to the wife. The bank is entitled, in the absence of a contrary indication, to assume that the solicitor has performed this task satisfactorily. The bank is unlikely to have detailed information about the relationship between the husband and wife. In practice the bank will have to take the required steps in any case where a person stands surety on a non-commercial basis.

---

14 [1994] 1 A.C. 180, HL.
15 *Barclays Bank plc. v. Boulter* [1999] 4 All E.R. 513, HL.

CHAPTER TWENTY-TWO

Illegality in the Law of Contract

Although the contract is complete in every respect, a party may be unable to enforce it because of illegality in the making, or in the performance, of the contract. The principle, traditionally expressed in the maxim, *ex turpi causa non oritur actio*, is one of law. The House of Lords held in *Tinsley v. Milligan*[1] that the court may not, as the Court of Appeal had thought it could, enforce the unlawful contract on the ground that to do so in the particular case would not be "an affront to the public conscience". Such a doctrine would, in effect, have given the courts a discretion to enforce the unlawful contract; and they have no such discretion.

WHERE THE MAKING OF THE CONTRACT IS PROHIBITED

Where the making of the contract is unlawful, neither party can sue on it, not even one who is unaware of the facts which make it illegal and has been deceived by the other. In *Re Mahmoud and Ispahani*[2] a sale of linseed oil was prohibited by legislation unless both the seller and the buyer had a licence. The plaintiff, who had a licence to sell, asked the defendant whether he had a licence to buy. The defendant replied untruthfully that he did. Relying on that representation, the plaintiff agreed to sell linseed

---

1 [1994] 1 A.C. 340, HL; S. & T. 685. Another aspect of the case is described below, p. 264–265.
2 [1921] 2 K.B. 716.

oil to the defendant. The defendant refused to accept delivery and, when sued for damages for non-acceptance, successfully pleaded the illegality of the contract. The contract was expressly forbidden and the court would do nothing to enforce it. In *Mohamed v. Alaga & Co.*[3] M, a Somali, contracted with the defendant solicitors that he would introduce Somali asylum-seekers to the firm and assist in the preparation of their cases by translating documents, etc., in return for half the fees received from legal aid. Such a fee-sharing agreement is unlawful under rules made by the Law Society. M was unaware of this but he could not recover under the illegal contract. It was held, however, that he could recover on a *quantum meruit* a reasonable sum for professional services—translation, etc.,—rendered. The court, somewhat generously perhaps, held that payment for these services was not part of the consideration payable under the unlawful contract. The court was much influenced by the fact that M was less blameworthy than Alaga, who either knew, or certainly ought to have known, of the illegal nature of the agreement.

It follows that an agreement to commit a crime is not enforceable. Every agreement to commit a crime, even an offence triable only summarily, is indictable as a conspiracy—*i.e.* the agreement itself is an offence.[4] An agreement to defraud, even where the fraud contemplated does not amount to a crime, is also the crime of conspiracy. In *Miller v. Karlinski*[5] an employer agreed to pay his employee £10 a week plus expenses and that his "expenses" should include the amount of income tax payable on his salary. The parties were agreeing to defraud the Revenue and consequently, the employee's action to recover arrears of salary failed. The fraudulent term was not severable and invalidated the whole contract. An agreement to deceive is not saved from the taint of illegality because it is shown to be a common practice in trade or business. In *Brown Jenkinson & Co. Ltd v. Percy Dalton (London) Ltd*[6] shippers of orange juice were advised by the shipowner that the barrels were old and leaking. The shipowner advised that a "claused" bill of lading should be issued but the shipper wanted a "clean" bill and agreed to indemnify the shipowner, if he would issue a bill stating that the barrels were "shipped in apparent good order and condition". The shipowner did so. When the barrels arrived, they were leaking and the shipowner had to compensate the holder of the

3 [1999] 3 All E.R. 699.
4 Criminal Law Act 1977, s.(1).
5 (1945) 62 T.L.R. 85.
6 [1957] 2 Q.B. 621, CA; S. & T. 698.

bill. His action under the indemnity failed. As Morris L.J. said, "the promise upon which the plaintiffs rely is in effect this: if you will make a false representation, which will deceive indorsees or bankers, we will indemnify you against any loss that may result to you." The majority were unimpressed by the claim that such practice was common. Lord Evershed M.R., dissenting, accepted the trial judge's view that the shipowners did not intend anyone to suffer any loss (presumably because any holder of the bill would be compensated) and that, though they may have been thoughtless and misguided, they were not dishonest.

Implied prohibition of contracts

In the *St John Shipping* case[7] and in *Archbolds (Freightage) Ltd v. S. Spanglett Ltd*[8] there was much discussion of the question of the implied prohibition by Parliament of contracts. In the former case Devlin J. said, *obiter* that since statute forbids the *use* of an unlicensed vehicle on a highway, "there may well be" an implied prohibition of all contracts for the use of unlicensed vehicles. It is surely possible to answer the question more categorically, on the assumption, which Devlin J. appears to have made, that both parties know the vehicle to be unlicensed. Of course the contract is prohibited because it is a conspiracy—it was a common law conspiracy when Devlin J. spoke and is now a statutory conspiracy contrary to section 1 of the Criminal Law Act 1977. If the hirer does not know that the vehicle is unlicensed then, surely, the contract is not prohibited because, as Devlin L.J. said in *Archbolds'* case, there is probably an implied warranty that the vehicle is licensed. The hirer could sue on the contract but the letter, of course, could not. In the *St John* case, Devlin J. said that contracts for the carriage of good by unlicensed vehicles or for the repairing or the garaging of unlicensed vehicles may well be different. Repairing and garaging would not in themselves involve any illegality and the agreements would not constitute conspiracies. Devlin J., in a passage approved by Pearce L.J., said, "The answer might be that collateral contracts of this sort are not within the ambit of the statute." Not only could the repairer or garager sue on the contract, but the owner of the vehicle also might enforce it, provided he did not invoke the illegal use, or proposed illegal use, of the vehicle in support of his claim, as by showing that it had broken down, or that he had been prevented from using it, on a road. It is arguable that, if the repairer or garager knew of the intention to use the vehicle

7 Below, p. 261.
8 [1961] 1 Q.B. 374, CA; S & T. 693.

on the road, he would be guilty of aiding and abetting that use if it occurred[9]; and in that case, he could hardly be allowed to enforce the contract.

In *Archbolds v. Spanglett* the contract was for the carriage of a load of whisky from Leeds to London which the carrier performed illegally by using a vehicle for which he did not hold the requisite "A" licence, entitling him to carry the goods of others for reward. The load was lost through the negligence of the driver. The plaintiffs' action for the loss of their whisky succeeded. They neither knew, nor ought to have known that the defendants did not have an "A" licence. The contract of carriage was not prohibited, expressly or impliedly, and the plaintiffs were guilty of no illegality. If they had known that the defendants had no "A" licence, they would have been aiding and abetting the offence and would have failed.

WHERE THE PURPOSE OF THE PARTIES IS CONTRARY TO PUBLIC POLICY

In the cases considered so far, where the contract was held to be illegal, either its making, or its performance necessarily involved the commission of crime or, at least, fraud. But "illegality" in the law of contract goes beyond this. Adultery, fornication and prostitution are not crimes in England but contracts made with the purpose of promoting them have been regarded as "illegal" and invalid. In *Pearce v. Brooks*[10] the contract was one of hire-purchase of a carriage, a miniature brougham, which seems harmless enough. But when the defendant returned the brougham in a damaged condition after paying only the second instalment, the plaintiff's action for breach of contract failed. The defendant pleaded successfully that the purpose of the hiring, as the plaintiff knew, was to enable her to pursue her calling as a prostitute. The plaintiff knew that he was assisting the defendant in her immoral purpose and that was enough. It was immaterial that it was not part of the contract that she should so use it and that it was not proved that he was to be paid out of the proceeds of the prostitution. The supplier of goods and services which he knows to be required solely for the purpose of prostitution cannot sue for the price and, if he receives it, is probably guilty of the crime of living, in part, on the earnings of prostitution.[11] The supplier of the ordinary necessities of life, however, can recover the price, notwithstanding his awareness of the fact that his

9 Smith & Hogan, *Criminal Law* (9th ed., 1999), Chap. 7.
10 (1866) L.R. 1 Ex. 213; S. & T. 686.
11 Smith & Hogan, *Criminal Law* (6th ed.), 460.

customer is a prostitute who could not carry on without them. Bramwell B., in argument in *Pearce v. Brooks*, instanced shoes sold to a streetwalker. The shoes will certainly assist in the practice of her profession but she must have shoes whatever her calling, so she may be required to pay for them. There is an exception where an excessive charge is made because the other party is a prostitute, as where a landlord charges an exorbitant rent for that reason. He is probably guilty of the offence of living on the earnings of prostitution and, if so, it is plain that he cannot sue on the contract.

Public policy is a changing concept. At one time a contract by a man to take a flat for his mistress was treated as illegal[12]; but changing attitudes to sexual morality are such that the decision is unlikely to be followed today.

WHERE THE CONTRACT IS LAWFULLY MADE BUT CARRIED OUT IN AN UNLAWFUL MANNER

In the cases considered so far, the contract was in some way tainted with illegality at the moment it was made. A contract, perfectly lawful when made, may be carried out in an illegal manner. If it is, the party or parties responsible for the illegal performance may be debarred from enforcing the contract. Whether a party is so debarred depends on whether the illegal act is central to the performance of the contract or merely incidental.

In *Anderson v. Daniel*,[13] the contract was for the sale of fertiliser. There is nothing wrong with that; but statute required the seller to deliver with the goods an invoice stating their composition. It was an offence to fail to do so. The seller delivered 10 tons of artificial manure but no invoice. His action for the price failed. The result is harsh. The seller is liable to such punishment in a criminal court as is appropriate to his offence. In addition he loses the value of the goods, though there may be nothing wrong with them. The buyer on the other hand, is unjustly enriched. He gets the goods for nothing. If the goods are defective, the seller's illegal performance of the contract does not debar the buyer from suing on it unless he has aided and abetted the seller's offence.

It is not, however, every illegality committed in the course of performing a contract which has this drastic effect. It would be

12 *Upfill v. Wright* [1911] 1 K.B. 506, not followed in *Heglibiston Establishment v. Heyman* (1977) 36 P. & C.R. 351.
13 [1924] 1 K.B. 138.

absurd if a carrier were to be debarred from recovering the cost of carrying goods from London to Newcastle because his driver exceeded the speed limit at one point on the journey; or that a manufacturer should be unable to recover the cost of goods made in his factory because one of his machines was not fenced as required by law. The offence in *Anderson v. Daniel* existed for the protection of the buyer. Speed limits exist for the protection of the public and factory legislation for the protection of the workers in the factory. In *St John Shipping Corporation v. Joseph Rank Ltd*[14] the contract was for the charter of a ship to carry grain. In the course of the voyage the master put into port and took on an additional load which submerged the ship's loadline. That was an offence under the Merchant Shipping Act 1932 for which the master was fined £1,200. The consignee withheld part of the freight due under the contract. Devlin J. held that the shipowner was entitled to recover it; the illegal act was merely incidental to the performance of the contract. In *Shaw v. Groom*[15] a landlord failed to provide a tenant with a rent book as required by the Landlord and Tenant Act 1962. Though this was an offence on his part, he was entitled to recover arrears of rent. The rent book clearly is for the protection of the tenant and the case is not easily distinguishable from *Anderson v. Daniel*. The court thought that the rent book, though it must be provided, is not an essential of the contract of letting. That may be true; but, then, is the invoice specifying composition any more essential to the contract of sale of fertiliser? The court attributes the result to the intention of the legislature; Parliament intended the landlord to be subjected to the prescribed penalty but did not intend that he should be precluded from recovering unpaid rent. This is really a fiction. The only intention expressed by Parliament in any of these cases is to impose the criminal penalty. The effect on a contract, if any, is invented by the court.

WHERE THE CONTRACT IS SO DEVISED AS TO ENABLE ONE PARTY TO PERPETRATE A FRAUD

Even though neither the contract nor the performance of it involves any illegality, it may be held to be illegal as against a party who has devised it in such a form as to enable him to perpetrate a fraud. In *Alexander v. Rayson*[16] the plaintiff let a service flat to the defendant. In one document he leased the premises at a rent of £450 a year; in another, he agreed to provide

14 [1957] 1 Q.B. 267.
15 [1970] 2 Q.B. 504, CA.
16 [1936] 1 K.B. 169, CA.

certain services for £750 a year. This looks somewhat eccentric, the flat being substantially undervalued and the services grossly overvalued; but the court is not interested in the adequacy of the consideration and there is nothing inherently wrong with such an arrangement. However, when the plaintiff sued for arrears of rent, it was alleged that his purpose, unknown to the defendant at the time, was to produce the lease to the rating authority as evidence that the premises were worth only £450 a year to get the rates reduced. The Court of Appeal held that, if that were so, the plaintiff could not sue on either agreement. If the defendant had been a party to the fraud, it would have been a conspiracy to defraud.[17] As the defendant was innocent, the agreement was not an offence but, at most, an act preparatory to the commission of an offence by the plaintiff.

WHERE ONE PARTY TO THE CONTRACT HAS AN ILLEGAL PURPOSE

Since only one party has the illegal purpose, the agreement does not amount to a conspiracy and is not prohibited as such; but, if the performance of the contract by A would assist B in the commission of an offence, A cannot be liable for breach of contract in refusing to perform when he learns of the illegal purpose. The law as a whole must be consistent and cannot hold that A is criminally liable as an aider and abettor if he performs the contract and is liable for breach of contract if he does not. Not only may he properly refuse to perform, he must refuse. If A has contracted to sell weedkiller to B—a contract perfectly lawful in itself—not only is he entitled to refuse to deliver, but he is bound to do so, on discovering that B's purpose is to administer the substance not to the weeds but to his wife. In *Cowan v. Milbourn*[18] the defendant agreed to let a room to the plaintiff for a series of lectures. He then discovered that the lectures were of a blasphemous—*i.e.* criminal—character and refused the plaintiff the room. It was held that he was not only entitled but bound to do so.

THE EFFECT OF AN ILLEGAL CONTRACT

Property may pass, notwithstanding illegality. It has been seen that, where a contract is void because of a mistake of identity, whether of the subject-matter of the contract or of a party to it,

17 *cf. R. v. Hollinshead* [1985] A.C. 975, HL.
18 (1867) 2 Ex. 230.

ownership does not pass to the buyer, even by delivery.[19] Although contracts tainted by illegality are commonly described as "void" it seems clear that property in the subject-matter may pass from one party to the other, whether it be full ownership, described as "the general property", or some lesser proprietary interest, designated "a special property". Parke B.'s dicta in *Scarfe v. Morgan*[20] concerning a bailee's lien—a variety of special property—were applied by the court of appeal in *Bowmakers Ltd v. Barnet Instruments Ltd*[21] where one, Smith, sold machine tools to the plaintiff finance company so that the finance company might let them on illegal hire-purchase contracts to the defendants. In *Singh v. Ali*[22] the Privy Council held that the property in a lorry passed when it was sold and delivered under an illegal contract; and in *Belvoir Finance Co. v. Stapleton*[23] the Court of Appeal held that the plaintiffs acquired a good title to cars under a contract of sale which amounted to a criminal conspiracy although the cars were never delivered to the plaintiffs but to the car-hire firm to which the plaintiffs let them on hire-purchase terms.

RECOVERY OF PROPERTY DELIVERED UNDER AN ILLEGAL CONTRACT

It is frequently said that, where the parties to an illegal contract are equally at fault, one cannot get his property back from the other: *in pari delicto potior est conditio defendentis*. If the plaintiff has to disclose the illegality in order to make out his case, he fails. But this proposition requires, at least, qualification. A leading case is *Taylor v. Chester*.[24] The plaintiff claimed the return of half of a £50 banknote, alleged to have been delivered to the defendant, to be returned on request. The defendant pleaded that the half note had been deposited with her by way of pledge to secure the repayment of money due from the plaintiff to the defendant and not paid. The plaintiff's reply was that the money due was for a debauch in a disorderly house kept by the defendant. The plaintiff's action failed but not only, as is often said, because he had to disclose his own iniquity. It failed because, following *Scarfe v. Morgan*,[25] the special property in the

19 Above, p. 00.
20 (1838) 4 M. & W. 270.
21 [1945] K.B. 65; S. & T. 702. The point was conceded by counsel and the court had no doubt that the concession was rightly made.
22 [1960] A.C. 167, PC.
23 [1971] 1 Q.B. 210.
24 (1869) L.R. 4 Q.B. 309; S. & T. 700.
25 Above.

half note had passed to the defendant. The question was not raised, and was left open, of the effect of a tender of the amount for which the note was pledged. Although the court referred to the maxim, *in pari delicto*, and the fact that the plaintiff was relying on the illegal nature of the transaction to recover his property, it seems that the principal reason why the defendant succeeded was that she had a special property in the note which entitled her to retain it until the money due was tendered. If the money due had been tendered, then the question would have arisen whether the plaintiff was debarred by the illegality from recovering his own property, now freed by the tender from the defendant's special property in it. *Bowmakers Ltd v. Barnet Instruments Ltd*[26] suggests that Taylor could then have sued successfully for the conversion of the half note. There were three agreements under which Bowmakers let machine tools to the defendants on hire-purchase. All were assumed to be illegal, as contravening a statutory instrument regulating hire-purchase transactions. The defendants, having, in breach of the agreements, fallen behind with the instalments, sold the machines which were the subjects of agreements 1 and 3 and refused to deliver up the one which was the subject of agreement 2. The plaintiffs sued successfully in conversion. The ownership in the tools had passed from the original owner, Smith, to the plaintiffs, notwithstanding the illegality of the transaction, and they were not debarred from asserting their proprietary rights against the defendants merely because the goods had come into possession of the defendants in the course of an illegal transaction. *Taylor v. Chester* was distinguished on the ground that there the defendant had a right in possession of the half note since she was holding it as a pledge for money which remained due. Now if Bowmakers had acquired the general property in the tools from Smith, notwithstanding the illegality of the whole transaction, it followed that the defendants had acquired a special property by reason of the bailment; but, in the case of agreements 1 and 3, this had been terminated by the sale of the tool. In respect of agreement 2, however, the defendants were still in possession of the tool. The plaintiffs could show that they were entitled to possession of it only by proving that the defendants were in breach of the illegal agreement. To that extent, they appear to have been allowed to rely on it; but the case is still different from *Taylor v. Chester* for there the plaintiff was relying not on a breach of the agreement but on the *illegality* of the agreement.

These cases were followed in *Tinsley v. Milligan*.[27] T and M

26 [1945] K.B. 65; S. & T. 702, above, p. 263.
27 Above, p. 256.

jointly bought a house for use as a lodging house but registered it in the sole name of T, so that M could make false claims to the Department of Social Security for benefit. When they quarrelled, T claimed that the house belonged to her alone. It was held (Lords Goff and Keith dissenting) that, since M had contributed to the purchase price, the presumption of a resulting trust applied so that she could establish an equitable interest in the property without relying in any way on the underlying illegality. She was not seeking to enforce an illegal contract but founding her case on a right of property acquired under the contract.

VOID CONTRACTS

Occasionally Parliament declares a particular type of contract to be not illegal or an offence but to be void. The most conspicuous example is the wagering contract which is so treated by the Gaming Act 1845, s.18. It is traditional to examine wagering contracts in some detail in general books on the law of contract but they are not central to the subject and are not pursued further here.[28]

Public policy also attributes the effect of voidness rather than illegality to certain agreements. The difference appears to be that an illegal term in an agreement is said to taint the whole contract, including collateral transactions. A merely void term does not have this effect. In appropriate circumstances it may be severed from the rest of the contract which remains valid. The most important examples are contracts in restraint of trade and contracts to oust the jurisdiction of the courts. Only the former category is discussed here.

CONTRACTS IN RESTRAINT OF TRADE

There are three principal categories of such agreements:

   (i)   The vendor of a business covenants that he will not compete with the purchaser.
  (ii)   An employee covenants with his employer that he will not compete with him on leaving his employment.
 (iii)   A group of traders contract to regulate their prices, output, etc.

The third type of agreement is regulated by the Resale Prices

---

28 See S. & T. 679–682 for a summary; *Cheshire, Fifoot & Furmston* (13th ed.), 334–351.

Act 1976[29] and is not examined here. The first two types are governed by the principles stated by Lord MacNaghten in *Nordenfelt's Case*[30] and Lord Parker in *Herbert Morris & Co. v. Saxelby*.[31] Since it is in the public interest that people should follow their calling and pursue their trades, all covenants in restraint of trade are prima facie contrary to public policy and void; but a covenant may be upheld if:

(a)   the covenantee shows that it is reasonable as between the parties to it and

(b)   the covenantor does not show that it is unreasonable in the public interest.

The courts take a less strict view of covenants between vendor and purchaser than of similar covenants between employer and employee. If the vendor of a business were free immediately to set up in competition next door, the purchaser would not get what he had paid for, so it will usually be fairly easy to establish that it is reasonable that some degree of restraint be imposed on the vendor. The restraint must, however, be no wider in terms of time and area, than is necessary to protect the proprietary interest acquired by the purchaser. A covenant by the vendor of the goodwill of a brewer's licence that he will not brew beer is invalid if the vendor has never brewed beer for there is no goodwill, in respect of beer, to protect.[32] If the vendor's business is worldwide, then a worldwide covenant may be upheld; but if the business has only a limited area of operation, a covenant precluding the vendor from carrying on business outside that area will be invalid. In *Ronbar Enterprises Ltd v. Green*[33] an agreement between partners in a weekly paper provided that, if one bought the other out, the vendor should not, for five years, "carry on or be engaged in any business similar to or competing with the business of the partnership." The words "similar to" were too wide because a "similar" business might be anywhere in the world, which would be far wider than was necessary to protect the purchaser's interest in a paper with a very limited circulation; but the court held that the offending words could be severed; and a covenant against joining a "competing" business was valid because the purchaser was entitled to be protected against competition from the vendor for a reasonable period of

---

29 See *Cheshire, Fifoot and Furmston* 358–361; Albery and Fletcher-Cooke, *Monopolies and Restrictive Trade Practices.*

30 [1894] A.C. 535.

31 [1916] A.C. 688.

32 *Vancouver Malt and Sake Brewing Co. Ltd v. Vancouver Breweries Ltd* [1934] A.C. 181, PC.

33 [1954] 2 All E.R. 266; S. & T. 716.

time. If the words "or competing with" had not been included in the covenant it would have failed altogether.

A restraint upon an employee will be upheld only where it is reasonably necessary to protect a proprietary right of the employer in the nature of a trade connection or trade secrets. The employer is not entitled to protect himself against mere competition by his former employees. But, if he can show that his former employee has acquired knowledge of a secret process or method of manufacture, he is entitled to enforce such restraint on him as will afford reasonable protection to that interest. Similarly, where the nature of the employment is such that the employee may acquire the trust of, or influence over, the customers, so that they may well take their business to him if he sets up in competition. In *Fitch v. Dewes*[34] it was held that a contract by a solicitor's clerk that he would not practise within seven miles of Tamworth town hall was valid, though it was unlimited in time. Of course, the wider the covenant in terms of time and place, the heavier the onus on the covenantee to prove that it is reasonable.

The courts will not allow an employer to achieve indirectly what he cannot do directly. In *Kores Manufacturing Co. Ltd v. Kolok Manufacturing Co. Ltd*[35] two companies agreed that neither would, without the consent of the other, employ any person who had been an employee of the other within the previous five years. Although the agreement was made between two employers its effect was to restrain employees and so was subject to the same tests. Both companies had trade secrets which they were entitled to protect. But the agreement applied to all employees, some of whom would have no access to secret information of any kind. The agreement then was far wider than necessary and it was impossible to sever it so as to render it applicable only to employees who were likely to learn the company's secrets. It was invalid. In *Bull v. Pitney-Bowes Ltd*[36] the offending provision was in the company's pension scheme which provided than any retired member who became employed in any activity in competition with the company and who failed to discontinue the activity when required to do so, would be liable to forfeit his pension rights. Thesiger J. held that the pension scheme was part of the contract of employment and the provision was void as an unreasonable restraint of trade.

The doctrine of restraint of trade affords no protection to a person who buys or leases land subject to a restrictive covenant.

34 [1921] 2 A.C. 158, HL.
35 [1959] Ch. 108, CA; S. & T. 709.
36 [1967] 1 W.L.R. 273, Q.B.D.

He has no right to be on the land, let alone trade there, before he gets possession under the contract. Even though his right to trade on the land is limited, or non-existent, he is deprived of no right which he previously enjoyed but acquires some new rights.[37] The doctrine does apply where a person already trading on a particular site accepts some restriction on his freedom to do so in future. In the *Esso* case[38] the owner of two garages entered into contracts (known as "solus agreements") with Esso that he would buy only their fuel and sell it at their retail prices and comply with various other conditions. This agreement was subject to the doctrine. It restricted the right previously enjoyed by the owner to buy petrol from whomsoever he pleased. But, since the application of the solus system in this case was for the benefit of both parties, the restraint was reasonable and enforceable.

In the *Alec Lobb*[39] case, Alec Lobb Ltd, in order to solve its financial difficulties, leased the site of its garage to Total Oil Ltd for 51 years at a peppercorn rent in consideration of the payment by Total of a premium of £25,000 and a sub-lease of the garage to Mr and Mrs Lobb, including a solus agreement. Mr and Mrs Lobb had no previous legal interest in the site, because it had belonged to their company; but the court would not allow the doctrine to be evaded by a device of this kind. Mr and Mrs Lobb were granted the sub-lease only because they were the proprietors of the company previously in occupation. The court has "ample power to pierce the corporate veil" and recognise a continuing identity of occupation. But, again, the restraints were reasonable and valid.

Similar principles apply to contracts for the entire services of another. In *Schroeder Music Publishing Co. Ltd v. Macaulay*[40] the plaintiff, a young and then unknown song-writer signed the defendant company's standard form assigning to them the copyright in anything produced by him for five years and, if the royalties reached a total of £5,000, for a further five years. The defendants did not undertake to exploit his work, though they did agree to pay royalties on any work in fact exploited. They could terminate the agreement at any time but there was no provision for determination by the plaintiff. The House of Lords held that this was an agreement in restraint of trade and unenforceable against the plaintiff because unreasonable.

37 *Esso Petroleum Co. Ltd v. Harper's Garage (Stourport) Ltd* [1968] A.C. 269; S. & T. 710.
38 Above, n.37.
39 *Alec Lobb (Garages) Ltd v. Total Oil G.B. Ltd* [1985] 1 W.L.R. 173; S. & T. 670, CA.
40 [1974] 3 All E.R. 616, HL; S. & T. 714.

INDEX